Love's Architecture

Devotional Modes in Seventeenth-Century English Poetry

THE GOTHAM LIBRARY
OF THE NEW YORK UNIVERSITY PRESS

The Gotham Library is a series of original works and critical studies published in paperback primarily for student use. The Gotham hardcover edition is primarily for use by libraries and the general reader. Devoted to significant works and major authors and to literary topics of enduring importance, Gotham Library texts offer the best in literature and criticism.

Comparative Literature and Foreign Language
Literature: Robert J. Clements, Editor
Comparative and English Language Literature:
James W. Tuttleton, Editor

Love's Architecture

Devotional Modes
in Seventeenth-Century
English Poetry

Anthony Low

New York · New York University Press · 1978

Library of Congress Cataloging in Publication Data

Low, Anthony, 1935–
    Love's architecture.

    (The Gotham library)
    Includes bibliographical references.
    1.   English poetry—Early modern, 1500-1700—History
and criticism.   2.   Devotion in literature.   I.   Title.
PR545.D47L6   821'.3'0935   77-94391
ISBN 0-8147-4984-4
ISBN 0-8147-4985-2 pbk.

The Phænix builds the Phænix' nest.
Love's architecture is his own.

Richard Crashaw,
"In the Holy Nativity"

Let mans Soule be a Spheare, and then, in this,
The intelligence that moves, devotion is.

John Donne, "Goodfriday, 1613"

Preface

Two conclusions may be culled from some major debates of modern criticism: that the seventeeth century produced much of England's best lyric poetry, and that its most significant practitioners were Milton and the Metaphysicals. These poets have spoken with peculiar force and relevance to our times. Yet oddly, the poetry they left us has a refractory characteristic that runs quite counter to modern tastes: most of it is irreducibly religious. That did not disturb our most influential critic, T. S. Eliot, nor does it much disturb specialist scholars seeking to reconstruct the past. But it has been an unacknowledged embarrassment to the main currents of modern criticism. Donne's *Songs and Sonnets* and Marvell's secular lyrics have been explicated and made new for each generation of readers, but many of the devotional poems have had only cursory or specialized treatment. Alternatively, efforts have been made to divorce such poets as Herbert or Milton from the religious elements in their verse and to treat them not as devotional writers but as pure poets—an elusive term. Book after book has put these writers in a "modern" light, which is to say a secular light, while critics who swim against the stream are cast in the role of traditionalists and dismissed as irrelevant to twentieth-century readers.

What amounts to a modern critical schizophrenia stems from a basic paradox in seventeenth-century poetry. Because it unites sense and feeling with intellect, is faithful to experience, is minutely responsive to the subtleties of mind and matter, has brilliant imagery and highly sophisticated control of structure, rhetoric, and rhythms, it fascinates us. Yet insistently it turns from the perceived world that we favor to the world of spirit. In modern eyes, the style and much of the substance is admirable, but the subject is outmoded. Yet it is chiefly twentieth-century critics, many of them modernists, who have explored the style and techniques of seventeenth-century poetry and enabled us to read it with an understanding that would otherwise be impossible.

A few important critics, like Douglas Bush, Helen White, and Helen Gardner, have devoted themselves to the religious dimension in the poetry. Yet even Helen Gardner surprisingly confesses, in her introduction to Donne's divine poems, that she thinks religious poetry inferior to secular poetry by its very nature. Milton scholars, a tribe sui generis, have long tried to perceive their poet as both Christian and relevant, but not without disagreements. Louis Martz may be the only critic successfully to have brought religious matters to the sympathetic attention of contemporary criticism. His findings concerning meditation are widely accepted as critical tools, probably because he analyzes the methods and techniques of devotion rigorously, like a New Critic working on a poem. Indeed, criticism of religious verse had lagged so far behind secular verse that Martz was almost the first to bring it into the twentieth century. Although less sympathetic to religious verse than its predecessors, it turns out that the present age, with its appreciation for technique, is in some ways better able to understand it.

At the threshold of "The Church" Herbert warns prospective readers:

Avoid, Profanenesse; come not here:
Nothing but holy, pure, and cleare,
Or that which groneth to be so,
May at his perill further go.

Herbert's attitude, not unique to him, raises obvious difficulties for us. Like Vaughan or Crashaw, he wrote for believers or candidates for belief. We may ignore his warning, of course.

Taken to its limits, the demand for belief would bar many from the century's best verse. An open mind, willingness to learn, and the suspension of disbelief will go far toward replacing the committed faith Herbert and his fellows expected, while doing better justice to the poetry than a resolute modernism will permit. In this study I try to balance the needs of modern readers and the standards of critical objectivity against the intractable demands of the poets and their poems.

As I explain in more detail in the introductory chapter, the aim of this book is to propose a broader and more comprehensive approach to devotional poetry than previous critics have attempted. Seventeenth-century poets employed at least four major devotional modes: vocal, meditative, affective, and contemplative. Most previous criticism (notably Martz's) has concentrated on the meditative mode. After an initial survey my chapters are chronological: Donne, Herbert, Crashaw, Vaughan, Herrick, Marvell, and Traherne. I prefer this approach to a four-part division based on devotional modes, as it allows a more inductive method and does more justice to the individuality of each poet.

While the account of meditation in Donne and Herbert covers some ground familiar to experts, it is necessary both as a base for what follows and for readers less familiar with the poetry and its criticism. Strong passions arise when the relationships between poetry and music are discussed; I should say that I do not attempt to prove anything mathematically about this difficult subject, but rather to show that some of the poetry was influenced by specific vocal and musical devotional methods, such as the singing of psalms and hymns.

Much of this book was written in 1974 and 1975 while I enjoyed a sabbatical leave in Cambridge. I owe the Master and Fellows of Jesus College a great debt for their hospitality, especially D. S. Whitehead and I. Gershevitch, whose pleasant rooms I shared, and H. H. Erskine-Hill. New York University gave me the sabbatical and several useful research grants.

Permission of Oxford University Press to quote from the following texts is gratefully acknowledged: John Donne, *The Divine Poems,* ed. Helen Gardner (Oxford: The Clarendon Press, 1969); George Herbert, *The Works,* ed. F. E. Hutchinson (Oxford: The Clarendon Press, 1964); Richard Crashaw, *The Poems, English, Latin and Greek,* ed. L. C. Martin (Oxford: The Clarendon Press, 1963); Robert Herrick, *The Poetical Works,* ed. L. C. Martin (Oxford: The Clarendon Press, 1963); Andrew Marvell, *The Poems,* 3d edn., ed. H. M. Margoliouth, rev. Pierre Legouis with E. E. Duncan-Jones (Oxford: The Clarendon Press, 1971); Thomas Traherne, *Centuries, Poems, and Thanksgivings,* ed. H. M. Margoliouth (Oxford: The Clarendon Press, 1958). The bibliography notes changes to these texts and lists other major editions consulted.

My old friend Murray Prosky sacrificed part of a vacation to read the typescript and suggested many useful changes. M. L. Rosenthal, who has unwittingly influenced my views about poetry through graduate students he has taught, also gave good advice. Herschel Baker offered encouragement while the work was in progress, and I thank him and the Harvard English Department for a subvention from the Hyder Edward Rollins Fund which has aided publication in difficult times. Finally, no one could write a book like this today without acknowledging a special debt to Louis Martz. His *Poetry of Meditation* especially has been an invaluable guide and a source of internal arguments for many years.

Cambridge and New York   A. L.

For my daughter:
Louise Marie Low

Contents

Abbreviations

ELH	*ELH: A Journal of English Literary History*
ELN	*English Language Notes*
ELR	*English Literary Renaissance*
ES	*English Studies*
JHI	*Journal of the History of Ideas*
JPC	*Journal of Popular Culture*
N&Q	*Notes and Queries*
PBSA	*Papers of the Bibliographical Association of America*
PMLA	*PMLA: Publications of the Modern Language Association of America*
PQ	*Philological Quarterly*
RES	*Review of English Studies*
SCN	*Seventeenth-Century News*
SEL	*Studies in English Literature, 1500–1900*
SP	*Studies in Philology*
TLS	*Times Literary Supplement*
UTQ	*University of Toronto Quarterly*

1.

Poetry and Devotion

1. The Importance of Technique   *I like this form!*

The seventeenth century saw a flowering of religious poetry in England that has never been equaled. Donne, Herbert, Crashaw, Vaughan, Milton: the roll is extraordinary, all the more so because so many figures were concentrated in so short a time. Many explanations might be given for the occurrence of this renaissance, the most obvious being that religion was a central preoccupation of the age.[1] Religious enthusiasm does not always produce great poetry—for example, Methodism bore different fruits—but this revival happened to coincide with the greatest outpouring of poetry of all kinds that England has yet seen, in the century from Spenser to Milton. Religious poetry requires genius of a special kind, since it combines two talents notoriously beyond rational control. As T. S. Eliot drily puts it: "The capacity for writing poetry is rare; the capacity for religious emotion of the first intensity is rare; and it is to be expected that the existence of both capacities in the same individual should be rarer still." [2] In the seventeenth century, many would have called religious genius a gift of God: "Not I, but Christ liveth in me" (Gal. ii.20). To a lesser degree,

1

the century also viewed poetic genius as a divine gift or at least an inborn talent. In Milton's words, it is nothing less than "the inspired guift of God rarely bestow'd," while even careful Ben Jonson gave credit to nature as well as art.[3]

Nevertheless, poetry is made as well as inspired; it is fashioned and refashioned on the Muses' anvil. All the significant English poetry of that time is characterized by reliance on the arts of the trivium—grammar, logic, and rhetoric—which were taught to all literate men from the primary schools onward. Even so comparatively "unlearned" a writer as Shakespeare reveals a thorough grounding in the arts of language. That the same holds true of the major seventeenth-century religious poets, all highly educated, goes without saying.[4] The best poets, such as Shakespeare, Milton, or Herbert, make their hard-learned technical methods seem natural to the reader. If, as is often the case with Donne, attention is called to learned techniques, they are made to seem more witty than labored. Because we are still influenced by the Romantics, who jettisoned many of the old technical methods in favor of originality, spontaneity, and unbuttoned naturalness, logic may seem to us a dead hand, dry and discursive, while poetry should be intuitive and organic; grammar may seem pedestrian, walking where poetry flies; and rhetoric may seem insincere, while poetry should flow from genuine observations and emotions. The distinction between poetic and rhetoric has been a shibboleth among prominent twentieth-century critics, despite their admiration for technique. But there is no escaping the tools of language. We still admire some devices, such as metaphor or irony; even a slight familiarity with others used by earlier poets will bring us closer to their poetry.

This book assumes that what is true of poetic techniques is also true of religious ones. Today one may be reluctant to admit that great religious poetry requires of its author not only strong faith but familiarity with elaborate technical systems if that faith is to be supported and conveyed to others. I refer not simply to poetic techniques or knowledge of theology, though Donne or Herbert could scarcely have spoken to us without them, but to devotional method. Again the Romantic influence intervenes.

Until recently, many critics were unwilling to admit that religious devotion could follow a controlled technical system yet still be authentic. As poetry was thought to be the gift of divine inspiration or the Muses, religious devotion has been thought a gift of God and not a matter for planning or systematization. In the post-Freudian era, many would prefer to say that poetry and religion are products of the unconscious, or reflect irrational currents in the cultural background. This is only another way of saying that neither is essentially rational or deliberate. It is symptomatic of our era that Eliot should say that "the capacity for *writing poetry* is rare"—a phrase that allows for the craftsman's competence as well as the poet's genius—but that he then spoils the symmetry of his sentence by continuing: "the capacity for *religious emotion of the first intensity* is rare." Why religious emotion? Is emotion more proper to religion than to poetry? Most authorities in Donne's time would say that emotion is a subsidiary element of devotion and that it should be controlled by the higher faculties of reason and will.

Many critics in the late nineteenth and earlier twentieth centuries, when our poets were revived, read them in terms of their own attitudes toward devotion. Whatever did not fit their preconceptions is referred to as quaint, eccentric, or outmoded. Such thoroughly learned craftsmen as Herbert or Vaughan are treated almost like uneducated primitives. Crashaw is still abused because his devotion was not ours. Probably most of us would now smile at W. L. Doughty's view that the Christianity of Vaughan and Traherne had not yet fully evolved and so their verse is inferior to Charles Wesley's.[5] Fewer among us may notice the more sophisticated distortions of such first-rate critics as Eliot.[6] The New Critics greatly illuminated Metaphysical Poetry by applying modern critical theories to it, yet lack of historical perspective sometimes introduced distortions correctable only by returning to the common assumptions of the Metaphysicals' own time.[7] The same is true of the devotional element. Much can be gained by returning to contemporary religious practices and devotional theories.

A decided breakthrough occurred in 1954, with the publication of Louis Martz's *The Poetry of Meditation,* which suggested that many poems of Donne, Herbert, Southwell, and others use techniques like those of meditative prayer.[8] Meditation was a highly developed art in the seventeenth century, thanks largely to numerous treatises. The *Spiritual Exercises* of Ignatius Loyola, though the best known, was only one of many such books by Catholic, Anglican, and Puritan writers. Their methodologies must have influenced the devotions of almost every literate Christian at that time. Further reinforcement was given by spiritual advisement or from the pulpit, and those not influenced by reading were copiously advised in sermons.[9]

Seventeenth-century thinkers felt that devotion, at least in its human part, ought to be systematic and deliberate, and the results seem to bear them out. It was a period of great and still influential devotional writing. Other times in Western history produced martyrs, theologians, or administrators, but this was the great age of devotional saints: mystics, spiritual advisers, preachers, teachers of prayer. One may instance Saints Teresa, John of the Cross, Francis de Sales, Ignatius, Philip Neri, Cardinal Bellarmine, Augustine Baker; or among English Protestants Lancelot Andrewes, John Donne, Jeremy Taylor, Nicholas Ferrar, Richard Baxter, George Fox. The devotional techniques of such men (and their predecessors) proved as useful technically to the religious poets of the period as, in a different way, the methods of the rhetoricians. Just as Dante relied heavily on the scholastic theologians in the *Commedia,* so Donne and Crashaw relied on the devotional writers.

Martz, who suggested in detail how pervasive meditative techniques and structures were in the poetry, has been overwhelmingly imitated and confirmed by other scholars.[10] Hardly a poet, religious or secular, has not been related to the meditative tradition. But although this tradition is diverse, and has been expanded to include what critics call "Augustinian meditation," "Bonaventuran meditation," "Protestant meditation," "Puritan meditation," "Salesian meditation," and so on (the term grows thin), other forms of devotion practiced in the seventeenth century have been almost ignored. Of these other forms, only mystical prayer has received much attention, and capable works examining its relation to English poetry are surprisingly few.[11] Other possible forms of devotion have been ignored.

Heavy concentration on the links between poetry and meditation, almost to the exclusion of other devotional modes, has meant that what began as a brilliant discovery and continued to shed light is now (to shift the metaphor) becoming a worked-out lode. Indeed, some derivative studies do readers a disservice by trying to apply this approach to poems it simply does not fit, concluding, as might be feared, that the poetry and not the critical methodology is at fault. There has been too exclusive a concentration on meditation as a source for English poetry; it is time to widen the inquiry.

2. Modes of Devotion

What other forms of devotion were available? The best spiritual writers agreed that, although elaborate systems might aid beginners in their prayer, each person must find his own path according to his nature, his unique psychology, or divine prompting. St. John of the Cross writes: "God raises every soul by different paths. Scarcely shall you find one soul that in half its way agrees with that of another." According to the English mystic, Augustine Baker: "Various, yea infinite, are . . . the ways of God. One may read all the ways that he finds written, but he is to follow that way—and no other—by which God calleth him." [12] The most influential method of the time, the *Spiritual Exercises*, threatened to become rigid and monolithic as it grew more popular, but even here the tendency was reduced because the exercises were often administered (in thirty-day retreats) by practiced spiritual advisers who tempered the system to individual needs.

As with literary genres, it is not always easy to draw clear lines between devotional forms: to say that one is meditative or another contemplative. The devotional literature is vast, multilingual, and sometimes difficult, while the devotional writers thought, perhaps with justice, that this kind of knowledge must be tasted and practiced before it can rightly be understood.

Augustine Baker, who was widely read in the field, speaks at length of four main categories of mental prayer.[13] With slight modification his distinctions are a useful guide. His four categories are vocal prayer, meditation, sensible affection, and immediate acts. Vocal prayer includes two main types: spoken prayer and song. Meditation is well-known to include many varieties, all, however, sharing certain characteristics of intellect and imagination. Sensible affection, or the prayer of emotions and feelings, was widely practiced but, as we shall see, little written about. Baker's "immediate acts" is his own term for the blind application of the will without reason or senses, a forerunner to mystical prayer. I prefer, however, to use the term "contemplation" when speaking of mysticism or the prayer that immediately precedes it. Since I adopt Baker as a guide, not a rigid authority, I also touch on other devotional manifestations he does not specifically mention, such as the use of iconographic materials as aids to meditation, or prayer that combines several devotional modes.

Religious devotion, like poetry, is not easily categorized, and it is well to avoid any illusion that distinctions can be watertight. Even more, one should avoid imposing a system of categories on the poetry from outside. As far as possible, therefore, the procedure in the following chapters is inductive: looking at what individual poets and poems actually seem to say and do and how they accomplish these effects. While the four categories—vocal prayer, meditation, sensible affection, and contemplation—are central to my thesis, I try to employ them only insofar as they help deepen and broaden our understanding of the poetry. The chief aim is to come closer to the English devotional poets by opening up paths into the highly variable and personal area where religion and poetry converge, joining two kinds of inspiration with two broad systems of technique.

3. Some Definitions

Before we proceed to specific cases, it may be helpful to discuss briefly some problems of definition that previous critics have raised. There are several useful approaches to devotional poetry. Louis Martz's view is that it is essentially active and meditative. To this Frank Warnke adds that it does not include "simple praise" or "simple exhortation of the faithful" but that it achieves and expresses "a personal and intense relationship between the protagonist . . . and God." [14] Certainly exhortation belongs only indirectly to devotion; one may also exclude simple theological formulations and religious polemics. There is, however, no good reason to exclude praise nor, as we shall see, those forms that are passive rather than active, affective rather than intellectual. Further, devotion may be public as well as private so long as, in the seventeenth-century phrase, the heart answers to the voice or the individual spirit answers to the ritual.

Like most terms, "devotion" has evolved through various meanings. Originally, "devoted" or "devout" meant that which was reserved as a sacrifice for God, as in Adam's lamenting cry to the newly fallen Eve in *Paradise Lost:* "How art thou lost, how on a sudden lost, / Defac't, deflourd, and now to Death devote" (IX.900–01). One broad definition from the *Oxford English Dictionary* summarizes its usual seventeenth-century and modern meaning: devotion is "religious worship or observance; prayer and praise; divine worship."

Put another way, devotion involves an inner movement, spiritual or intellectual, affective or sensitive. In Donne's words: "Let mans Soule be a Spheare, and then, in this, / The intelligence that moves, devotion is." Profane or parodic devotion might be directed toward a mistress or even toward some evil, but in its usual sense devotion is directed away from the world or evil toward those things that are considered good. If a devotional poem stresses departure from evil, the thing in view may be sin, death, or hell. In other poems, nature or its creatures, an angel or a saint might be focused on. But the ultimate goal of a Christian devotional poem in the seventeenth century, explicit or implied, is God. The focus is finally on the relationship between man and God, whether public or private, whether spoken, sung, or silent, and whether it involves self-analysis, petition, or praise. This focus on relationship as well as object, on the observer, lover, and worshiper, as well as the God who is worshiped, is, of course, characteristic of the period. It was

Donne, the lover of women, who turned his poetic eye not so much on them as on his own love and its interior processes, who gave major impetus to the English devotional poem.

The nearest that the devotional mode comes to effacing the worshiper is in the hymn or psalm of praise. Even here, however, the seventeenth-century devotional poet usually preserves a viewpoint and a subjective reaction. Donne's hymns refer constantly to himself. It was Herbert but it might have been Vaughan who began his Easter hymn, "I got me flowers to straw thy way." We never lose sight or sound of the singers in Marvell's "Bermudas," as they row along the paradisal shores. A verse from Crashaw's Nativity hymn illustrates a typical balance between praisers, with their viewpoints and feelings, and the divine object of their praise, with his splendor and beauty. Two shepherds sing:

> We saw thee in thy baulmy Nest,
>   Young dawn of our æternall *Day!*
> We saw thine eyes break from their *Easte*
>   And chase the trembling shades away.
> We saw thee; and we blest the sight
> We saw thee by thine own sweet light.

Devotional poetry takes many forms, but usually, as in the Metaphysical love lyric, there is an element of the dramatic: a speaker, singer, praiser, petitioner; someone reforming himself or being regenerated; a recipient of divine grace or mystical visitations; a viewpoint; a heart, mind, or soul in the process of removing itself from evil and seeking out or responding to God.

Of course, the best definition of devotional poetry is given by the example of the devotional poems. The element of judgment enters in selecting particular poets and poems for interpretation. Those poems we shall look at in this study are representative members of the family of devotional poetry as briefly defined here. They suggest some of the many forms devotional poetry takes and some of its many techniques. In Baker's words, "various, yea infinite . . . are the ways of God";

or as we might prefer to put it, various are the devices in the religious poet's armory of praise and self-analysis, and various his techniques for communicating his experience to his readers.

In the course of examining the relationship of one devotional method, meditation, to English poetry, Louis Martz argues that there is a meditative genre in English poetry; Isabel MacCaffrey prefers to speak of mode.[15] Presumably whatever term one chooses for meditation applies to the other devotional methods as well. Since one is borrowing terms from one area and applying them to another, the choice is somewhat arbitrary. I prefer to speak of devotional modes, mainly because the four main kinds treated in this study are kinds, or modes, or methods of devotion rather than of poetry. Also, while "genre" may refer to an object (poem) or a method (poetic style), "mode" more properly signifies method than object, and the devotional modes are essentially devotional methods or techniques. There are, of course, confusions. The hymn, for example, is a well-established genre of poetry as well as the reflection of a devotional method, with classical antecedants as well as a long history of employment in the Church.[16] The metrical psalm too is both a poetic form and the reflection of a popular devotional method. By analogy, one might say that various genres and subgenres of meditative, affective, and mystical poetry were well established in England by the end of the seventeenth century. Poetry and devotion could not be so closely intertwined without cross-pollenation.

A poem can be a sonnet and a meditation at the same time, or even a sonnet and a variant of the metrical psalm. The recognized as well as the developing genres of the time were seldom pure or unmixed. Nevertheless, it is reasonable to argue that vocal devotion, meditation, sensible affection, and contemplation are modes of devotion first, and poetic genres or influences upon genre only second.

Notes

1. See Helen C. White, *English Devotional Literature 1600–1640* (Madison: University of Wisconsin Press, 1931), p. 10.

2. Eliot, *After Strange Gods* (London: Faber & Faber, 1934), p. 31.

3. Milton, *The Reason of Church Government, The Works of John Milton,* ed. F. A. Patterson (New York: Columbia University Press, 1931–1940), III, 238; Jonson, "To the Memory of . . . Shakespeare."

4. For an overview of rhetoric and further citations, see Brian Vickers, *Classical Rhetoric in English Poetry* (London: Macmillan, 1970).

5. Doughty, *Studies in Religious Poetry of the Seventeenth Century* (1946; Port Washington: Kennikat Press, 1969).

6. On Herbert's religion see Joseph H. Summers, *George Herbert: His Religion and Art* (London: Chatto and Windus, 1954), pp. 49–69.

7. For cogent examples see Rosemond Tuve, *Elizabethan and Metaphysical Imagery* (Chicago: University of Chicago Press, 1947); and *A Reading of George Herbert* (Chicago: University of Chicago Press, 1952).

8. (New Haven: Yale University Press).

9. On meditation and preaching, see Barbara Lewalski, *Donne's Anniversaries and the Poetry of Praise* (Princeton: Princeton University Press, 1973), pp. 73–107. What Lewalski says of meditation is true of the other devotional modes; I believe, however, that there is nothing uniquely Protestant about these cross-connections.

10. Martz, *The Paradise Within* (New Haven: Yale University Press, 1964); *The Poem of the Mind* (New York: Oxford University Press, 1966). Among others, see John M. Wallace, "Thomas Traherne and the Structure of Meditation," *ELH,* 25 (1958), 79–89; Anthony Raspa, "Crashaw and the Jesuit Poetic," *UTQ,* 36 (1966), 37–54; U. Milo Kaufman, *The Pilgrim's Progress and Traditions in Puritan Meditation* (New Haven: Yale University Press, 1966); Melvin E. Bradford, "Henry Vaughan's 'The Night': A Consideration of Metaphor and Meditation," *Arlington Quarterly,* 1 (1968), 209–222; Terence Cave, *Devotional Poetry in France, 1570–1613* (Cambridge: Cambridge University Press, 1969); William H. Halewood, *The Poetry of Grace* (New Haven: Yale University Press, 1970); Lewalski, *Donne's Anniversaries,* see note 9 above.

11. Two recent studies are R. A. Durr, *On the Mystical Poetry of Henry Vaughan* (Cambridge: Harvard University Press, 1962); and A. L. Clements, *The Mystical Poetry of Thomas Traherne* (Cambridge: Harvard University Press, 1969).

12. St. John of the Cross, cited by E. I. Watkin, *The Philosophy of Mysticism* (London: Grant Richards, 1920), p. 209; Baker, *The Confessions of Venerable Father Augustine Baker,* ed. Justin McCann (London: Burns Oates & Washbourne, 1922), p. 109.

13. Baker, *The Inner Life and Writings of Dame Gertrude More,* ed. Benedict Weld-Blundell, 2 vols. (London: R & T Washbourne, 1910–1911); *Sancta Sophia,* 2 vols. (Douai: John Patte and Thomas Fievet, 1657), esp. II, 3–15 (III.i.1–2). For more on Baker, see my *Augustine Baker* (New York: Twayne, 1970).

14. Martz, esp. "The Action of the Self: Devotional Poetry in the Seventeenth Century," *Metaphysical Poetry,* Stratford-Upon-Avon Studs.11, ed. M. Bradbury and D. Palmer (London: Edward Arnold, 1970), pp. 101–121; Warnke, *Versions of Baroque* (New Haven: Yale University Press, 1972), p. 131. See also Miriam Starkman, *"Noble Numbers* and the Poetry of Devotion," *Reason and the Imagination,* ed. J. A. Mazzeo (New York: Columbia University Press, 1962), pp. 1–27.

15. Martz, *The Poetry of Meditation,* pp. 321–330; MacCaffrey, "The Meditative Paradigm," *ELH,* 32 (1965), 388–407. On "mode" see also Earl Miner's three books on seventeenth-century poetry.

16. See Philip Rollinson, "Milton's Nativity Poem and the Decorum of Genre," *Milton Studies,* 7 (1975), 165–188.

2.

Divine Song

1. Metrical Psalms

Vocal prayer is, as the frequent gloss in the Book of Common Prayer puts it, either "said or sung"; but as Baker among others insists, unless it is accompanied by mental prayer it is "no Prayer at all." [1] In effect, vocal prayer is a method of focusing the mind and heart toward God by speaking or singing words. Although it is the most elementary form of prayer, it need not remain so. In the early Christian era, as Baker notes, the desert Fathers customarily used spoken prayers and psalm recitations to achieve mystical heights. A little later, the monastic movement of St. Benedict, the effects of which reverberated through European history, was built on what was called the *Opus Dei*. In essence, this consists of cooperative labor and joint singing of the divine office. The custom of singing or reciting the offices in community spread to other religious orders as they were founded. By the sixteenth century the secular clergy too were required to recite daily offices. When the new Jesuit order sought permission to say the offices privately and not in community, in keeping with its stress on mental prayer, the innovation was strongly contested. The divine offices evolved over the centuries, but always at their center were the psalms, together

12

with scriptural canticles, hymns going back to the Church Fathers, and biblical readings.

The laity were not neglected either. Gradually there grew up around the clerical offices a variety of books of hours, primers, and psalters, to be used by devout laymen in or out of church as devotional guides. Some were in Latin, others partly or entirely in the vernacular. The typical primer in England just before the Reformation gave the psalms and most prayers in Latin but provided extensive English glosses. The history of the psalmbook in England is typical of these devotional aids. The Paris Psalter of King Alfred has parallel columns in Latin and Old English. After the Conquest, French versions appeared. In the fourteenth century, Sternhold was anticipated by an English metrical version:

> Seli bern, that noght is gan
> In the rede of wicked man;
> And in strete of sinfulle noght he stode,
> Ne sat in setel of storme um-gode.[2]

Richard Rolle of Hampole produced a popular translation and commentary on the psalms in the fourteenth century, of which twenty copies in various dialects survive.[3] But a Church decree of 1408 against the Lollards forbade translation of any part of the Bible into English without permission. Vernacular psalmody suffered, and the first printed English psalter did not appear until 1530.

The century-long gap in the production of English vernacular psalms, together with major changes in the language, may explain why most literary critics ignore the psalm's earlier history. The singing of psalms and hymns often is portrayed as peculiarly Protestant. But their use in devotion goes back to the earliest Christian periods. The interruption was an exceptional event. It also helps to account for the eagerness with which English reformers took up the psalms. Sometimes slanted translations or interpretive headings gave the psalms a polemical or Reformist air. "If thou wouldest have Christ to come conquere and beate downe the Sirians, Idumeans, Ammonites, Papistes,

Antichristians, Nullifidians, Neutralles, and ungratious Pelagians, use the 68. Psalme." [4] Nevertheless, the psalms would not have enjoyed such enormous popularity for two centuries had they not fed their users' positive devotional needs.

The prose psalms, englished in various Bibles, psalters, and editions of the Book of Common Prayer, were widely used and came to permeate the very language of religion and prayer. No one could attend church (which was compulsory) without hearing or reciting them. In cathedrals and college chapels, the prose psalms provided texts for sung anthems. Even more influential, if that were possible, were the metrical psalms, whose popularity was incredible. There were some 280 editions of Sternhold and Hopkins alone down to 1640.[5] It was the setting of these psalms to popular tunes that made them so effective. The evidence reveals an intense devotion fed by music and the act of singing. Sometimes the psalms were sung in groups of the faithful, sometimes privately or at work. Such had been the hope of the translators. Miles Coverdale (1488?–1569), one of the earliest writers of metrical psalm texts, reveals his intentions:

O that mens lippes were so opened, that theyr mouthes myght shewe the prayse of God. Yee [yea] wolde God that oure mynstrels had none other thynge to playe upon, nether oure carters and plow men other thynge to whistle upon, save Psalmes, hymnes, and soch godly songes as David is occupied with all. . . . Therefore to geve oure youth of Englonde some occasion to chaunge theyr foule and corrupte balettes into swete songes and spirituall Hymnes . . . I have . . . set out certayne comfortable songes grounded on Gods worde, . . . specyally out of the Psalmes of David, At whom wolde God that oure Musicians wolde lerne to make theyr songes.[6]

Like Coverdale, Thomas Becon, another translator of the psalms into verse, devoutly wishes that "all Mynstrels in the world, yea and all sorte of parsons both olde and yonge, woulde ones leave theyr lascivious, wanton and unclene balades, and

syng such godly and vertuous songes, as David techeth them." [7]
Likewise Matthew Parker, afterward Archbishop of Canterbury, prefaced his version of the metrical psalms (c. 1567) with
a verse wish:

The singyng man: and Poete must,
with grave devine concurre:
As Davids skill: all three discust,
when he his harpe did sturre.

Depart ye songes: lascivious,
from lute, from harpe depart:
Geve place to Psalmes: most vertuous,
and solace there your harte.

Ye songes so nice: ye sonnets all,
of lothly lovers layes:
Ye worke mens mindes: but bitter gall,
By phansies pevishe playes. [8]

The verses, heavily pointed for singing, might themselves help
drive out "lothly lovers layes."

In the next century, Charles I published a metrical psalter
translated by his father, the learned King James I, and noted
that we "doe allow them to be song in all the Churches of our
Dominions, recommending them to all oure good subjects for
that effect." [9] The Stuart kings, who will not be suspected of
canting Puritanism, recognized the value of singing the psalms.
(In Scotland, verse psalters were attached to the Book of Common Prayer.) Like others before them, however, they failed to
displace what came to be called the "Old Version" of Sternhold
and Hopkins.

At about the same time, Nicholas Ferrar was presiding over
the community of Little Gidding, where considerable use was
made of hymns and psalms in the daily gatherings for prayer.
Ferrar, a great believer in memorizing the psalms, gave the
children of nearby towns small presents for doing likewise.
Each week he heard these "Psalm Children" at their recitations.
As a result, one might hear:

the houses, and doores, and Streets Sound out the Sweet
Musick of Davids harp in all places and at all times of the
day, the weomen hearing and the Children repeating and
conning the Psalms with out Book as they Sat a Spinning
and Knitting: when as before time those Childrens mouths
and tongues were exercised dayly . . . in Singing of
naughty, leaud, and at least Vain Songs and Ballets.

Ferrar's friend Herbert was of like mind. He recommends in *A
Priest to the Temple* that the country parson encourage his
parishioners to sing "Psalms at their work, and on holy days." [10]

Toward the end of the seventeenth century, Anthony à
Wood recollected in *Athenae Oxonienses* (1691) an old story that
Sternhold, greatest of the metrical psalmists, "being a most
zealous Reformer," "became so scandaliz'd at the amorous and
obscene Songs used in the Court, that he forsooth turn'd into
English meeter 51 of *Davids Psalms,* and caused musical notes to
be set to them, thinking thereby that the Courtiers would sing
them instead of their sonnets, but did not, only some few ex-
cepted. However the Poetry and Musick being admirable, and
the best that was made and composed in those times, they were
thought fit afterwards to be sung in all Parochial Churches, as
they do yet continue." [11] The story in its precise details may be
apocryphal,[12] yet it is true in its essence. Sternhold, like Coverdale, Parker, and Ferrar, knew well the power of song in furthering religious devotion. Naturally he did not succeed in driving all profane songs from the traditional haunt of immorality,
the court. In spite of all the Reformers' efforts, housemaids and
plowmen continued to whistle love ditties and sing ballads. Yet
if the psalms failed to drive out all other music, they succeeded
remarkably in taking a powerful hold on people of many classes
and sectarian persuasions.

The intentions of the metrical psalmists (like the writers of
hymn texts) proved more than pious dreams. According to
Bishop John Jewell, writing in 1560: "You may now sometimes
see at Paul's Cross after the service, six thousand persons old
and young of both sexes, all singing together and praising

God." [13] A Roman Catholic writer complained in 1616: "There is nothing that hath drawne multitudes to be of their Sects so much, as the singing of their psalmes, in such variable and delightful tunes: These the souldier singeth in warre, the artizans in their shoppes, and wayfaring men in their travaile, litle knowing (God wotte) what a serpent lyeth hidden under these sweet flowers." [14] Even the numerous attacks on the literary quality of the Old Version psalms and the jokes made by Shakespeare, Jonson, and others at the expense of psalm-singing confirm the popularity of this devotional practice.

England was not alone in its enthusiasm for vocal praise and sung devotion. The metrical psalm texts in French by Clement Marot proved highly popular at the court of Henry II. The King himself set some of them to music and sang them to orchestral accompaniment. In Spain, Luis de León and Malón de Chaide wrote metrical translations of the psalms during the sixteenth century, while numerous poets, major and minor, wrote pious words to popular tunes. Fray Ambrosio Montesino, for example, wrote verses on the Nativity to be sung to the tune of "Who is it that made you angry, my good Love?" [15] The austere Calvin, who like John Knox in Scotland was highly favorable to congregational singing, commissioned Marot and later Theodore Beza to assemble a psalmbook for use in Geneva. They completed their famous verse psalter in 1562.

Over the years, psalm texts reflected the various kinds of music to which they were set. In the Middle Ages, devotion was fed by plainsong or Gregorian chant, later replaced by various kinds of part music. By the fifteenth and sixteenth centuries, Gregorian was replaced by the liturgical music of such composers as Dunstable and Dufay and then by the Netherlandish and Italian schools represented by Ockeghem, Josquin des Prez, Willaert, and Palestrina (who with St. Charles Borromeo reformed the liturgical music of Rome). This new music was variously called the *ars nova*, *ars perfecta* and (later) the *prima pratica*: a more inclusive term is Renaissance. Toward the end of the sixteenth century it was in turn succeeded by the *seconda pratica* of Monteverdi, Heinrich Schütz, and other Baroque compos-

ers. Increasingly the composers of the late Renaissance and the
seventeenth century sought for a music that imitated and
stirred in its auditors the feelings and emotions of the text. The
ars nova as well as the *seconda pratica* witnessed an intertwined
development of new musical forms with new poetry. Musicians
and poets often worked closely together, at the Italian
academies and the English court alike.

Although, with some exceptions outside England, the metrical psalms were cruder than most of the new musical texts,
they were meant to work in the same way: to reinforce their
texts with the power of music to sway and move. Those concerned with composing and spreading this form of devotion
never lost sight of their spiritual purpose. Becon writes: "What
so ever David singethe, it is excellent and incomparable. He
wyth his songes exciteth, provoketh and enflameth the myndes
of the faythefull and diligent hearers unto the love and desyre
not of transitory but of heavenly thynges." [16] Calvin proclaims
in the *Institutes* (1536) that "unless voice and song . . . spring
from deep feeling of heart, neither has any value . . . with
God. But they arouse his wrath against us if they come only
from the tip of the lips and from the throat. . . . If the singing
be tempered to that gravity which is fitting in the sight of God
and the angels, it . . . has the greatest value in kindling our
hearts to a true zeal and an eagerness to pray." In the mind of
Thomas Cranmer, music was almost necessary for vocal devotion to be fully effective. He writes to his master, Henry VIII, in
1545 concerning some liturgical translations he has made: "Yf
Your Grace commande some devoute and solemnpe note to be
made thereunto . . . I truste it woll moche excitate and stirre
the hartes of all men unto devotion and godlynes." [17] Like
Baker and many spiritual teachers of earlier ages, the Reformers saw no merit in sung or spoken prayers if the lips were
unaccompanied by inward devotion. Yet verse and music could
contribute greatly to raising that necessary inward spirit.

Of course, the psalms were not used only for vocal devotion. Writings of the period often connect them with meditation. At Little Gidding, for example, surviving records show

that meditation, recitation, and song all contributed to the totality of worship.[18] Primers, prayerbooks, and psalters could be used privately as bases for purely mental prayer. Nevertheless, there is clear evidence of a widespread habit of vocal prayer in England during the sixteenth and seventeenth centuries, which made use of hymns, psalms, and other forms of verse set to music.

2. Literary Psalms

In a sense, all religious poetry might be called a form of vocal prayer, since poetry consists of spoken words that focus the mind and feelings, and in religious poetry this focus points, directly or indirectly, toward God. But certain kinds of English religious poetry have closer, more direct connections with the traditions of vocal prayer, among them the metrical psalms. Something has already been said about the popular metrical psalms, whose authors were less concerned with poetry as such than with the immediate need to adapt scripture to popular devotion. Other efforts were made to replace old Catholic devotions with something worthier of the English Reformation. Many of England's major poets contributed. Wyatt and Surrey translated groups of psalms. Sidney and his sister, the Countess of Pembroke, produced an entire psalter in the style of Marot and Beza. Milton turned his hand to the task several times during his life. King, Herbert, Crashaw, and Vaughan all wrote metrical psalms. In a poem in praise of the Sidneian psalms that deserves to be better known than it is, Donne remarks that until they were written the English Church sang in a voice "more hoarse, more harsh," than any other nation's.[19]

The psalms of Wyatt and his successors are worth knowing, although few of them have high poetic quality or even approach the force of the magnificent contemporary prose translations. Their chief advantage was that they could be sung; without music much of their virtue is lost. A stanza from Sidney's Psalm III suggests the genre's limitations:

Salvation doth belong
   Unto the lord most strong:
   He is he that defendeth;
And on those blessed same,
   Which beare his people's name,
   His blessing he extendeth.[20]

Solemnly sung or chanted as a focus for religious devotion, this verse has a certain power, but simply as poetry it fails. The chief interest of the Sidneian psalms lies in their experimentation with verse forms. They constitute in their variety what has been called "a School of English Versification."[21]

Not even Milton could rise to the heights more than occasionally. Parts of Psalm VI (1653) suggest what might be accomplished:

And thou O Lord how long? turn Lord, restore
   My soul, O save me for thy goodness sake
For in death no remembrance is of thee;
   Who in the grave can celebrate thy praise?
Wearied I am with sighing out my dayes,
   Nightly my Couch I make a kind of Sea;
My Bed I water with my tears; mine Eie
   Through grief consumes, is waxen old and dark
Ith' mid'st of all mine enemies that mark.[22]

There are some powerful lines, but others are weak. Devout translators of the psalms felt obliged to put faithfulness to the original above other considerations, for to do otherwise would be to set up their work in place of God's. Milton had a gift for finding English poetry in biblical texts, as is evident in *Paradise Lost,* but not even he can translate whole passages into good poetry.

The greatest fruits of the English metrical psalm movement are not the psalms themselves but other poems that were influenced by them. Sternhold and Hopkins have been credited with helping to re-establish iambic accentual verse as the English norm. The varied stanza forms of Donne, Herbert, and

Vaughan owe as much to the Sidneian psalter.[23] Thus the psalm texts, as poems, had an important technical influence. They also influenced English poetry as examples of vocal devotion. Milton's Piedmontese sonnet is a powerful instance:

> Avenge O Lord thy slaughter'd Saints, whose bones
>   Lie scatter'd on the Alpine mountains cold,
>   Ev'n them who kept thy truth so pure of old
>   When all our Fathers worship't Stocks and Stones,
> Forget not: in thy book record their groanes
>   Who were thy Sheep and in their antient Fold
>   Slayn by the bloody *Piemontese* that roll'd
>   Mother with Infant down the Rocks. Their moans
> The Vales redoubl'd to the Hills, and they
>   To Heav'n. Their martyr'd blood and ashes sow
>   O're all th' *Italian* fields where still doth sway
> The triple Tyrant: that from these may grow
>   A hunder'd-fold, who having learnt thy way
>   Early may fly the *Babylonian* wo.

Clearly this is a religious poem: but what kind? Although there are vivid pictures in it, it has little in common, in structure or tone, with the meditative poetry of Southwell or Donne. Nor does it resemble the contemplative poetry of Vaughan or Traherne.

Although recognizing its emotional and spiritual force, most critics ignore its devotional implications and concentrate on historical background or polemical and political meaning. But the poem is more than a verse version of Cromwell's letter to the Duke of Savoy. It is addressed not to the Piedmontese or the reader, but to God the Father.[24] Formally a sonnet, it also falls into the broad genre of prayer. Like many prayers in the period, it is full of biblical phraseology.[25] There are echoes from many parts of the Bible, from Genesis to Revelation; but the poem's form and tone are basically those of a psalm. Its closest analogues are the psalms of lamentation and vengeance.[26] The editorial directions in the Sternhold-Hopkins psalter of 1567 would serve with only slight modification as a headnote to Milton's sonnet: "If thou wouldest have Christ to come conquere and beate down the . . . Papistes . . . use the 68. Psalme."

Making use of all his possible models, Milton recreated Greek tragedy in *Samson Agonistes* but gave it new Christian meaning. What he did in the Piedmontese sonnet is analogous. Relying on no single psalm or scriptural passage, borrowing from many, he produced a contemporary re-creation of the Hebrew psalm. Like its originals (as theorists of the time recognized) Milton's psalm is a poem. Like the English verse psalm texts, it is a devotion that relies chiefly on sound to focus the hearer's spirit. The use of sound in the poem has frequently been admired.[27] The most obvious effect is the long *o*, especially in the prominent rhyme words, resulting in a groaning, relentless progression from "bones" in the first line to the last Babylonian woe. The poem is full of cries and groans from the martyred victims. The visual images are kaleidoscopic; it is in the realm of sound that the sonnet achieves unity and gathers cumulative emotional force. Many of Milton's predecessors in the sonnet form made good use of sound too, but their poems lie closer to lyrical song. Milton's has all the powerful sonority of Reformation church music.

3. Hymns and Musical Texts: Donne

The psalms were not, of course, the only kind of poetry used for vocal devotion. Throughout Europe, Catholic and Protestant, it was a great age of religious music. In England, though the metrical psalms were first in popularity, texts and music for anthems, hymns, and other kinds of divine song were still written. Byrd, Tallis, and Morley wrote Latin masses, antiphonal motets, anthems, and music for English services. In the parishes one might hear Sternhold and Hopkins, but other music survived and was performed at the Chapel Royal and the cathedrals.

The close connection between music and secular lyrics has often been demonstrated.[28] The poetic hymn, too, had its origins and, in some cases, kept its contacts with music. Almost the only writer who attempted to author hymn texts for liturgical use was George Wither. He dedicated *The Hymnes and Songs of the Church* (1623) to James I, who (he writes) commanded "that these *Hymnes* should be annexed to all *Psalme-Bookes* in English Meeter." If the king in a moment of aberration ordered this, he was unsuccessful. The problem was that people were suspicious of hymns without biblical texts. After all, as Wither is forced to admit, the psalms and canticles were "written and left for our instruction, by the Holy Ghost." His counterclaim, that "the *Spirit* of *God* was first moover" of his own poetry, is unpersuasive.[29]

Still, hymns could be written for private use or on occasion be sung publically. According to Izaak Walton, Donne's "A Hymn to God the Father" was set to music at the poet's command:

> I have the rather mentioned this *Hymn,* for that he caus'd it to be set to a most grave and solemn Tune, and to be often sung to the *Organ* by the *Choristers* of St. *Pauls* Church, in his own hearing; especially at the Evening Service, and at his return from his Customary Devotions in that place, did occasionally say to a friend, *The words of this* Hymn *have restored to me the same thoughts of joy that possesst my Soul in my sickness when I composed it. And, O the power of Church-musick! that Harmony added to this Hymn has raised the Affections of my heart, and quickned my graces of zeal and gratitude;* and I observe, *that I always return from paying this publick duty of* Prayer *and* Praise *to God, with an unexpressible tranquillity of mind,* and a willingness *to leave the world.*[30]

Whether the exact wording of Donne's remark to his friend is his, the friend's, or Walton's, the passage suggests how hymns were used devotionally. The music, working with the poetry, "raised the Affections" of the hearer's heart. Even the act of listening to a hymn being sung is *"Prayer* and *Praise* to God." Donne, among the most private and meditative of England's religious poets, still valued the devotional power of music suffi-

ciently to order his poem set and sung at public services in St.
Paul's.[31]

Donne's views on the devotional power of poetry set to
music are not his only. Milton celebrates the power of the
"Sphear-born harmonious Sisters, Voice, and Vers" in "At a
Solemn Musick." They raise the listener to a state in which he
hears the heavenly music itself, sung by the angels and saints
around God's throne. Milton returns again and again to this
theme; the well-known passage from "Il Penseroso" is typical:

> There let the pealing Organ blow,
> To the full voic'd Quire below,
> In Service high, and Anthems cleer,
> As may with sweetness, through mine ear,
> Dissolve me into extasies,
> And bring all Heav'n before mine eyes.

The poetry is devotional as well as descriptive. Through the
sound of its words the reader is swayed as he might be by
hearing the organ and choir in church. Milton often captured
the effects of religious music—just as he imitated the effects of
secular music in parts of "L'Allegro."

Printing of music began late in England. Among the com-
mercially successful books of madrigals and airs were only a few
collections of religious music. These were edited not by poets
but by composers and sometimes publishers. As a result, most
settings were for services or scriptural texts, which would sell
most readily. Few contemporary settings for privately written
hymns survive, and those mostly in undated manuscripts. Since
so little has come down, it is hard to tell how much of the
period's religious poetry was set to music. Yet, if not actually
sung, many of the literary hymns and other poems show their
origins in song and retain their function: lifting the hearer's
heart by harmonious sound or (on occasion) piercing it with
deliberate discord.

Donne's interest in singing religious verse, aside from Walton's testimony, is attested to by his poem in praise of the Sidneian psalms and by his translation of "The Lamentation of

Jeremy" into metrical verse. Helen Gardner suggests he was following the Sidneys' example, hoping to enrich the Church's liturgy. When George Wither wrote his metrical version of Lamentations, set to music by Orlando Gibbons, he chose the same meter as Donne.[32] The Lamentations were long a popular source for anthems and sacred songs. Thomas Ford composed music for Donne's version but set only the first two verses, employing complicated, three-part music not suited to Donne's poem as a whole. The stanza Donne chose, four-line iambic pentameter, is one of his simplest and the closest he came to Sternhold and Hopkins. Metrically it is suitable for public worship.

In a letter to Sir Henry Goodyer, written about 1608, Donne says that he was inspired to write another potentially liturgical poem, "A Litanie," by two early Latin litanies. The use of litanies was frowned on by the reform-minded, which may be why he implies it is for private use. An early pope, he tells Goodyer, canonized the Latin litanies "and commanded them for publike service in their Churches: mine is for the lesser Chappels, which are my friends." Donne also speaks of his poem as a "meditation in verse," but it is not meditative in form.[33] He may have called it so because it was a product of his meditations while ill in bed, or because opinion would keep any litany but the one in the Book of Common Prayer from liturgical use. In the poem, Donne touches introspectively on meditative themes. At the same time, four stanzas are dominated by the metaphor of music. In Stanza 8, the prophets are the "Churches Organs," who harmonize the old and new covenants, "heavenly Poets" who express God's will "in rhythmique feet." In Stanza 14 The Church is a "universall Quire" that prays "ceaslesly" to God's ever-listening ear. In Stanza 23 the prayers of a repentant sinner are "more musique" than "spheares, or Angels praises bee, / In Panegyrique Allelujaes." And in Stanza 24 Donne prays that "intermitting aguish Pietie," like the "sighes, teares, thoughts" of the previous stanza, be changed to "evennesse" by the "musique of thy promises." These musical themes within the poem are less important than its structure as a whole, which takes the form of a vocal devo-

tion. Perhaps none of Donne's poems is untouched by meditation. The hymns, "A Litanie," and "The Lamentation of
Jeremy," however, subordinate this element to vocal devotion.
It may be that in some of the "Holy Sonnets" meditation is also
secondary, but that must await consideration in the next chapter.

4. Sacred Song: Herbert

Like Donne, George Herbert has often been discussed in
the context of meditation. Many of the poems in *The Temple* are
characterized by the privateness and introspection of mental
prayer. Some, like "The Agonie," are meditative set pieces. Yet
most of Herbert's poetry has strong lyrical qualities as well.
Joseph H. Summers has discussed music in *The Temple* at
length, and Alicia Ostriker suggests that it balances "song" and
"speech," lyrical and colloquial.[34] There is a corresponding balance between vocal and mental forms of devotion. Some poems
are predominantly meditative, some a mixture of meditation
and lyric, others almost purely lyrical. It was not eccentricity
that led Vaughan to speak of Herbert's poems as hymns.[35]

Herbert's love of music is well known. Walton reports that
he went twice a week from Bemerton to the Cathedral of Salisbury (once the home of the famous Sarum Rite) to play with a
group of friends. Music so effectively raised up his soul he
called it his "Heaven upon Earth." We do not know if Herbert
and his friends played any of his own compositions at Salisbury.
Walton does tell us, however, that Herbert composed "many
divine *Hymns* and *Anthems,* which he set and sung to his *Lute* or
Viol."[36] What were these hymns and anthems? Walton does not
say; yet either their texts are now printed in *The Temple* or
Herbert simply discarded them. We know he set at least one
poem in *The Temple* to music. Walton is describing Herbert on
his sickbed:

> The *Sunday* before his death, he rose suddenly from his
> Bed or Couch, call'd for one of his Instruments, and took it
> into hand, and said—

> *My God, My God,*
> *My Musick shall find thee,*
>   *And every string*
> *shall have his attribute to sing.*

And having tun'd it, he play'd and sung:

> *The Sundays of Mans life,*
> *Thredded together on times string,*
> *Make Bracelets, to adorn the Wife*
> *Of the eternal glorious King:*
> *On Sundays, Heavens dore stands ope;*
> *Blessings are plentiful and rife,*
>   *More plentiful than hope.*

Thus he sung on Earth such Hymns and Anthems, as the Angels and he, and Mr. Farrer, now sing in heaven.[37]

The verse is from Herbert's poem "Sunday."

Walton also tells us that Herbert instructed his congregation concerning "the use of the *Psalms,* and the *Hymns* appointed to be daily sung or said in the Church-service." [38] The *Life* makes it clear how much he valued the hymns and psalms and the regular round of the Church year for singing them. He wrote a number of poems related to this yearly hymn cycle and two on the daily cycle: "Mattens" and "Even-song." Such poems as "A Dialogue-Antheme," the two "Antiphons," "A True Hymne," and "Mans medley" all reveal connections with religious music. Musical metaphors run suggestively through "The Temper (I)," "Employment (I)," "Praise (II)," and "Josephs coat." Summers notes the frequent use of technical terms from musicology: subtle puns on such terms as "broken consort," "strain," "discord," "relish." [39] Whole poems, such as "Church-musick," are predominantly aural rather than visual. These stanzas from "Providence" typify his use of musical imagery:

> Beasts fain would sing; birds dittie to their notes;
> Trees would be tuning on their native lute
> To thy renown: but all their hands and throats
> Are brought to Man, while they are lame and mute.

Man is the worlds high Priest: he doth present
The sacrifice for all; while they below
Unto the service mutter an assent,
Such as springs use that fall, and windes that blow.

The universal hymn of nature and harmony as an expression of the divine order were commonplaces. Yet these metaphors still kept their close connections with the music that gave them birth.

Two of Herbert's poems have other relations to Church liturgy. "The Sacrifice" derives from the Good Friday reproaches.[40] "The 23d Psalme" is in the Common Meter, with the debt that implies to Sternhold and Hopkins. An early setting by Henry Lawes survives in manuscript (BM Add. MS. 53723). Seven other psalms were attributed to Herbert in the seventeenth century by John Playford, but with doubtful authority. Playford also printed a musical setting of his own composition for "The Altar" in 1671. Henry Playford printed Herbert's "Longing" in 1688 with music by Henry Purcell, to which he later added a version of "Grieve not the Holy Spirit" set by John Blow. Six early and possibly contemporary settings by John Jenkins also survive in manuscript.[41] Much later, John Wesley adapted many of Herbert's poems for use as Methodist hymns; versions are still in use.[42] Thus while the surviving evidence that Herbert's poems were suited for musical setting is fragmentary, it is not inconsiderable.

To understand the basic role music may have played in shaping the poems of *The Temple,* another brief look at the historical background may be helpful. It is often pointed out that there were two basic kinds of metrical psalms (as also of hymns) in the period. One was the Common Meter, Short Meter, or folk psalm, which in England came to be dominated by the Old Version, with simple, ballad-like stanzas. The other was the literary or court psalm, of which the best examples are Marot-Beza in France and in England the psalms of Sidney and his sister. The court psalms had complex stanzas, which varied from one psalm to the next. One reason for their characteristic complexity and variety is that they were written for audiences

with sophisticated poetic tastes. There is another, musical reason. The meter of the Sternhold-Hopkins psalms was determined by the simple ballad tunes to which they were sung and
further limited by the Reformers' conviction that music should
not interfere with scriptural meaning. For this reason Cranmer
and Elizabeth repeatedly enjoined that music in the Established
Church should be plain and distinct, and that as nearly as possible, composers should set "for every sillable, a note; so that it
may be songe distinctly and devoutly." [43]

Court or cathedral music, in contrast, could be more complicated and could be played and sung in parts. Composers
sought poetic texts with varying line lengths and longer stanzas,
which could be set to more challenging tunes. In the realm of
secular music, Bruce Pattison convincingly argues, it was the
interaction of musicians and poets, the simultaneous development of new music and new poetry in Italy, France, and
England, that was primarily responsible for the outburst of new
stanza forms during the period.[44] Pattison does not discuss religious poetry, but one may suggest that Wyatt (for example)
wrote his psalms, like his secular lyrics, to be sung. Likewise the
Sidneys probably chose to write their psalter in a variety of
stanza forms not for poetic reasons only, nor in simple imitation
of Marot, but in order to fit them to the new styles of music.
Indeed it is misleading to speak of "literary" psalms or hymns
except as a judgment on their quality, since many of them were
shaped by, as well as set to, music.

Although the stanza can become a purely literary device, its
origins are musical. Poetry only develops stanzas when it is sung
to tunes of more than a line's length. Typically there is a line of
poetry for each musical phrase, and a stanza for each repetition
of the tune. As music grows more sophisticated, stanza forms
grow more varied, from simple songs and dance rhythms like
the ballad to texts of great complexity like the air or madrigal.
Such poets as Donne and Herbert, in their fruitful experimentation with stanza forms, did not need to draw on sources like
the Sidney psalms in a literary vacuum because the music originally responsible for stanzaic variety was still an active force.

Half a dozen of Donne's *Songs and Sonnets* have musical

settings by composers whom he may have known personally. Much of the music is presumably lost and those tunes that survive may not be the earliest. Originally many—perhaps all—of the *Songs and Sonnets* may have been shaped by interaction with the music of the period. In some cases—such as "The Baite," written after Marlowe and Raleigh—the music preceded the poem. In most cases the setting would come afterward, as Donne indicates in "The Triple Foole": "But when I have done so, / Some man, his art and voice to show, / Doth set and sing my paine." Writers of stanzaic poems like Donne might well have one eye on the composer. Some of Donne's poems have been called harsh and unmusical, but, paradoxically, precisely this quality gave them interest to musicians at this particular time, when chromatic harmony and dissonance were increasingly popular. One might not choose "The Apparition," one of Donne's bitterest poems, as a likely candidate for a song, yet part of a setting by William Lawes, Henry's brother, survives in manuscript. Significantly, *Grove's Dictionary* describes William Lawes as the period's most passionate and "discordant" composer.[45] The harshly satiric "Goe, and catche a falling starre" was likewise set to music. If Donne seldom speaks of his lute or song, that may be attributed to his revolt against conventionality.[46]

What the background of music and poetry suggests is that the notable variety of stanza forms in *The Temple* probably is not due simply to literary experimentation. Like Campion, Herbert had the advantage of being his own composer. We may presume from various statements he made that he used common Anglican psalms, hymns, and services in the church at Bemerton, sung to the simpler kinds of music recommended by the authorities. The same probably was not true of his private music. His Easter hymn is suggestive: it speaks of parts, of harmony between instruments and voice, and (like "L'Allegro") of the twisting of music and words to a pleasant length suggesting contrapuntal structure. Even as an undergraduate, Walton tells us, Herbert was a "great Master" of music.[47] He continued to compose and perform it for the rest of his life. Proofs are fragmentary, but probabilities urge that *The Temple* was vitally influenced by music, that music is present not merely in many references and musical analogies, but that it informs the sounds and rhythms of the poetry and everywhere influences stanzaic structure. Poetically, the poems of *The Temple* are mixtures of speech and song; devotionally, they are skillful blends of mental devotion and vocal prayer.

5. Poetry and Song

Donne and Herbert were not the last English religious poets deeply influenced by music, although as the century progressed that influence may have grown more indirect. Henry Vaughan entitled his introduction to the second edition of *Silex Scintillans* the "Preface to the following Hymns." Richard Crashaw called his second collection *Carmen Deo Nostro* and subtitled it "Te Decet Hymnus." But enough has been said for now to suggest the importance of sung devotion to English seventeenth-century poets.

Generally, modern critics ignore the musical and sometimes even the vocal element in metaphysical poetry. To appreciate the devotional poetry to the full, however, we should resist the temptation to prefer meditation to song or metaphysical weight to lyrical ease. Very likely these preferences have come about because the more intellectual methods of devotion and poetry are more readily dissected. A primary aim of New Critics and historical critics alike is to explicate and analyze. Even Louis Martz, who has played a unique role in rediscovering the devotional element in the poetry, is not immune to this tendency. In *The Poetry of Meditation* he describes all nonmeditative devotional materials in post-Reformation England as "collections of scattered prayers, scraps of liturgy, and bundles of precepts," which are "ineffectual when compared with the rich imaginative exercises" of the Counter-Reformation treatises on meditation.[48] Does this include the psalms? The hymns set by William Byrd? Does it even do justice to the collections of daily prayers Martz is primarily referring to? The Reformation, with its polemics and political upheavals, damaged English devotional life. But it never destroyed it entirely or prevented a resurgence of many different kinds of devotion.

John Playford, in his introduction to *Psalms and Hymns in Solemn Musick* (1671), tells his readers that "I have done but one half in Setting the *Musick,* which yet remains but as a dead letter: It being your part to Complete it, and add Life to its *Harmonious Body,* by your Sweet According Voyces." [49] Regrettably we cannot often follow this advice literally, since the music for most of the hymns and song texts of Donne, Herbert, Crashaw, and Vaughan is lost. Yet it is well at least to keep in mind the spirit of Playford's words. George MacDonald, in *England's Antiphon,* portrays English religious verse, from the earliest carols to the nineteenth century, as a chorus of praise, to which he plays the part of "listening-master." [50] Perhaps this major metaphor of his book is apter than he realized.

Notes

1. Baker, *Sancta Sophia* (Douai: John Patte and Thomas Fievet, 1657), II, 7 (III.i.l.9); see also II, 3–15.
2. Helen C. White, *Tudor Books of Private Devotion* (Madison: University of Wisconsin Press, 1951), p. 35. See also White's *English Devotional Literature 1600–1640* (Madison: University of Wisconsin, 1931).
3. White, *Tudor Books of Private Devotion,* p. 37.
4. Sternhold, Hopkins, and others, *The Whole Booke of Psalmes* (1567), sig. A4^v.
5. Hallett Smith, "English Metrical Psalms in the Sixteenth Century and their Literary Significance," *Huntington Library Quarterly,* 9 (1946), 251.
6. Myles Coverdale, *Goostly Psalmes and Spirituall Songes* (c. 1538), sigs. *2, *3^r.
7. Thomas Becon, *Davids Harpe ful of moost delectable armony* (London, 1542), sigs. a6^v–a7^r.
8. Matthew Parker, *The Whole Psalter Translated into English Metre* (London: John Daye, 1567?), sig. B2^r, cited by Smith, p. 266.
9. *The Psalmes of King David, Translated by King James* (Oxford: William Turner, 1631); another edition with music was printed by Thomas Harper, London, 1636.
10. *The Ferrar Papers,* ed. B. Blackstone (Cambridge: Cambridge University Press, 1938), p. 36; Herbert, *The Works,* ed. F. E. Hutchinson, p. 248.

11. Col. 62.

12. As Hallett Smith argues, pp. 250–251.

13. *Zurich Letters*, ed. Robinson, Hastings (Cambridge, 1842), I, 71; cited by J. C. A. Rathmell, ed., *The Psalms of Sir Philip Sidney and the Countess of Pembroke* (New York: New York University Press, 1963), p. xiii.

14. *Tessaradelphus, or the Foure Brothers,* ed. Thomas Harrap (n.p., 1616), sig. D2ᵛ, cited by White, p. 44.

15. Edward M. Wilson, "Spanish and English Religious Poetry of the Seventeenth Century," *Journal of Ecclesiastical History,* 9 (1958), 38–53.

16. Becon, *Davids Harpe* (1542), sig. a6ᵛ.

17. Calvin, cited by Coburn Freer, *Music for a King* (Baltimore: Johns Hopkins University Press, 1972), p. 27; Cranmer, in E. H. Fellowes, *English Cathedral Music* (London: Methuen, rev. ed. 1969), p. 24.

18. See *The Ferrar Papers:* meditation, pp. 55, 57, 76, 90; recitation and psalm-singing, pp. 33–46, 55–58, 66, 87, 102.

19. Donne, "Upon the translation of the Psalmes by Sir Philip Sydney, and the Countesse of Pembroke his Sister."

20. *The Poems of Sir Philip Sidney,* ed. William A. Ringler, Jr. (Oxford: Clarendon Press, 1962).

21. Smith, p. 269.

22. Other superior metrical psalms include Psalm 23 by Herbert and Psalm 121 by Vaughan; Wyatt's excellent penitential psalms are more paraphrase than translation.

23. Hallett Smith, Coburn Freer.

24. See Lawrence Hyman, "Milton's 'On the Late Massacre in Piedmont,' " *ELN,* 3 (1965–1966), 26–29.

25. Problems of viewing devotional poetry from a Romantic standpoint are illustrated by Mark Pattison in his edition of the Milton's sonnets (1883), pp. 58–60. He cannot understand how the poem can be so powerful when it borrows every thought and image from the Bible and is wholly composed of "hackneyed biblical phrases."

26. See, e.g., Psalms 10, 37, 54, 68, 94, 137, 141, 142, 143.

27. See Mark Van Doren, *Introduction to Poetry* (New York, 1951), pp. 121–125.

28. See John E. Stevens, *Music and Poetry in the Early Tudor Court* (London: Methuen, 1961); Bruce Pattison, *Music and Poetry of the English Renaissance* (London: Methuen, 2d edn. 1970); also Denis Stevens, *Tudor Church Music* (London: Faber & Faber, 1966), and Fellowes, *English Cathedral Music.*

29. Wither, *The Hymnes and Songs of the Church* (London, 1623), sig. A2; music by Orlando Gibbons. As Coburn Freer notes (p. 32), Wither also fell afoul of the Company of Stationers, who were jealous of their prerogatives.

30. Walton, *The Lives of John Donne*, etc., The World's Classics (London: Oxford University Press, 1927), p. 62.

31. H. J. C. Grierson, ed., *Donne's Poetical Works*, II, 252–253, prints music for this hymn by John Hillton (d. 1657) from Brit. Mus. Egerton MS. 2013.

32. Gardner, ed., *The Divine Poems*, p. 104; Wither, *The Hymnes and Songs of the Church*. Other settings of Lamentations are by Byrd, White, and Tallis, in *Tudor Church Music*, ed. P. C. Buck, Fellowes, et al., IX, 153; V, 14, 35; VI, 102, 110; it was a popular song text.

33. Donne, *Letters to Several Persons of Honour* (London, 1651), p. 33.

34. Summers, *George Herbert* (London: Chatto & Windus, 1954), pp. 156–170; Ostriker, "Song and Speech in the Metrics of George Herbert," *PMLA*, 80 (1965), 62–68; see also Roberta Schleiner, "Herbert's 'Divine and Moral Songs' . . . ," Diss. Brown University 1973.

35. Preface to *Silex Scintillans* (1655).

36. Walton, *Lives*, p. 303.

37. Walton, pp. 316–317.

38. Walton, p. 298.

39. Summers, *George Herbert*, pp. 158–160.

40. See Rosemond Tuve, *A Reading of George Herbert* (Chicago: University of Chicago Press, 1952), p. 44.

41. John Playford, *Psalms and Hymns in Solemn Music* (London, 1671); Purcell in Henry Playford, *Harmonia Sacra* (London, 1688); Blow in Henry Playford, *The Divine Companion* (London, 1701); John Jenkins, Christ Church MSS. 736–38; the two latter cited by Vincent Duckles, "John Jenkins' Settings of Lyrics by George Herbert," *Musical Quarterly*, 48 (1962), 461–475, the two former by Hutchinson and Summers.

42. See F. E. Hutchinson, "John Wesley and George Herbert," *The London Quarterly and Holborn Review*, 161 (1936), 439–455.

43. Letter from Cranmer to Henry VIII, quoted in Fellowes, *English Cathedral Music*, p. 24. Queen Elizabeth repeated this direction.

44. Pattison, *Music and Poetry of the English Renaissance*, esp. pp. 61–88.

45. *Grove's Dictionary of Music and Musicians*, 5th ed. (London: Macmillan, 1966), V, 94b.

46. Music for Donne's poems is given by Gardner in an appendix to *The Elegies and the Songs and Sonnets* and by J. T. Shawcross in *The Complete Poetry of John Donne* (New York: Doubleday, 1967). A setting by Ferrabosco, "The Expiration," appeared in his *Ayres* (1609), another by Corkine, "Breake of Day," in the *Second Book of Ayres* (1612). Four settings in MS cannot be dated exactly. Thomas Ford, who set "The Lamentations of Jeremy," published *Musicke of Sundrie*

Kindes in 1607, became musician to Prince Henry in 1611 and to Charles I in 1626; he died in 1648. John Coprario or Cooper, who set "The Message," was born c. 1575, active from c. 1604. He taught William and Henry Lawes. Like Donne he contributed a lament on the death of Prince Henry, and music for two masques at the marriage of Frances Howard and Robert Car, for which Donne wrote an epithalamium. He died in 1626.

47. Walton, p. 269.
48. Martz, pp. 8–9.
49. Playford, sig. a2^v.
50. MacDonald, *England's Antiphon* (London: Macmillan, 1869), p. 2.

3.

John Donne: Liturgy, Meditation, and Song

1. Meditation

Precise definition of meditation is difficult: it is a protean form, often adjusted to suit different times and temperaments. Its historical roots go back through many devotional writers to St. Augustine and earlier. In the sixteenth and seventeenth centuries, however, meditation came to have a fairly specific ✓ meaning. The most influential figure in this revitalization was Ignatius Loyola, author of *The Spiritual Exercises* and a major force in the Catholic Counter-Reformation. There were other important authorities, such as Luis de la Puente, or in England the Jesuit Robert Persons and, among Protestants, Richard Rogers, Joseph Hall, and Richard Baxter.[1]

Meditation is a discursive form of mental prayer, in which, ideally, all the faculties are engaged. Augustine Baker gives a good preliminary definition:

✓ *Meditation* is such an Internall Prayer, in which a Devout Soule doth in the first place take in hand the consideration

36

of some particular *Mystery of Faith,* to the end that by a serious and exact search into the severall points and circumstances in it with the Understanding or Imagination, she may extract Motives of good Affections to God, and consequently produce suitable Affections in vertue of the said Motives, as long as such vertue will last.[2]

Ordinarily the matter to be meditated on would be found in the Bible or other religious writings. Treatises on meditation often speak of a threefold process in the meditation itself. *Memory* recalls the particular mystery to mind. *Understanding* considers it in detail. The *will* then produces good motives such as revulsion from sin or love toward God. These, according to St. Augustine and most scholastic theologians, are the three higher faculties of the soul. Memory, however, is rarely dwelt on by devotional writers or faculty psychologists. Instead, most meditative treatises emphasize the second stage, exact and discursive use of the understanding. Baker also mentions *imagination*—the power of the mind that takes images from the senses and manipulates and rearranges them internally.

What particularly characterizes seventeenth-century meditation is complex and subtle intellectual analysis (to feed and persuade the understanding) and vividly realized imagery (for the imagination and passions to work on). Emphasis on imagination and understanding led to such techniques as "composition of place." For instance, if one is to meditate on a biblical incident or mystery, the scene is vividly, even painstakingly, imagined. The English Jesuit Richard Gibbons suggests reading geographies, noting well "the distance from one place to another, the height of the hills, and the situation of the townes and villages." [3] If this seems trivial advice, we may remember how much attention Milton paid to similar matters in preparing himself to write *Paradise Lost*—even buying new geographies after he went blind. Similarly, Henry Vaughan created an inner biblical landscape for himself, so he can walk among sacred events in his poetry.

Another technique resulting from emphasis on imagination is called "composition by similitude." When one meditates, he should not try to analyze an abstraction but embody his subject in concrete terms. Thus to meditate on death, hard to picture in itself, Gibbons advises us to imagine "our selves laied on our bed, forsaken of the Physitians, compassed about with our weeping friends, and expecting our last agony." [4] These techniques can be further intensified if the meditator puts himself into some relation with the event being meditated on. Martz notes that the treatises suggest three ways of doing this. One may put himself into the scene—kneeling off to one side of the hill at Golgotha, for example. Or he may move the event, imagining it taking place before his eyes in the present world. Or he may imagine the mystery taking place in his heart. The application or fulfillment of biblical events within oneself was a particular favorite of Puritan writers and preachers.

Instead of using books, an alternative was to meditate on the "Book of Creatures," as the natural world was sometimes called. Nature was viewed as the great complement to Scripture. In it traces of the Creator might everywhere be seen. Sir Thomas Browne writes: "The world was made to be inhabited by beasts, but studied and contemplated by man." [5] Meditation on the creatures is based on the ancient analogical view, which presupposes elaborate correspondences between the world's parts and assumes a divine harmony and order in nature. The "law of cause and effect," just beginning to displace this analogical way of perceiving things, as yet lacked the force given it by mechanistic science and the theories of Newton and Laplace. Hobbes was already proclaiming the new era, but old ways lingered.[6]

Many spiritual treatises speak of a ladder or scale that the soul climbs toward God. One common division concerns the subject matter of one's meditations. Progress begins with the "purgative way," meditation on such subjects as sin, death, judgment, and hell. Baker, like St. Ignatius and others, advises most individuals to start here: "Let her begin with the matter of the *Purgative way* . . . And let her abide in the Exercises of that way, till she finds in her selfe *an aversion from Sin,* and that much of the *Feare* and remorse that were formerly in her, are deposed, so that she is come to have some good measure of Confi-

dence in God." [7] The purpose of such meditations is not simply
to raise up fears of sin, death, and judgment but (as in tragedy)
to purge these fears. Not everyone is alike, however: "Therfore
scrupulous and fearefull souls even in the beginning a[r]e to be
forbidden the Exercises of Terrour." [8] Perhaps Donne, in his
"Holy Sonnets" and elsewhere, was attempting to purge himself
of the fear of death and judgment, raising in order to exorcise
the terrors to which he was prone.

After the soul passes through the purgative way, it progresses to the "illuminative way." According to Baker, this way
involves meditations "whose matter or argument is some *Mystery of Faith* touching *our Lords Life, Passion* etc. and which are
apt to beget and encrease *Humility, Patience* and other Vertues
in her." [9] Within the illuminative way there are also traditional
progressions: for example, from the testament of law to the
testament of spirit (a favorite with Protestants) or from the
blessed mysteries of the Annunciation and Nativity, through
the sorrowful mysteries of Christ's Passion and death, to the
glorious mysteries of his Resurrection and Ascension (the pattern on which the rosary is based). By "illuminative" is meant
not merely intellectual understanding but engagement of all
the faculties and gradual incorporation of the mysteries or
meditated materials into the inner life of the soul: or, to put it
another way, an *imitatio Christi* or inward regeneration. When
the illuminative way is followed for some time it changes insensibly into the "unitive way." But at this point, properly speaking, the soul transcends meditation and enters the realm of
contemplation.

The goal of a meditative exercise, it was generally agreed,
is in its last stages: emotions, acts of the will, determinations of
amendment, colloquies with God. Without this kind of outcome
the exercise would be meaningless. Inevitably, as methods grew
more complex and manuals of devotion proliferated, the ends
were sometimes lost sight of among the techniques. Baker protests against "the too common Practise, in which *Meditation* is
made rather a study and speculation, then an exercise of the
spirit." There should, he writes, be no more time spent on
"inventing *Motives*" and "internall discoursings"—that is, use of

imagination and understanding—"then shall be necessary to move the will to good Affections." [10] St. Francis de Sales, in *The Introduction to the Devout Life,* urges that meditations be kept "as simple as possible" and states that unless they issue in practical results they are "useless," even "harmful." [11] In a similar vein many English Puritans and Anglicans wrote impatiently of technical methods and stressed practical, heartfelt application to the self.[12]

The main drawbacks of meditation, as perceived by both Catholics and Protestants, were twofold. First, it was in danger of becoming too elaborate or intellectual, of existing for its own sake. With devotion, as with poetry, technique is ideally subordinated to a larger end. Second, meditation was not for everyone. Jean-Pierre Camus argues in *The Spiritual Combat* (1631) that most people find a "kind of simple contemplation" easier and more natural than formal meditation.[13] Augustine Baker argues again and again that contemplation is often possible to those who cannot meditate. Meditation, he writes, "is a Prayer to the exercise whereof all sorts of Persons are neither disposed, nor enabled. . . . the more that a Soule doth abound with Devotion and good Affections to God, the lesse is she enabled or disposed thereto." [14] If the purpose of meditation is to arouse affections and direct the will, then those who already "abound with devotion and good affections" need not trouble themselves with laborious intellectual or imaginative exercises. A less formal kind of meditation, such as the Salesian method, might be appropriate, or they might find meditation of any kind irrelevant and even harmful. Baker was not alone in making this point: that different souls follow different paths was a spiritual commonplace, though occasionally lost sight of through enthusiasm for one method or another.

2. Donne and Meditation

Except for relatively minor writers like Alabaster or Southwell, Donne is the most purely meditative of the English devotional poets. Two reasons may be postulated: training and natural disposition. Donne came of a devout and stubbornly Catholic family. His brother died in prison for religion, his uncle was head of the Jesuit order in England, his mother remained faithful to the old religion. Donne himself eventually and rather painfully became an Anglican. But as was often the case, his devotional methods maintained a continuity that bridged his religious conversion. Thus (if Donne wrote the "Holy Sonnets" in 1609 as Gardner convincingly argues) he found no difficulty in using Ignatian devotional methods at the very time he was helping Morton with his anti-Roman polemics and writing *Pseudo-Martyr,* and only a year before his violently anti-Jesuit tract *Ignatius His Conclave.* No paradox is involved: Donne was simply following the well-worn practice of spoiling the Egyptians, or as Gardner puts it, "taking the corn and leaving the chaff." [15]

While religious training sufficiently accounts for Alabaster's sonnets, it cannot wholly explain those poems where the method takes fire. Donne's "Holy Sonnets" are a witness not only to his training in Ignatian meditation but to his personality and poetic genius. Reading his poetry, secular and sacred, one is likely to have a strong impression of poetic personality, which has seemed to many critics to be both passionate and intellectual: fusing, at its best, strong feelings and precise rationality and vivid, wide-ranging imagination. These gifts, especially suited to a "Metaphysical" poet, reveal a personality also suited to the Ignatian method of meditation.

If one compares the religious poetry of Donne and Herbert, certain differences are immediately apparent. This may in part be an accident in devotional training, especially Donne's early exposure to Jesuit methods. Probably it also results from a difference in devotional personalities. Herbert, in spite of aridities and counter-impulses, looks very much like one of those people described by Baker, who abound in good affections and natural devotion and need not whip themselves up to produce proper feelings. Donne, however, in spite of obviously strong emotions, seems to need deliberate efforts of intellect and imagination before his feelings are raised or his will rightly directed. This seems true of many of the love poems as well as most of the religious poems. Neither Donne nor Herbert is necessarily superior from a devotional standpoint, or more advanced; rather, they take different paths.

3. "La Corona"

Not all of Donne's religious poems are primarily meditative. Those dominated by the Ignatian method seem to have been written between 1609, when Donne began the "Holy Sonnets," and 1613, when he finished "Goodfriday, 1613." The two Anniversaries, also influenced by meditation, were published in 1611 and 1612. *"La Corona,"* among the earliest of Donne's divine poems, reveals a mixture of devotional methods. In a letter to Mrs. Herbert printed by Walton, Donne writes: "I commit the inclosed *Holy Hymns* and *Sonnets* . . . to your judgment." There follows Donne's sonnet "To the Lady *Magdalen Herbert,"* which concludes by urging her to "Harbour these *Hymns"* addressed to the "dear name" of Christ. Walton dates the letter 11 July 1607, though the correct date may be a year later.[16] Although Walton says "these *Hymns* are now lost to us," editors since Grierson agree that letter and poem probably refer to *"La Corona."* These sonnets, Gardner argues, unlike the later ones "may properly be called hymns, since they unite the elements of prayer and praise." [17]

"*La Corona*" is neither a group of poems nor a single poem, but a tightly woven "crown" of sonnets more closely related than the traditional sonnet sequences. Martz and Gardner exaggerate only slightly when they insist that "properly speaking, there are no individual sonnets here. We have one poem, one corona." [18] This unity is achieved both by subject and technique. Technically, the poems are drawn together by interlocking first and last lines and by alternating rhyme schemes in the sestets, so Sonnets 1, 3, 5 have one form and 2, 4, 6, 7 another. In the text of 1633 the sonnets are separately numbered and (except the first) titled. They cannot stand separately yet are not precisely a single poem. The obvious analogy, of structure and subject, is the rosary. Gardner cites the traditional rosary, while Martz proposes the "corona of our Lord," a rosary of thirty-three aves and a sevenfold division of subject.[19]

The rosary was a popular devotion among Catholics, but most Protestants were suspicious or scornful of it. They objected to the use of beads and crucifix and condemned the rote repetition of words. Spenser characteristically gave a set of beads to his sinister hermit Archimago. But Catholic practices were often modified and adopted by the Church of England. Donne abandons the objectionable features of the rosary— beads, verbal repetitions, and too-great attention to the Virgin—yet retains much of his original. What chiefly characterizes the rosary as a devotion is that it is at once vocal and meditative. That is also what is most noticeable about the devotional technique of *"La Corona"*: it is part vocal prayer or "hymn," part meditation.

The first sonnet might be called "Advent." As Gardner points out, "its leading ideas and much of its phrasing are derived from the Advent Offices in the Roman Breviary." [20] Like Advent, the poem is a preparation, which poet and reader undergo in order to ready themselves for the mysteries of the remaining sonnets. Determination and dedication are stressed: "With a strong sober thirst, my soule attends." Some critics find these poems cold and passionless; they are not, but their mode is less personal and more nearly liturgical than the later "Holy Sonnets." The first sonnet dedicates the cycle to Christ, whom it addresses, and prays that poem and poet be accepted. It ends with the voice of Isaiah or John the Baptist, crying in the wilderness and making straight the path of the Lord:

'Tis time that heart and voice be lifted high,
Salvation to all that will is nigh.

These lines recall the vocal nature of this prayer, which (recalling conventional descriptions of divine song) is a lifting up of heart and voice together.

The second sonnet, addressed to Mary, is a meditation on the Annunciation, but not discursive or visual in the Ignatian manner. Instead, it consists of the traditional Christmas

paradoxes, as celebrated in primers and ancient hymns to the
Virgin.

> That All, which alwayes is All every where,
> Which cannot sinne, and yet all sinnes must beare,
> Which cannot die, yet cannot chuse but die,
> Loe, faithfull Virgin, yeelds himselfe to lye
> In prison, in thy wombe.

Although the speaker addresses Mary, the emphasis is on
Christ and the mystery of the Incarnation. Paradox follows
paradox, with increasing wonder and gratitude. Intellect is
used to produce intellectual humility:

> Ere by the spheares time was created, thou
> Wast in his minde, who is thy Sonne, and Brother,
> Whom thou conceiv'st, conceiv'd; yea thou art now
> Thy Makers maker, and thy Fathers mother,
> Thou'hast light in darke; and shutst in little roome,
> *Immensity cloysterd in thy deare wombe.*

As the weight of the first poem falls on salvation, announced to
all who will hear, here it falls on the "immensity" of God and of
this mystery. Yet, in characteristic seventeenth-century fashion,
the humanity of mother and child are never lost sight of. Immensity is cloistered in "thy dear womb."

The third poem, again addressed to Mary, begins in a similar devotional style with continued paradox:

> *Immensitie cloysterd in thy deare wombe,*
> Now leaves his welbelov'd imprisonment,
> There he hath made himselfe to his intent
> Weake enough, now into our world to come.

The second quatrain moves toward a more imaginative form of
meditation:

> But Oh, for thee, for him, hath th' Inne no roome?
> Yet lay him in this stall, and from the Orient,

Starres, and wisemen will travell to prevent
Th' effect of *Herods* jealous generall doome.

This quatrain, which visualizes slightly and puts the reader into
a slight relation with the scene by speaking of *"this* stall," is
transitional. The sestet is formal meditation. Turning from the
Virgin, the speaker addresses his own soul, directing it to look
with feeling on the Nativity events:

Seest thou, my Soule, with thy faiths eyes, how he
Which fils all place, yet none holds him, doth lye?
Was not his pity towards thee wondrous high,
That would have need to be pittied by thee?
Kisse him, and with him into Egypt goe,
With his kinde mother, who partakes thy woe. ✓

Donne is using the highly developed meditative technique of
putting himself (and the reader) into the scene. Not only does
he look on it with "faiths eyes," but he goes right up to kiss the
threatened child and accompanies him and his sorrowing
mother into Egypt.

The fourth poem, "Temple," addresses Joseph, who is
told, "turne backe; see where your child doth sit." But if "see"
leads us to expect a visual picture, we are disappointed. What
we and Joseph see is not an object but a metaphor: the child
Jesus blowing out "sparks of wit" among the Doctors. The
poem returns to the earlier mode of paradox and wonder,
abandoning visual meditation for a more vocal mode.

The fifth poem, "Crucyfying," begins without a specific
address—the only place in the cycle that this occurs. The
speaker assumes a narrative mode and describes Christ in the
third person. Paradoxes continue, quietly for a few lines, then
suddenly bursting into violent emotion:

By miracles exceeding power of man,
Hee faith in some, envie in some begat,
For, what weake spirits admire, ambitious, hate;
In both affections many to him ran,
But Oh! the worst are most, they will and can,

Alas, and do, unto the immaculate,
Whose creature Fate is, now prescribe a Fate,
Measuring selfe-lifes infinity to'a span,
Nay to an inch.

As in the "Holy Sonnets," the closing in of time before death moves Donne powerfully. At this point, he turns from narrative to address an unspecified audience which can only be the reader or himself. In a brief but intense meditation Christ is seen carrying his Cross toward Golgotha:

Loe, where condemned hee
Beares his owne crosse, with paine, yet by and by
When it beares him, he must beare more and die.

The meditation is not primarily visual: The brief image of Christ carrying his Cross is immediately drawn into further paradoxes. The senses are not evoked at length, yet the paradoxes have great emotional weight.

The last three lines of "Crucyfying" describe the Crucifixion itself. Still no time is spent on visualizing the scene or raising emotions by imaginative effects. These elaborate measures are unnecessary, for the emotions are there without them:

Now thou art lifted up, draw mee to thee,
And at thy death giving such liberall dole,
Moyst, with one drop of thy blood, my dry soule.

For the second time in this sonnet the speaker changes his mode of address and speaks directly to Christ on the Cross. Most readers—especially the practiced meditators of the seventeenth century—could not help but have some sort of visual picture in their minds when reading these lines. But it is the reader's creation without much help from the poem. The last lines are more vocal prayer than meditation; or they are the colloquy to a meditation that never takes place.

The nature of the Crucifixion sonnet may be better grasped by comparing its last lines with a similar scene in

"Goodfriday, 1613." [In "*La Corona*," the speaker prays for a
single drop of blood to moisten his dry soul. In "Goodfriday,"
he cannot bear to see Christ's blood, the seat of men's souls,
"Make durt of dust."] If this reading (supported by the best
manuscripts but not 1633) is correct, Donne gives his reader a
powerful picture, visual and even tactile, of the drops of
Christ's blood falling to the ground below the Cross, turning
dust to dirt with their moisture. [Both poems make the same
theological point about salvation through atonement, but one
uses a meditative approach to drive its point home and the
other does not. This does not mean the earlier poem is missing
something or expresses less passion; only that its method is
different.]

The sixth sonnet continues to address Christ, but now an
indefinite Christ no longer hanging on the cross. Although its
title is "Resurrection," that mystery is scarcely mentioned.
Donne turns instead from Christ to his own inner life and follows the drop of blood from the crucified Christ of the previous
sonnet into the depths of his own heart:

> *Moyst with one drop of thy blood, my dry soule*
> Shall (though she now be in extreme degree
> Too stony hard, and yet too fleshly,) bee
> Freed by that drop, from being starv'd, hard, or foule,
> And life, by this death abled, shall controule
> Death, whom thy death slue; nor shall to mee
> Feare of first or last death, bring miserie,
> If in thy little booke my name thou enroule.

Resurrection is ordinarily a "glorious" mystery, but Donne
characteristically dwells instead on death and the fear of dying.
For him, resurrection is apprehended by passing first through
death, a theological truism here felt as well as thought:

> If in thy little booke my name thou enroule,
> Flesh in that long sleep is not putrified,
> But made that there, of which, and for which 'twas;
> Nor can by other meanes be glorified.

May then sinnes sleep, and deaths soone from me passe,
That wak't from both, I againe risen may
Salute the last, and everlasting day.

Resurrection finally appears: not Christ's, however, as one might expect in a sequence of sonnets on his life, but the speaker's.

The glory and exultation of the crowning mysteries of faith, held back in "Resurrection," find full expression in the last sonnet of the sequence: "Ascention." It opens with an address to the triumphant saints, blessed martyrs who have passed through suffering and death to emerge in glory. They (and the reader) are told to "Behold the Highest": to look on Christ in Majesty as he will appear at the Second Coming. No exact picture of this event can be given. Instead, what the saints "behold," following on their sorrow being turned to joy, their filth to cleanliness, is the apocalyptic metaphor, expressed mainly by darkness being transformed to an inconceivable light. This is more a matter for direct emotional or spiritual apprehension than discursive reason. The octave is less a meditation than a paean or hymn. So too the sestet, which closes both sonnet and sequence with a last address to Christ, now in triumph:

O strong Ramme, which hast batter'd heaven for mee,
Mild lambe, which with thy blood, hast mark'd the path;
Bright torch, which shin'st, that I the way may see,
Oh, with thine owne blood quench thine owne just wrath,
And if thy holy Spirit, my Muse did raise,
Deigne at my hands this crowne of prayer and praise.

The titles of Christ—"strong Ramme," "Mild lambe," "Bright torch"—though they include pictorial qualities, do not build an imaginary scene. Rather they are evocations of the Christ who is addressed and sought and of the wished-for responses of the heart, which, softened and purified by the sequence and the drop of blood, responds now to this exultant lifting up of heart and voice. The strong affections are reinforced by powerful rhythms, pauses, and elisions. Only two words in six lines are

so med creates risval image
(hymn has aural force)

not monosyllables. The result is a sonnet best described as a potent and triumphant hymn. Outside of the sermons there is nothing else like it in Donne.

One continuing subject of *"La Corona"* is close to the nature of devotion itself: the relationship between God and man and especially the human response to the entry of God into the world. This response is presented throughout as potentially or actually double. Either man accepts or he rejects. The theme is broached in the first sonnet, when the speaker confronts the "All changing unchang'd Antient of dayes" and asks him to accept his "muses white sincerity." He seeks not earthly bays but an eternal crown and prays to achieve the correct stance toward earth and heaven. Then comes the Annunciation, made not to all but "all that will." In "Nativitie," the stars and wise men come to worship but Herod reacts oppositely with his "jealous generall doome." The Holy Family must flee into Egypt, and all the poet as spectator can do is show his allegiance by kissing the baby and joining them in exile. Back in the Temple, the child is found both blowing and blowing out the "sparks of wit" which he, as *Logos,* created in the Doctors' souls. A two-sided reaction to his wisdom is implied. His miracles too cause a double reaction of increasing intensity. In some faith is begotten, in others envy. Some admire, some hate. Filled with strong affections, men are pictured running toward Christ, their passions transformed into violent motion. Tragically, of those who come running, "the worst are most." Because the response of hate is commoner than that of love, Christ must die.

When the poet turns from the outward scene in the sixth poem and probes within himself, it is to follow the drop of Christ's blood into his stony and sinful heart. He too is potentially one of those who react against divine intervention. Instead of celebrating the Ascension with a "white sincerity," perhaps he is among those who brought about the Crucifixion. This marks a turning point in the sequence. Up to this moment, none of the poems (even "Annunciation," which dwells on sin, death, and imprisonment) is free of man's dark and violent state. But through violence, suffering, and death the triumphant mood of the glorious mysteries is finally reached. Those who throughout the sequence respond to Christ with hatred disappear from the last sonnet, their judgment omitted from the final vision. Only those responding with love are seen, a company whom the poet hopes to join.

Although Donne speaks frequently of "I," these are the least personal of his divine poems and among the least personal of any he wrote. In this respect, *"La Corona"* is uncharacteristic of Donne, whose constant focus is introspectively upon himself. Usually concerned with his own thoughts and feelings, he seldom turns to an outward event or another person without soon turning back inward to examine his reactions to that event or person. In *"La Corona,"* however, Donne introduces himself differently, with complete objective control. He first appears in order to dedicate himself to right intentions. Next he kisses the baby and follows him into Egypt. Then he presents his soul to be moistened by Christ's saving blood. Finally, he prays that Christ will lead him to eternal life. Nowhere do we find either the biographical or the role-playing Donne so often at the center of his poems. (Even his late hymn, publicly sung, puns on his name and addresses his peculiar spiritual difficulties.) There is none of that in *"La Corona."* Instead, the "I" is a kind of Christian everyman, with whom the reader can assimilate and identify.

What might appear an exception is the "I" as poet who appears in the first sonnet. But this is a generalized poet, not expressing himself idiosyncratically but (he hopes) acting as mouthpiece and channel for divine inspiration. We find Donne, in the first and last sonnets, speaking seriously of his muse, as if he were Spenser or Milton and not the man who banished the classical gods with all they represent. If the poet fails, "muse" will be only another name for himself. If he succeeds, his muse will be raised and animated by the Holy Spirit, and the poems will be a worthy gift for Christ, a "crowne of prayer and praise," God's work and not his. He will be rewarded not with a poet's bays, the fruit of earthly ambition, but a saint's eternal crown. The corona of sonnets, which moves forward through Christ's life to its triumphant outcome, also moves upward through the stages of the soul's regeneration to the same end. At the same time, the last sonnet circles back to the first. At the close, the poet's soul, having passed through the mysteries, encounters the fullest expression of divine grace which it sought all along. His muse, inspired by Christ's triumph and raised by the Spirit, is ready to make a true beginning.

Not much is gained by arguing whether the sonnets of "La Corona" are superior or inferior to the better-known later sonnets. Certainly they have had less critical attention, and probably most readers of Donne come to them late if at all. They are less striking than the "Holy Sonnets" and less readily separable from the context of their sequence, thus disappointing the modern preference for brief and passionate lyrics. Yet they have a peculiar excellence among Donne's poems, which resides in their impersonality. This makes them seem less immediately powerful or disturbing, yet more durable as devotional exercises or poems read repeatedly. Their language, method, and tone are liturgical or hymnlike.

Though intended for private use, the Corona sonnets are close to public discipline and communion of feeling. The "Holy Sonnets," more dramatic and idiosyncratic, sometimes direct attention to themselves instead of serving as vehicles for meditation. Feelings find a vehicle in the Corona sonnets: more vivid use of meditative imagery might stir them more strongly at first, but would not work so well after many readings. The emotions in "La Corona" are ordered and objectified in such a way that the sequence bears repetition and may be used like a liturgical prayer or a hymn that is sung many times yet keeps its potency for lifting up the heart with the voice. The Corona sonnets are not, of course, literally hymn or song texts, but they share the pronounced vocal and liturgical qualities of these forms.

4. "A Litanie"

Donne's major religious poem between the two groups of sonnets, "A Litanie," was probably written during an illness in 1608. Traditionally, a litany is a liturgical prayer, intended for public use./\Donne's poem, as he tells Goodyer, is designed for the private use of his friends. There are degrees of privacy. Some poems are written for self-expression and the poet's personal use, others, like *"La Corona,"* are sent to friends. These poems, like the office books and primers, may be semi-liturgical. To be effective in this role they require a certain objectivity and universality. If an "I" appears in them, it must be an "I" with whom others can identify.

So far as they can be dated, all Donne's earlier religious poems share this semi-liturgical quality. That Donne intended them for the use of others is supported by the letters to Mrs. Herbert and Goodyer: both from what he says and from the fact that he encloses copies for his friends' use. Helen Gardner has described the personal circumstances in which Donne composed the poems.[21] It was a period of illness and spiritual dejection, reflected by *Biathanatos,* his tract on suicide, and *Pseudo-Martyr,* his argument that English Recusants who died for their faith (among them his brother) were not true martyrs. Donne had abandoned the Roman Catholicism of his youth but was not yet entirely sure of his motives in converting to Anglicanism. His scruples and searchings of conscience are reflected in "A Litanie." Yet from them Donne succeeded in creating what Gardner rightly calls his most characteristically Anglican poem. Anti-asceticism, reasonable piety, acceptance of a middle way, development of a right attitude toward the saints (neither idolatrous nor iconoclastic): these are the interrelated themes running through the poem.

A traditional litany consists largely of prayers to the saints, and for that reason it was not an easy form for the Anglican Church to adapt. Donne could not say *ora pro nobis* to a saint without violating his Church's articles. He gets around the problem not (as Gardner suggests) by continuous and precarious ingenuity, but by the simplest method possible. He pays the saints their due respects but avoids praying for their intercession simply by addressing the entire litany to God. Donne, plainly aware of speaker and audience in his poems and always handling them for the best dramatic effect, could be expected to find this solution. He constantly alerts the reader to the position by addressing God directly with the words "thy" and "thou" near the beginning of most of the stanzas on the saints. And he speaks of, but not to, "thine Angels," "thy Patriarches," "Thy Eagle-sighted Prophets." Yet at the same time these saints are always found praying for the speaker, warding off evils, begging, obtaining favors for him. The subtle but firm handling of saintly intercession is summed up in the stanza that concludes this section:

> And whil'st this universall Quire,
> That Church in triumph, this in warfare here,
>   Warm'd with one all-partaking fire
> Of love, that none be lost, which cost thee deare,
>   Pray ceaslesly, 'and thou hearken too,
>   (Since to be gratious
> Our taske is treble, to pray, beare, and doe)
> Heare this prayer Lord, O Lord deliver us
> From trusting in those prayers, though powr'd out thus.

The distinctions Donne makes are certainly subtle, but his tone is not that of a hair-splitter. Feelings of warmth and love, of wished-for community with the "universall Quire" of the Church, pervade these lines. If Donne cannot give more, he could scarcely find a more gracious way of saying so.

Another significant aspect of Donne's rhetorical strategy is his use of "I" and "we." Liturgical prayer can employ either form. In the creed the tradition is "I believe," while in the Lord's prayer and the litany it is "our Father" and "pray for us." "I" is not necessarily private nor "we" public. Their interchangeability is suggested by current Roman Catholic practice: "credo" in the Latin creed and "we believe" in English. Donne, in "A Litanie," uses both forms with what appears to be considerable care. The result is to call indirectly to mind by the use of "we" the universal relationship between God and the corporate Church or all mankind, and by the use of "I" the individual relationship between God and the soul—the speaker's or the reader's. Donne's usage in the first part of the poem is illustrated by the first stanza:

Father of Heaven, and him, by whom
It, and us for it, and all else, for us
Thou madest, and govern'st ever, come
And re-create mee, now growne ruinous:
My heart is by dejection, clay,
And by selfe-murder, red.
From this red earth, O Father, purge away
All vicious tinctures, that new fashioned
I may rise up from death, before I'am dead.

When Donne moves from the plural pronoun to the singular, he is not shifting from mankind to John Donne but from a universal to a personal relationship. There is nothing peculiar to Donne or necessarily autobiographical in the "I" of "A Litanie"; any reader can equate it with himself. What Donne accomplishes by the shift is to internalize and drive home to the reader matters that might otherwise seem external to him. The method of the second stanza is similar:

O Sonne of God, who seeing two things,
Sinne, and death crept in, which were never made,
By bearing one, tryed'st with what stings
The other could thine heritage invade;
O be thou nail'd unto my heart,
And crucified againe,
Part not from it, though it from thee would part,
But let it be by applying so thy paine,
Drown'd in thy blood, and in thy passion slaine.

Donne uses a recognized meditative technique, imagining that the Crucifixion is occuring within himself, but embodies it in a metaphysical conceit as forceful as the famous "bracelet of bright haire about the bone."

"A Litanie" recurrently employs the imaginative techniques of meditation, though seldom as formally as here. These meditations occur, however, within a context that, appropriate to the genre, is primarily vocal. The personal and meditative is outweighed by the liturgical. Though not a song text, the poem often approaches song:

Thy Eagle-sighted Prophets too,
Which were thy Churches Organs, and did sound
That harmony, which made of two
One law, and did unite, but not confound;
Those heavenly Poëts which did see
Thy will, and it expresse
In rythmique feet, in common pray for mee,
That I by them excuse not my excesse
In seeking secrets, or Poëtiquenesse.

The public mode of this stanza is appropriate because it balances what is otherwise the most nearly autobiographical of the self-references in "A Litanie." "I" refers here not to everyman or potential readers but to the poet who is writing the poem.

As in "La Corona," Donne is concerned with the problem of religious poetry, which should be written not for ambition or personal advantage but, in the Jesuit phrase, ad majorem Dei gloriam. If such poetry has a worldly purpose, it is as a vehicle for devotion, either for the poet or for his readers. Herbert and Marvell both reveal themselves aware like Donne of the problem of eliminating self-interest from sacred poetry. One way would be to eliminate "I" entirely, but that would be foreign to Donne's genius as it is revealed in poetry and sermons alike. The other Metaphysical Poets, and Milton too, made the same choice: not to eliminate the poet but to objectify him. Donne appropriately appears as poet in the stanza on the prophets because they are the perfect models for him to emulate, "heavenly Poëts" who channel God's word through the "rhythmique feet" of poetry, as Donne himself would wish to do.

In the second part, Donne turns from his description of the praying saints to a series of direct petitions to God:

From being anxious, or secure,
Dead clods of sadnesse, or light squibs of mirth,
From thinking, that great courts immure
All, or no happinesse, or that this earth
Is only for our prison fram'd,
Or that thou art covetous

> To them whom thou lov'st, or that they are maim'd
> From reaching this worlds sweet, who seek thee thus,
> With all their might, Good Lord deliver us.

As the litany grows more personal and inward, Donne abandons his double use of "I" and "we" and speaks only of "we." He may, of course, have been guided by the traditional refrains on which he plays changes: "Lord deliver us" and "Lord hear us." But the function of these phrases as congregational responses to the priest no longer obtains; the poem, though conceived as vocal prayer, is to be recited not antiphonally but in the single voices of his private friends. Probably Donne retained only "we" in the last part because he was still concerned with balance: the more corporate form balances the more inward nature of the devotion. When speaking of the angels and saints the important thing was to internalize; poet and reader are led to relate these outward matters to themselves. When the focus turns inward, however, Donne logically shifts from internalization to objectification.

In keeping with its genre, "A Litanie" remains to the end in the world of sin, sorrow, and petition. The note of glory is heard not in its conclusion but earlier, when the speaker turns from himself to the saints. It is heard in the rhythmic feet of the eagle-sighted prophets, seen in the "illustrious Zodiacke" of the Twelve Apostles, triumphs in the "Virgin Squadron of white Confessors" and the universal choir of the whole Church. In *"La Corona,"* the poet is enabled by the drop of blood to participate in the mysteries of the Resurrection and Ascension, with the full note of triumph coming at the end. Christ's blood appears again at the close of "A Litanie":

> Sonne of God heare us, and since thou
> By taking our blood, owest it us againe,
>   Gaine to thy selfe, or us allow;
> And let not both us and thy selfe be slaine;
>   O lambe of God, which took'st our sinne
>   Which could not stick to thee,
> O let it not returne to us againe,
> But Patient and Physition being free,
> As sinne is nothing, let it no where be.

Petition and self-abasement persist to the last. While the subject of the final stanza is salvation, the glories of heaven and the Church Triumphant have no part in it. Donne concludes not that God is all but that sin is nothing. One need not assume, however, that Donne's "dejection" has grown more despairing than the "low devout melancholie" of the previous year. The triumphant evocation of the saints contradicts such a theory. The difference is rather one of poetic genre and devotional mode. *"La Corona,"* a rosary poem, takes the reader through the full cycle of blessed, sorrowful, and glorious mysteries in the life of Christ, who appears in the end as the strong ram and mild lamb of apocalypse. The emphasis is on him, and the speaker is swept up in his victory. In "A Litanie," a petitionary poem, the closing emphasis is on the speaker. The "lambe of God" is invoked but not seen. Greater distance is preserved between the glories of heaven and the petitioner; what closeness there is is mainly in suffering and sorrow: Christ and the speaker touch in the mystery of blood. Donne may have chosen to write in such a genre for personal reasons, when his life had ebbed low, but having made his choice he wrote appropriately to the genre of poetry and mode of devotion to which "A Litanie" belongs: vocal and petitionary, with local admixture of meditation.

5. "Holy Sonnets"

The "Holy Sonnets" mark a new departure in Donne's religious poetry. Those poems that can be dated earlier show a balance between liturgical and private forms, vocal prayer and meditation. In the "Holy Sonnets" this balance is abandoned, and Donne turns to Ignatian meditation for the structure and texture of his poetry and the primary method of his devotion. No gradual increase in the meditative mode is observable in the poems leading up to the "Holy Sonnets." The change is abrupt. Even a casual reader, knowing nothing about devotional modes, senses something quite different when he comes to these poems. Why Donne should have turned so enthusiastically to Ignatian meditation in 1609 can only be speculated on.

His primary inspiration need not have been the *Spiritual Exercises,* since other sources, Catholic and Protestant, were many. Doubtless the Jesuits who stayed at his home during childhood were an influence on him. Paradoxically, it may have been a re-reading of Jesuit materials during his controversial attacks on them at this time that led to renewed interest in their method of prayer.

As Gardner notes, most critics and readers prefer the "Holy Sonnets" to Donne's earlier religious verse because they "give an immediate impression of spontaneity." [22] They seem more intensely emotional and more genuinely self-expressive than *"La Corona"* or "A Litanie." What has appealed to readers, however, is really less a matter of greater genuineness than a shift in technique. All these poems are vehicles for passion, all of them perhaps equally genuine. But the meditative techniques of the "Holy Sonnets" appeal more openly and powerfully to the imagination than the mixed techniques of the earlier poems. Technically, this accounts both for their peculiar strengths and weaknesses. They appeal especially to the imagination. They are designed to stimulate emotion. Their kind of devotion is immediately accessible to unpracticed readers. At the same time, as Gardner suggests, they are in danger of falling into exaggeration, emotional violence, and strain. The "deliberate stimulation of emotion" may overdramatize and falsify the very feelings it attempts to stir up.[23] Moreover, they may appeal more quickly but wear less well. Imagery calculated to shock and carry the reader by storm may not be so effective the second time, or the third, or the tenth. More than one critic has said that *"La Corona"* and "A Litanie" improve with long and close acquaintance: one would not think (or perhaps need) to say that about the "Holy Sonnets."

The "Holy Sonnets" are not all poetically equal. Yet in spite of an occasional falling off in the poetry or the devotional method, at their best they are unexcelled. As so often, Gardner puts her finger on the precise quality of their greatness:

> No other religious poems make us feel so acutely the predicament of the natural man called to be the spiritual man. None present more vividly man's recognition of the gulf

that divides him from God and the effort of faith to lay hold on the miracle by which Christianity declares that the gulf has been bridged.[24]

If emotions are sometimes forced, that too seems genuine; it is the predicament of natural man, who, as Fulke Greville complains, is born to one law, to another bound. It detracts nothing from the poetic or even the devotional quality of Donne's "Holy Sonnets" to say that they represent a protagonist on a low rung of the spiritual scale—perhaps even a protagonist striving to catch hold of the bottom rung. Donne, of course, was not beginning a devotional life in 1609, as his earlier poems sufficiently witness. But he seems to have been laying new foundations for a new start. Spiritual advisers of his time recommend such a course in times of doubt and uncertainty.

The first of the "Holy Sonnets" is a "preparatory prayer" to the main cycle of twelve sonnets.[25] In it, Donne touches on the many reasons why he owes God a debt of allegiance and love. Similar considerations are found at the beginning of many meditative methods: for example, the first meditation on "our creation" in the *Introduction to the Devout Life*. Donne, however, chooses a form more vocal than meditative. The imagery is developed much as it was in *"La Corona"*:

> As due by many titles I resigne
> My selfe to thee, O God, first I was made
> By thee, and for thee, and when I was decay'd
> Thy blood bought that, the which before was thine,
> I am thy sonne, made with thy selfe to shine,
> Thy servant, whose paines thou hast still repaid,
> Thy sheepe, thine Image, and till I betray'd
> My selfe, a temple of thy Spirit divine.

The poem is addressed to God, partly (line 4) in his person as Christ. The octave is not so immediately effective as in some of the other sonnets, because it does not attempt to construct an imaginary scene. Yet it would be an unsympathetic reader who found these lines merely theological or intellectual. As vocal or semi-liturgical prayer they could scarcely be bettered.

The sestet drives home the speaker's predicament with a lament:

> Why doth the devill then usurpe in mee?
> Why doth he steale, nay ravish that's thy right?
> Except thou rise and for thine owne worke fight,
> Oh I shall soone despaire, when I doe see
> That thou lov'st mankind well, yet wilt'not chuse me,
> And Satan hates mee, yet is loth to lose mee.

Donne asserts for the first time the theme that dominates the whole sequence: that the only exit from his predicament is in the hands of God. He himself can do nothing. Whether this is orthodox Augustinian Christianity, Calvinist rigor, or a personal tendency to despair must remain in dispute. There is nothing unorthodox in saying that man can do nothing without God's grace, but much depends on how it is said or qualified. Spenser stresses grace as emphatically as Donne and portrays despair as vividly, but he also reminds us continually of hope. In his poetry the positive prevails at last over the negative, and prevails convincingly. Donne's sermons reach toward such a balance, but his "Holy Sonnets" do not really attempt it.

Sonnet 2 begins with a combination of traditional methods: composition of place and composition by similitude or "congruous thoughts." [26] The soul is summoned by an illness that is like the herald of death. The prospect of death and judgment is made vivid by two interlinked analogies. The soul is like a pilgrim who has committed treason abroad and dares not answer a summons to return home; it is like a condemned thief, haled to the place of execution, desperately wishing himself back in the prison from which he once hoped for deliverance. The sestet still addresses the soul and so is neither petition nor colloquy. It is, however, an attempt to make a resolution based on the foregoing meditation. Faced with its terrible predicament, the soul must seek Christ's grace and wash in his blood. But it is paralyzed by the thought that it cannot seek grace without "grace to beginne"—still further grounds for despair that must somehow be escaped.

The third sonnet draws even closer to death and the judgment that lies beyond:

> This is my playes last scene, here heavens appoint
> My pilgrimages last mile; and my race
> Idly, yet quickly runne, hath this last pace,
> My spans last inch, my minutes latest point,
> And gluttonous death, will instantly unjoynt
> My body, and soule, and I shall sleepe a space,
> But my'ever-waking part shall see that face,
> Whose feare already shakes my every joynt.

Donne combines three traditional methaphors: life as a play, life as a pilgrimage or exile from heaven, and life as St. Paul's footrace. This conventional material is transformed by extreme extension—a method almost synonymous with metaphysical conceit. The last pace, the last inch, the latest point; the images are like a mathematical series converging on zero, the very opposite of the "houres, dayes, months" of the love poems, which suggest expansion to infinity. At the zero point, when the end is reached, death acts "instantly." Donne's figure of death, like the first metaphors, is based on a conventional image: all-devouring, "gluttonous death." But Donne re-creates this image too, not by picturing death in some new detail but by making the act of devouring vivid in a new way. What death does, in a last grimly violent metaphor, is "unjoynt" Donne's soul and body—like someone eating a chicken. The image is not, of course, so specific as that: like Milton's Death, Donne's is all the more disturbing for being left pictorially vague. Its force is felt not by the eyes but by the deeper kinesthetic sense of bodily integrity. The octave does not end here, however. After a moment's false sense of relief—"and I shall sleepe a space"—it moves on inexorably to confront Donne's worst fear of all: the Judgment, the inescapable confrontation with "that face, / Whose feare already shakes my every joynt." Here too visual detail is unnecessary: "that face" is enough.

The octave, employing mainly composition by similitude, is an instance of purgative meditation at its most effective. Its aim is to raise terror by directing the imagination toward the Last Things. The sestet takes this emotion and uses it to motivate a resolution: in this case, a petition for a safe issue from death.

> Then, as my soule, to'heaven her first seate, takes flight,
> And earth-borne body, in the earth shall dwell,
> So, fall my sinnes, that all may have their right,
> To where they'are bred, and would presse me, to hell.
> Impute me righteous, thus purg'd of evill,
> For thus I leave the world, the flesh, and devill.

Critics find this second part less effective than the first. Several differences may account for this reaction, but far from being flaws, they are necessary to the total effect. The major difference results from devotional and consequent poetic technique. Imaginative meditation gives way to vocal petition, and therefore the imagery is less vivid. Accompanying this change is a shift in feeling. It is not a slackening, which would rightly be called a flaw, but a redirection to another end. The mood is no longer frantic but sober and resolute, though hardly extending so far as hope. Donne has no intention of raising terror in his reader and then leaving him in that state. Such a proceeding might be expected from Poe or Baudelaire, but for a seventeenth-century religious poet to write poetry of such a kind would have seemed evil. Donne raises up and confronts death not for its own sake but in order to lead the reader or himself to repentance and spiritual progress. Fear is evoked not to be lingered over but purged. The first part is an act of the imagination that raises uncontrolled emotions, the second an act of will that channels them and brings them under control.[27]

Sonnet 4 is a meditation on the Last Judgment, which begins with a classic composition of place:

> At the round earths imagin'd corners, blow
> Your trumpets, Angells, and arise, arise
> From death, you numberlesse infinities
> Of soules, and to your scattred bodies goe,
> All whom the flood did, and fire shall o'erthrow,

All whom warre, dearth, age, agues, tyrannies,
Despaire, law, chance, hath slaine, and you whose eyes,
Shall behold God, and never tast deaths woe.

Although the imagination is stirred and a scene evoked, Donne
does not follow the advice *ut pictura poesis*. Most readers reconstruct a scene, perhaps remembering the Sistine Chapel, but
there are few visual details in this passage. How then does it
work so effectively? The obvious answer is that this too is vocal
poetry, which would lose most of its sensible force if it were not
heard in the mind's ear. The sound of trumpets is evoked, the
repeated exhortation "arise, arise" affects one like a loud cry.
The enjambment that sweeps the reader forward is essentially
an aural device. So too the catalog of ways to die, which does
not linger descriptively but suggests an infinite multitude by its
onward rush and its forceful, gathered stresses. All the "Holy
Sonnets" should be read aloud, but especially this and the
tenth.

The sestet of Sonnet 4 further emphasizes the tumultuous
octave by its contrasting quietness:

But let them sleepe, Lord, and mee mourne a space,
For, if above all these, my sinnes abound,
'Tis late to aske abundance of thy grace,
When wee are there; here on this lowly ground,
Teach mee how to repent; for that's as good
As if thou'hadst seal'd my pardon, with thy blood.

The technique resembles "A Litanie," as the scene shifts from
the general to the specific, the objective to the personal, the
exterior to the interior. The theological point is that it is too late
to repent after death; from this is drawn a more immediate
devotional point: Repent now. The point is reinforced by the
structural contrast, which Donne repeats in miniature at the
center of the sestet in two contrasting words separated by a
semicolon: "there; here."

In Sonnet 5 Donne employs a fresh technique that Herbert
later made much use of: deliberate arousal of impious emotions

in order to purge them. Martz traces this method to the
Spiritual Combat of Lorenzo Scupoli (1589). "We must deliberately bring to mind whatever moved us to a given vice. Then,
'when you recognize the same emotion rising in your lower
appetite, mobilize the entire force of your will to suppress
it.' " [28] Such a technique has obvious dangers; of course, one
cannot tell if Donne deliberately stirred up his emotions when
he wrote Sonnet 5 or wrote it in response to emotions spontaneously felt. There are similar doubts about such poems as
Herbert's "The Collar." What is certain is that Donne and Herbert passed on their poems and thus chose to raise and allay
such emotions in their readers.

> If poysonous mineralls, and if that tree,
> Whose fruit threw death on else immortall us,
> If lecherous goats, if serpents envious
> Cannot be damn'd; Alas; why should I bee?
> Why should intent or reason, borne in mee,
> Make sinnes, else equall, in mee, more heinous?
> And mercy being easie, and glorious
> To God, in his sterne wrath, why threatens hee?

The octave is meditative insofar as its purpose is to raise an
emotion that a colloquy will direct. But the usual techniques of
composition are not used. Images abound: poisonous minerals,
deadly tree, fruit, lecherous goats, envious serpents, but the
real interest is less in these objects than in the feelings and
character of the meditator. Significantly he classifies himself
with poisonous and malignant creatures and protests any
difference—not, of course, intending the conclusion that this
classification suggests.

In a sense, any poem in which a poet introduces an "I" of
some kind involves masking or role-playing. The speaker in
Sonnet 5, however, differs in degree or even in kind from the
speakers in the other sonnets. He is like the protagonists of
some of Donne's love poems; he strikes a pose that the poem as
a whole deliberately undercuts. The trembling fear of the first
sonnets must be purged and transformed into love, but there is

nothing wrong with fear as such: it is the natural response to the situation in which the speaker finds himself. Such is not the case in the octave of Sonnet 5, which presents a speaker trying not to face but to wriggle out of his predicament—but who only succeeds in condemning himself further with each addition to his argument. The point is driven home by the sestet, in which he realizes what he has been doing:

> But who am I, that dare dispute with thee?
> O God, Oh! of thine onely worthy blood,
> And my teares, make a heavenly Lethean flood,
> And drowne in it my sinnes blacke memorie.
> That thou remember them, some claime as debt,
> I thinke it mercy, if thou wilt forget.

To the frantic ravings of the octave Donne opposes an intense remorse. The couplet concludes more quietly and deliberately. As in the earlier poems, the resolution rests with God.

The sixth sonnet, "Death be not proud," was a favorite of Wordsworth's and probably the best known of the "Holy Sonnets." Donne's recent critics have not placed it so high. It is suggested that the challenge to death is shrill and unconvincing, that the speaker is a dramatic persona whose views the reader is expected to reject. That may be, but it seems to me that while Romantic criticism went astray by identifying the poet too closely with his protagonists, modern critics may err by over-preoccupation with dramatic masks. Sonnet 5 shows us a speaker with whom we are meant to disagree, as the sestet confirms. Nothing like this is found in Sonnet 6. Such interpretations please our modern taste for complexity, irony, and separation of poet and poem, but should not be pressed too far.

The victory over death certainly is not easy. The images form a powerful undercurrent working against the assertions of the speaker. For example, there is little comfort that death is "slave to Fate, chance, kings, and desperate men" and lives with "poyson, warre, and sicknesse." An imaginative reader may feel queasy. But that is not to imply the speaker is simply fooling himself, rather that the poem gives death its due. A balance is struck between natural fear and supernatural triumph, but there is no doubt where the victory lies: "One short sleepe past, wee wake eternally, / And death shall be no more, Death thou shalt die." The speaker is a natural man, trembling with human fears which he is striving to overcome; but the last couplet is based not on his self-confidence but on Christ's victory over death and the saving grace that ensues. The poem is not a traditional devotion but balances indirect meditation on death with vocal thanksgiving for salvation.

In Sonnet 7, Donne returns to meditation. At this point, halfway through the sequence, he moves from the purgative to the illuminative way, though the change is not immediately noticeable since the emphasis is still on sin and death.

> Spit in my face yee Jewes, and pierce my side,
> Buffet, and scoffe, scourge, and crucifie mee,
> For I have sinn'd, and sinn'd, and onely hee,
> Who could do no iniquitie, hath dyed.

The speaker wants to take Christ's place, because it would seem more just for the guilty and not the innocent to suffer. Yet it cannot be:

> But by my death can not be satisfied
> My sinnes, which passe the Jewes impiety:
> They kill'd once an inglorious man, but I
> Crucifie him daily, being now glorified.

Crucifixion of the innocent is unjust, yet paradoxically only the innocent Christ can satisfy Justice for the speaker's sins. At first he identified himself with the victim and imagined himself scourged and crucified. Now he realizes he is to be identified with the persecutors, for he is daily a worse sinner than they. The octave is grim and self-accusing, yet Douglas Peterson rightly points out that this is the first expression of sorrow in the sequence "not motivated by fear." [29]

The speaker has progressed from personal fear of death and damnation to outward-directed sorrow. His gesture of offering himself in Christ's place is futile yet reveals an admirable impulse. It is like Eve's offer to take all the punishment on her head in *Paradise Lost.* Adam points out that she cannot bear this burden, yet her offer is a vital step in their repentance and regeneration. Sonnet 7 is also the first to speak of God's love, save for the brief reference in the first sonnet in which the speaker excludes himself: "thou lov'st mankind well, yet wilt'not chuse me." The difference is clear:

> Oh let mee then, his strange love still admire:
> Kings pardon, but he bore our punishment . . .
> God cloth'd himselfe in vile mans flesh, that so
> Hee might be weake enough to suffer woe.

Sonnet 8 reverts to the creatures, not to complain as in Sonnet 5, but to wonder at their subjection to sinful man. Its conclusion reverts to the greater wonder of Sonnet 7: "But their Creator, whom sin, nor nature tyed, / For us, his Creatures, and his foes, hath dyed."

Sonnet 9 also reverts to an earlier subject, the Last Judgment. Now the personal terrors of judgment give place to a vision of the Crucifixion. Donne employs what may be called double composition of place: first imagining himself on the brink of judgment, then shielding himself from that awful brink by imagining a picture of the crucified Christ in his heart. His technique resembles the contemporary practice among Catholics of holding a crucifix before the eyes of the dying. Christ was the fearful judge of Sonnet 3; now Donne replaces that image of terror with one of love and mercy:

> What if this present were the worlds last night?
> Marke in my heart, O Soule, where thou dost dwell,
> The picture of Christ crucified, and tell
> Whether that countenance can thee affright,
> Teares in his eyes quench the amasing light,
> Blood fills his frownes, which from his pierc'd head fell,
> And can that tongue adjudge thee unto hell,
> Which pray'd forgivenesse for his foes fierce spight?

√ This surely is meditation at its most effective. It is instructive to compare this imaginative devotion with the different method of approaching the same topic in *"La Corona."*

In the sestet too Donne allows himself a more personal, imaginatively shocking approach than would have been fitting in the earlier, more liturgical sequence.

> No, no; but as in my idolatrie
> I said to all my profane mistresses,
> Beauty, of pitty, foulnesse onely is
> A signe of rigour: so I say to thee,
> To wicked spirits are horrid shapes assign'd,
> This beauteous forme assures a pitious minde.

Love between Christ and the soul is traditionally pictured in human terms, but only Donne could have suggested this particular analogy. Love, mercy, goodness might come to mind as fitting words to describe the crucified Christ pictured in the octave. Beauty, the unexpected ground of the comparison, is both more shocking and more convincing.

In Sonnet 10, Donne turns from Ignatian meditation back to vocal prayer. Imagination has plenty to work with, but little in the poem is pictorial. Instead, Donne's chief tool is sound, used both to convey strong feelings and to give the poem its dynamic structure. The first quatrain sets up an elaborate rhetorical pattern, which would seem artificial if it were not so powerful:

> Batter my heart, three person'd God; for, you
> As yet but knocke, breathe, shine, and seeke to mend;
> That I may rise, and stand, o'erthrow mee, 'and bend
> Your force, to breake, blowe, burn and make me new.

The structuring devices are so obvious they scarcely need comment: strong *b* alliteration, verbs grouped in triplets to reflect the Trinity, correspondence between each verb in the second group and the first, the gathering of strong stresses together at the climaxes. The very obviousness of these tech-

niques contributes to the quatrain's success: it batters its way to
its goal with no attempt at subtlety.

The second quatrain, the "usurpt towne," flows naturally
from the first but abandons its methods; four more lines in the
same style would be too many. In the sestet, a third image
complex is used, again different from its predecessor but flow-
ing from it logically and emotionally:

> Yet dearly' I love you, and would be loved faine,
> But am betroth'd unto your enemie,
> Divorce mee, 'untie, or breake that knot againe,
> Take mee to you, imprison mee, for I
> Except you' enthrall mee, never shall be free,
> Nor ever chast, except you ravish mee.

As often, Donne takes a traditional metaphor, the soul as the ✓
bride of God, and creates a vivid conceit by extending and
twisting it. The sonnet seems to conclude as pessimistically as
the earlier sonnets. Donne can do nothing, all the initiative is
God's, he must be totally annihilated, not married but raped
against his will. Yet there is a difference: the theme is not fear
but love.

The last two sonnets in the sequence form a pair. In Sonnet
11, Donne addresses his soul (as the reader may address his):
"Wilt thou love God, as he thee! then digest, / My Soule, this
wholsome meditation. . . ." Certainly this is the proper question after "Batter my heart." If only it can be answered, the
tortured predicament of a soul unable to respond to love will be
solved. The first lines imply that such an answer can be found
by digesting a "wholsome meditation" that will follow. But this
"meditation" proves to be a theological statement, not an
imaginative realization. The distant, terrifying God of the first
sonnets assumes a new relationship with the poet. The Father,
who in Sonnet 1 would not "chuse" him, now "Hath deign'd to
chuse" him as son and coheir of Christ's glory. The Holy Spirit
makes a temple in his breast. Climactically, and making the rest
possible, the Son of God has come down, become man, and
died for him. These are the essential facts which, fully "di-

gested," are all he needs to transform his relationship with God and truly to love him. But the sonnet is not a meditation, though Donne himself uses the term, nor does Donne succeed this time in finding a suitable alternative form. Sonnet 11 has a crucial position in the sequence—like that moment when we learn that Lycidas is not dead—but fails poetically and devotionally to measure up to what is needed.

Sonnet 12, a colloquy to the preceding theological statement and the sequence as a whole, addresses the Father. Donne's theme is still love and the effort to put fear of justice behind him. But this last prayer is a petition and not a thanksgiving, as it might have been had greater progress been made. Death and life, fear and love, justice and mercy, law and spirit, old covenant and new: these are the contrasts on which the sequence has been built, and they are made explicit in the concluding poem. It is not a celebration that the better has conquered the worse, but a petition that it may be so:

> Father, part of his double interest
> Unto thy kingdome, thy Sonne gives to mee,
> His joynture in the knottie Trinitie,
> Hee keepes, and gives mee his deaths conquest.
> This Lambe, whose death, with life the world hath blest,
> Was from the worlds beginning slaine, and he
> Hath made two Wills, which with the Legacie
> Of his and thy kingdome, doe thy Sonnes invest,
> Yet such are those laws, that men argue yet
> Whether a man those statutes can fulfill;
> None doth, but all-healing grace and Spirit,
> Revive againe what law and letter kill.
> Thy lawes abridgement, and thy last command
> Is all but love; Oh let that last Will stand!

The metaphors are tangled and difficult at a first reading. This is the Donne who, in Coleridge's phrase, wreaths pokers into love knots. The style appropriately reflects the difficult questions of law, justice, and love that Donne is considering. The mode is impersonal and in that respect resembles *"La Corona,"* but in keeping with the difficulties and emotional intensities confronted earlier the resolution is knottier and more complex. Nothing is extraneous or gratuitously complicated. It is, I think, fully as good a poem as any that precede it, but for reasons now familiar it is less immediately accessible than the great meditations. Readers looking for the appearance of self-expression will find little in it; those alive to how precise placement of words can make liturgical prayer, like the language of the Authorized Version, potent and proof against repetition, will judge otherwise.

Meditation is the dominant method of the "Holy Sonnets." It gives the sequence its characteristic feeling, its chief moments of brilliance, and its bravura effects. But Donne avoids tedium by using a variety of meditative methods and by including several sonnets that are not meditative at all, as well as others that balance meditation against vocal and liturgical techniques. Taken together, the poems form a sequence, but their individual structures and the ties connecting them are not mechanically predetermined by adherence to a single method. The sequence does not, as one might expect, present the soul's journey from the depths to the heights. Rather it describes only such progress as there can be between a soul desperately evading the assaults of fear and death and a soul longing with equal passion for love and salvation. By one measure a beginning is scarcely made; by another, an essential revolution has taken place. If Donne has won a victory, it is not an easy one nor one to rest happily in for long. Yet, if nothing else, the end of the sequence is utterly convincing.

6. "Goodfriday"

The last of Donne's three occasional poems on the Christian year, "Goodfriday, 1613. Riding Westward," is also the last and perhaps the best of his verse meditations. The poem is in three parts. In the first, Donne proposes an extended metaphorical hypothesis: "Let mans Soule be a Spheare." The inward intelligence that moves this sphere, like the angels who move the planets, is devotion, which bends his soul toward the East. At the same time, the metaphorical primum mobile, for most men turned by business or pleasure rather than God, hurries him westward. The poem plays on traditional moral interpretations of the two astronomical motions, planetary and stellar, as well as on Christian directional symbolism.[30] East is the direction of Christ, whose name is Oriens and whose rising begets eternal day. It is the direction of Jerusalem, toward which churches face, so the crucifix at the back of the sanctuary is against the eastern wall. Westward motion, traditionally the direction of death, carries Donne away from the imagined crucifix. The poem also implicitly questions the propriety of riding at all, doing business or seeking pleasure on Good Friday, properly a time for meditation on the sorrowful mysteries.

While his body moves west, his "Soules forme bends toward the East," under the pull of devotion. The second part of the poem considers this alternative direction:

> There I should see a Sunne, by rising set,
> And by that setting endlesse day beget;
> But that Christ on this Crosse, did rise and fall,
> Sinne had eternally benighted all.

The poem proceeds through a series of further paradoxes, underlining the central meanings of this sorrowful mystery. The method is similar to *"La Corona,"* which likewise uses the traditional paradoxes to underline the Christian mysteries, but in "Goodfriday" the meditating imagination plays a far larger role:

> Could I behold that endlesse height which is
> Zenith to us, and to'our Antipodes,
> Humbled below us? or that blood which is
> The seat of all our Soules, if not of his,
> Make durt of dust, or that flesh which was worne
> By God, for his apparell, rag'd and torne?

A. B. Chambers remarks that the speaker is "physically unable but spiritually compelled to look" at the event he describes.[31] The very questions themselves, the implied inability to face the mystery, become more and more paradoxical. Donne cannot bear to look yet is totally absorbed mentally in that very act of looking from which he shrinks.

The central part of the poem is just such an Ignatian meditation as one might make in church on Good Friday, kneeling in front of the crucifix or the east window. Reformers might remove the crosses (and how Donne felt about that is told in "The Crosse"). Business might take him away. Nevertheless, memory and the other powers of the mind can restore the picture to him and enable him to make an appropriate act of meditative devotion. The poem is a metaphor for the difficulties of meditating in less than ideal circumstances—before a crucifix, cloistered from the world, perhaps belonging to a religious order. The man who meditates is a man of the world, devout and wishing to do his duty but unable to escape the press of business and the distractions of life. The poem's achievement is that these common problems are not ignored but turned to account, poetically and devotionally. The resulting meditation seems more natural than any of the "Holy Sonnets," more a spontaneous outpouring and less a calculated assault, yet carried out with greater urgency and power than if more conventional methods were employed. It is art concealing art. If the world and its demands cannot be evaded, they can be used, transformed by the meditating mind.

In the last part, Donne returns to his westward motion. Like a witty lover, who has made some dreadful gaffe while speaking to his mistress but with a quick stroke of ingenuity turns it into a compliment, he converts his situation, the failure to keep this day holy, into a virtue. "I turne my backe to thee, but to receive / Corrections." His purpose in turning away from God was not really to receive stripes, however: as he said earlier, pressing business called him out. Of course God, unlike a human mistress, can read his heart and perceive the sophistry. Can sophistry, insincerity, even an outright lie be appropriate in a devotional poem? Ben Jonson, in "Inviting a Friend to Supper," tells his friend he will go so far as to lie about the food if that will persuade him to come. In such a situation, lying is a kind of compliment, and admitting the lie is a greater one. So with Donne.

Besides, a lie can become the truth, as any poet knows. The essence of Ignatian meditation is conscious effort of the will, construction of opportunities and manufacture of emotions. The aim is conversion or metamorphosis, pretending to be something and then becoming it. If business takes Donne to the West, that is only the outward cause. Inwardly, he can make something quite different of it, and so he does, transforming the journey in the crucible of devotion.

7. *"Upon the Psalmes"*

"Goodfriday, 1613" is the last poem in which Donne makes a dominant use of meditation. His poems to Herbert and Tilman reveal something of his religious development in the next few years but are not devotions. The poem praising the Sidneian psalms is another matter. Although partly a literary compliment, it is primarily an act of devotion inspired by the Sidneys' work. Throughout, the poem addresses "Eternall God." While its couplet form might lead one to expect polite epistolary praise, its primary genre is vocal prayer, a mode that reflects the psalms it praises. Thus it further compliments the translators while fulfilling the true purpose of their work.

Donne also honors the man his age considered the greatest sacred poet: David, who stood to his successors as Homer stood to would-be writers of epic. Donne portrays him as divinely inspired by a "cloven tongue" of fire, appropriately borrowing his image from Acts ii.3 which describes the descent of the Holy Spirit to the Apostles at Pentecost. This divine inspiration is twofold:

> For 'twas a double power by which he sung
> The highest matter in the noblest forme.

As a religious poet David needed double inspiration, as prophet and maker. The rest of Donne's poem confirms the need of such double inspiration.

By their example, the Sidneys teach English poets the same twofold lesson:

> Two that make one *John Baptists* holy voyce,
> And who that Psalme, *Now let the Iles rejoyce,*
> Have both translated, and apply'd it too,
> Both told us what, and taught us how to doe.

Repeated emphasis on high matter and noble manner— religious and poetic inspiration—becomes the poem's major theme. Indeed, that the Sidneys have taught Donne what and how to write may be more than mere praise, for Donne underlines the point by his own use of music. The poetry is unmistakably the mature Donne's, with his characteristic "strong lines" and intellectual urgency. At the same time it is more musical in subject and technique than anything he had written up to this time. The *Songs and Sonnets* reflect music of a kind, but often a bitter, discordant music suited to the new dissonant styles. The poem on the psalms reflects music of another sort. In it, Donne gives himself wholeheartedly to divine and poetic harmonies that sound at times almost like the Milton of the "Nativity Ode." Perhaps reading the Sidney psalms inspired him at a time when his poetry was ready to take a new devotional form.

> They shew us Ilanders our joy, our King,
> They tell us *why*, and teach us *how* to sing;
> Make all this All, three Quires, heaven, earth, and sphears;
> The first, Heaven, hath a song, but no man heares,
> The Spheares have Musick, but they have no tongue,
> Their harmony is rather danc'd than sung;
> But our third Quire, to which the first gives eare,
> (For, Angels learne by what the Church does here)
> This Quire hath all. The Organist is hee
> Who hath tun'd God and Man, the Organ we:
> The songs are these, which heavens high holy Muse

Whisper'd to *David, David* to the Jewes:
And *Davids* Successors, in holy zeale,
In formes of joy and art doe re-reveale
To us . . . .
So though some have, some may some Psalmes translate,
We thy Sydnean Psalmes shall celebrate,
And, till we come th' Extemporall song to sing,
(Learn'd the first hower, that we see the King,
Who hath translated these translators) may
These their sweet learned labours, all the way
Be as our tuning, that, when hence we part
We may fall in with them, and sing our part.

The poem is an extraordinary praise of sung devotion, which itself mimics the psalms of praise and becomes a vocal prayer. It also points in the direction Donne's last poems will take.

8. The Hymns

In "Upon the Translation of the Psalmes," Donne speaks of Christ as "The Organist . . . Who hath tun'd God and Man." At the close, in a variation on this conceit, the Sidneian psalms become the agents that put their users into tune, preparing them to sing their parts in heaven. A similar conceit begins Donne's "Hymne to God my God, in my sicknesse," and underlines a continuity of devotional method. Only one of Donne's hymns is known definitely to have been set to music in his lifetime, but all three are eminently suitable hymn texts. Unlike Donne's meditative poems, which typically are dramatic, narrative, or introspective, the hymns are direct prayers to God. Though full of vivid images, many of which deserve to be called metaphysical conceits, they make no attempt to build coherent scenes or achieve more than fleeting compositions of place.
Many of the psalms contain passages on which one might meditate while singing or reciting them. Similarly, there are meditative passages in Donne's hymns:

We thinke that *Paradise* and *Calvarie,*
    Christs Crosse, and *Adams* tree, stood in one place;
Looke Lord, and finde both *Adams* met in me;
    As the first *Adams* sweat surrounds my face,
    May the last *Adams* blood my soule embrace.

This stanza and the next embody traditional meditations on the two Adams and the Passion; but they are brief meditations within a larger structure. Moreover, they consider public themes with liturgical connections, often pictured in stained glass, recited in Good Friday reproaches, or sung in hymns. The hymn begins with an image of music:

Since I am comming to that Holy roome,
    Where, with thy Quire of Saints for evermore,
I shall be made thy Musique; As I come
    I tune the Instrument here at the dore,
    And what I must doe then, thinke now before.

This, the most continually conceited of Donne's devotional poems, owes much to traditional meditations on one's deathbed and other meditative subjects. But its overarching structure and mode are vocal prayer and by genre it is a hymn text: a meditative hymn. Having begun with music, Donne returns at the close to another public, liturgical form, the sermon: "And as to others soules I preach'd thy word, / Be this my Text, my Sermon to mine owne, / Therfore that he may raise the Lord throws down." The hymn combines two devotional methods, but vocal prayer predominates.[32]

    When he wrote the hymns, late in his career, Donne still confronted death and judgment. "A Hymne to God the Father," probably the last, evokes a powerful image of the ultimate ground for despair: "I have a sinne of feare, that when I have spunne / My last thred, I shall perish on the shore." But the hymn recovers from this abyss and, as J. B. Leishman says, "ends on a note of peace and security that is scarcely found in his earlier religious poetry."[33] This is a penitential hymn that, in marked contrast with the penitential sonnets, ends happily, confident that God will grant the sinner forgiveness:

> Sweare by thy selfe, that at my death thy Sunne
> Shall shine as it shines now, and heretofore;
> And, having done that, Thou hast done,
> I have no more.

Set to music several times during the seventeenth century, once at Donne's command, this hymn is actually the least musical of the three. But it is not meditative. Appropriate to its vocal mode, and uniquely among Donne's works, it employs an aural device, the pun, not simply in passing but as the poem's most notable figure and structural lynchpin.

"A Hymne to Christ, at the Authors last going into Germany," solemn and authoritative in its rhythms, is the closest Donne came to the somber but confident style of the great Protestant hymns. He begins by evoking and allegorizing a succession of visual details. The first stanza is a microcosm of what may be called an emblematic hymn:

> In what torne ship soever I embarke,
> That ship shall be my embleme of thy Arke;
> What sea soever swallow mee, that flood
> Shall be to mee an embleme of thy blood;
> Though thou with clouds of anger do disguise
> Thy face; yet through that maske I know those eyes,
>   Which, though they turne away sometimes,
>   They never will despise.

After this, emphasis on visual perception ceases. What gives the poem continuity is the voice of a man engaged in prayer, overheard like one of Donne's lovers addressing his beloved. The difference is that in the *Songs and Sonnets* the reader is a spectator, whatever his engagement in the situation, whereas in the hymns as in the other devotional works he is invited to participate in the prayer.

All three hymns reveal Donne's new, hard-won confidence in God, but "A Hymne to Christ" is his greatest poem on the subject of reciprocated love between God and the soul, a goal toward which his earlier poems pointed without ever quite arriving.

I sacrifice this Iland unto thee,
And all whom I lov'd there, and who lov'd mee;
When I have put our seas twixt them and mee,
Put thou thy sea betwixt my sinnes and thee.
As the trees sap doth seeke the root below
In winter, in my winter now I goe,
   Where none but thee, th' Eternall root
    Of true Love I may know.

Nor thou nor thy religion dost controule,
The amorousnesse of an harmonious Soule,
But thou would'st have that love thy selfe: As thou
Art jealous, Lord, so I am jealous now,
Thou lov'st not, till from loving more, thou free
My soule: Who ever gives, takes libertie:
   O, if thou car'st not whom I love
    Alas, thou lov'st not mee.

Seale then this bill of my Divorce to All,
On whom those fainter beams of love did fall;
Marry those loves, which in youth scattered bee
On Fame, Wit, Hopes (false mistresses) to thee.
Churches are best for Prayer, that have least light:
To see God only, I goe out of sight:
   And to scape stormy dayes, I chuse
    An Everlasting night.

Characteristically, Donne achieves his goal of love in the hymns by confronting the imminent prospect of his death. Again and again in the earlier poems he confronted the same threat without achieving a convincing victory. But he returned to the attack to the end in sermons and poetry. This constant reiteration of an early theme or what might be thought an early stage of spiritual development did not signify an inability to progress poetically or devotionally, still less a regression to old fears and doubts. In a paradox typical of Donne, it represents progression by circularity, continued preoccupation with spiritual underpinnings—guilt, fear, sorrow, penitence—finally enabling him to love. Thus he reached tranquility through violent struggle and gained the heights by retreating to his roots. The same pattern is seen in miniature in single poems and sonnets, on a larger scale in the sonnet cycles or "A Litanie," and on a larger scale still in his devotional poetry as a whole.

This poetry moves from liturgical to meditative back to liturgical forms, from confidence to doubt and back to confidence, from vocal praise to introspection back to vocal praise. In many ways his last religious poems are more like his first than those that came between. The late sonnets and hymns are closer to *"La Corona"* in poetic and devotional technique than to the Ignatian poems of Donne's middle period of *Sturm und Drang*. But what Donne gained, technically and devotionally, during that period was not so much relinquished as subsumed. Although not all the dates are known, a distinct pattern emerges nonetheless: a corona of prayer and praise.

Notes

1. For fuller discussion and bibliography see Louis L. Martz, *The Poetry of Meditation* (New Haven: Yale University Press, 1962); on English Protestant meditation see Barbara K. Lewalski, *Donne's Anniversaries* (Princeton: Princeton University Press, 1973), pp. 73–107, and Frank L. Huntley's forthcoming book, *Bishop Joseph Hall.*

2. Baker, *Sancta Sophia* (Douai: John Patte and Thomas Fievet, 1657), II, 100–101 (III.ii.2.2).

3. Gibbons, *An Abridgement of Meditations* (1614), cited by Martz, p. 27.

4. Martz, p. 28.

5. Browne, *Religio Medici,* i.13.

6. Lest we feel superior to earlier times it may be noted that the same thing is happening today. Cause and effect as an absolute law, which dominates our thinking, is discredited in those very sciences that gave it birth. As earlier, the humanities may be the last to change. See F. Waismann, "The Decline and Fall of Causality," *Turning Points in Physics,* ed. A. C. Crombie (Amsterdam: North-Holland Publishing, 1959).

7. Baker, *Sancta Sophia,* II, 110 (III.ii.3.11).

8. Baker, II, 111 (III.ii.3.15).

9. Baker, II, 110 (III.ii.3.11).

10. Baker, II, 113 (III.ii.3.20).

11. Francis de Sales, *Introduction to the Devout Life*, ii.2–8, trans. M. Day (London: Burns & Oates, 1962), pp. 50–58, esp. pp. 53, 56.

12. See Lewalski, pp. 90, 98. Her work amplifies Martz, but I disagree that practical self-application was uniquely Protestant.

13. Martz, p. 57.

14. Baker, II, 101 (III.ii.2.3).

15. Gardner, ed., *The Divine Poems*, p. lv. On "spoiling the Egyptians," see commentaries on Exod. iii.22.

16. Izaak Walton, *The Lives* (London: Oxford University Press, 1927), p. 266; for 1608 see David Novarr, "The Dating of Donne's *La Corona*," *Philological Quarterly*, 36 (1957), 259–265. "Goodfriday" may have been begun 1610–11: see *TLS* (16 August 1974), pp. 870–873; this would narrow the meditative period still further.

17. Gardner, ed., *The Divine Poems*, p. 55.

18. Martz, pp. 110–111; cf. Gardner, p. xxii.

19. Martz, pp. 107–108.

20. Gardner, p. 57.

21. Gardner, pp. xxiv–xxvi.

22. Gardner, p. xxix.

23. Gardner, pp. xxx–xxxi.

24. Gardner, p. xxxi.

25. Gardner, p. xl. Gardner restores the sonnet order of 1633 and the relevant MSS; I use her numbering which differs from Grierson and prior editors.

26. Gardner, p. lii.

27. On this pattern see William H. Halewood, *The Poetry of Grace* (New Haven: Yale University Press, 1970), pp. 79–83.

28. Cited by Martz, p. 132.

29. Peterson, *The English Lyric from Wyatt to Donne* (Princeton: Princeton University Press, 1967), p. 341.

30. See A. B. Chambers, " 'Goodfriday, 1613. Riding Westward': The Poem and the Tradition," *ELH*, 28 (1961), 31–53.

31. Chambers, p. 50.

32. Cf. Lewalski, pp. 73–107, on combinations of meditation and sermon which she calls "Protestant" meditation but I would call a mixed form (found also among Catholics).

33. Leishman, *The Monarch of Wit* (New York: Harper & Row, 1965), p. 266.

4.

George Herbert: Varieties of Devotion

1. Hymns for the Church Year

Although George Herbert was inspired by Donne's religious verse, he early developed his own characteristic poetic and devotional techniques. The most important lesson he learned from his predecessor was simply that poetry could fruitfully be linked with personal religious devotion. Success bred emulation. The younger poet adopted some of Donne's techniques with minimal change: for example, the use of a dramatic speaking voice or an abrupt opening. At the same time, his detailed technical procedures often differ. Donne is flamboyantly personal and given to over-statement, while Herbert, even in the act of introspection, is self-effacing and favors understatement. These differences are related to devotional as well as poetic technique. Nevertheless both poets were in one respect children of their age. They both share a conviction that method and technique are the apt tools of poetry and devotion alike.

Something has been said in Chapter 2 about Herbert's lifelong interest in music and the generally musical nature of his poems. Often their titles are suggestive: "A true Hymne," "Mans medley," "Mattens," "Even-song," "A Dialogue-Antheme," "Antiphon," "Church-musick." Musical imagery

pervades Herbert's poems, musical sounds balance their speech
rhythms, and musical accompaniment, whether potential or actual, shaped their stanza forms. There are hymns for Holy
Communion, for morning and evening prayer, for Sundays.
There are songs of praise, balanced by groans of tribulation
and penitence. With this embarassment of riches it is hard to
know where to begin a discussion of the vocal and musical
element in Herbert's poetry and harder to know where to leave
off. A reading of "The Church" reveals music's virtual omni-
presence. But one series of poems illustrates this side of Herbert well: the hymns on the Christian year. Hymn cycles based
on the Christian calendar were traditional. In the seventeenth
century, Puritans inside and outside the Established Church
intensified their attack on these holy-day observances. One result was that convinced Anglicans grew more firmly committed
to them. As the century progressed, these hymns assumed passionate and sometimes defiant Anglican connotations. Herbert's works in this tradition include "Christmas," "Lent," "Easter," "Whitsunday," and "Trinitie Sunday."

  "Christmas" is in two parts. The first, a sonnet, begins in
the narrative mode. Tired of riding after pleasure, the poet
stops at an inn. There he encounters his "dearest Lord," who
expects his arrival. He asks Christ, briefly characterized by the
traditional Christmas paradoxes, to cleanse and refurnish his
soul and dwell in it. In the second part, Herbert turns from this
preparatory poem, with its exposition, meditation, and petition,
to what amounts to a Christmas hymn. In its present form, with
a lengthened last line, it does not seem to be an actual hymn
text. Yet the abrupt shift in the poetry from speech to song and
in devotional method from meditation and petition to sung
vocal praise could not be more obvious:

> The shepherds sing; and shall I silent be?
>   My God, no hymne for thee?
> My soul's a shepherd too; a flock it feeds
>   Of thoughts, and words, and deeds.
> The pasture is thy word: the streams, thy grace
>   Enriching all the place.

Shepherd and flock shall sing, and all my powers
     Out-sing the day-light houres.
Then we will chide the sunne for letting night
     Take up his place and right:
We sing one common Lord; wherefore he should
     Himself the candle hold.
I will go searching, till I finde a sunne
     Shall stay, till we have done;
A willing shiner, that shall shine as gladly,
     As frost-nipt sunnes look sadly.
Then we will sing, and shine all our own day,
     And one another pay:
His beams shall cheer my breast, and both so twine,
Till ev'n his beams sing, and my musick shine.

Most of the poem is in psalm-like alternating rhythms, with heavy midline pauses in the longer lines. Typical of Herbert, the visual element of the hymn is as striking and pervasive as the aural. Pasture, streams, shepherd, flock are presented vividly, not so much in detail as in bright, archetypal generality. Above all these shines the image of the sun. The two most prominent words in the poem, underlining its method, are *sing* and *shine*. At the close, sight and sound converge harmoniously, so the sun's beams seem to "sing" and Herbert's music to "shine."

Not every hymn can be filled with musical references. "Lent," in keeping with its season, is a more sober poem than "Christmas." Its purpose is partly devotional, to put the user in the right frame of mind for fasting, and partly polemic, because fasting and Lent are under Puritan attack. As one might expect, Herbert is the gentlest of polemicists, holding firmly to his views but urging them charitably. The line between devotion and polemic is sometimes difficult to draw, because Herbert's method of dispute is not only to reason but to encourage a proper devotional attitude:

Who goeth in the way which Christ hath gone,
Is much more sure to meet with him, then one

That travelleth by-wayes:
Perhaps my God, though he be farre before,
May turn, and take me by the hand, and more
    May strengthen my decayes.

The rhythm, built on a pattern of two long lines and a short, is
sober and resolute. It resembles the pattern found by Daniel
and Marvell to recreate the Horatian ode in English. One can
imagine an appropriate tune that would underline the basic
and massively developed emotions.

Like "Christmas," "Easter" is in two parts, but in this case
both appear to be hymns. First is an opening paean celebrating
this most joyful of the Church's feasts. The first line of each
stanza could be set appropriately to a rising tune:

Rise heart; thy Lord is risen. Sing his praise
        Without delayes,
Who takes thee by the hand, that thou likewise
        With him mayst rise:
That, as his death calcined thee to dust,
His life may make thee gold, and much more, just.

Awake, my lute, and struggle for thy part
        With all thy art.
The crosse taught all wood to resound his name,
        Who bore the same.
His stretched sinews taught all strings, what key
Is best to celebrate this most high day.

Consort both heart and lute, and twist a song
        Pleasant and long:
Or, since all musick is but three parts vied
        And multiplied,
O let thy blessed Spirit bear a part,
And make up our defects with his sweet art.

Herbert's reference to his lute may be more than a dead con-
vention. We know from Walton that when he set and sang his

hymns he accompanied them on the lute or viol. The references to heart and lute struggling for their parts, to their eventual consort, to the twisting of a song, "pleasant and long," from this harmony are unmistakably in the language composers use to describe part music and counterpoint. One may speculate further. There are three stanzas, which, as the last suggests, honor the Trinity. In the first, the heart rises and sings, representing a single voice. In the second, the lute enters, playing counterpoint to that voice, which presumably repeats the initial tune. In the last, the Holy Spirit like a second instrument bears a part and makes up the full, three-part harmony to round off the conceit. The poem, constructed on this musical metaphor, seems also to provide us with a program for its musical setting.

The second part of "Easter" is the simplest and most lyrical of Herbert's songs. The measure, four lines in tetrameter or Long Meter, was a favorite of hymn and psalm writers. It could be sung to many established tunes. Its three-stanza structure links it to the first part, but its simpler style allows a harmonious contrast that music would underline:

> I got me flowers to straw thy way;
> I got me boughs off many a tree:
> But thou wast up by break of day,
> And brought'st thy sweets along with thee.
>
> The Sunne arising in the East,
> Though he give light, and th' East perfume;
> If they should offer to contest
> With thy arising, they presume.
>
> Can there be any day but this,
> Though many sunnes to shine endeavour?
> We count three hundred, but we misse:
> There is but one, and that one ever.

With radiance of vision, sweetness of scent, harmonious sound, as often, Herbert appeals to more than one of the senses. He employs a meditative technique, putting his singer into the

Palestinian landscape where he gathers flowers for his offering. But this is done not with the conscious effort and strain that characterize a "Holy Sonnet" or a formal Ignatian exercise, but with an ease that allows meditation to blend with harmony and results in a small but perfect specimen of the meditative hymn.

"Whitsunday" is not so striking. Like the other hymns, it is addressed to God. Its opening invocation sufficiently indicates its musical nature:

> Listen sweet Dove unto my song,
> And spread thy golden wings in me;
> Hatching my tender heart so long,
> Till it get wing, and flie away with thee.

The measure is close to the second Easter poem, with an extra foot to the fourth line.

"Trinitie Sunday" is predictably celebrated by another trinitarian poem, three stanzas of three lines each. To two events often linked in tradition, creation by the Father and redemption or re-creation by the Son, Herbert adds a third: sanctification by the Holy Spirit. The third stanza overgoes the first two with tripled triplets:

> Enrich my heart, mouth, hands in me,
> With faith, with hope, with charitie;
> That I may runne, rise, rest with thee.

The poem is not especially lyrical, but its form is suitable as a hymn text. Music would help flesh out its rather intellectual structure.

After a brief dedication, "The Church" begins with a Good-Friday poem. It proceeds through Easter to a number of the other feasts, but it is unclear how closely the whole sequence of poems matches with the Christian calendar. Several images recur in the holy-day hymns and help link them together. The main images in "Christmas" are the singing poet and the shining sun. In "Lent," Christ takes the poet by the hand to assist him along the way. In "Easter," the risen Lord again takes him by the hand to assist him in rising. Singing, harmony, and rising pervade the first "Easter" poem, while the second is dominated by sun imagery. "Whitsunday" too mentions singing, describes an upward flight assisted by God, and is presided over by sun imagery. "Trinitie Sunday," though short, recalls the main events of Good Friday, Easter, and Pentecost and looks forward to that final apocalyptic Sunday when the soul will "rest." Running and rising are activities familiar from the other hymns. By ending on rest in this poem, last in the calendar, the sequence concludes fitly. The parallels among these hymns may have no special significance. Most of the images arise naturally from the occasions being celebrated, while similar connections between images run from poem to poem throughout "The Church." Yet there are enough poems in "The Church" celebrating holy days, suitable for musical setting, and in vocal devotional modes, to make up almost a full sequence of hymns on the Christian year.

2. *Music in* The Temple

A number of poems in "The Church" may be confidently classified as hymns by poetic genre and devotional intent, especially those that fall into recognized divisions of the genre. Among them are the seasonal hymns, and a variety of liturgical hymns for matins, evensong, Holy Communion, and the like. Typical of these is "An Offering." Like several of the holy-day hymns it has a meditative or possibly spoken first part, which ends: "Then bring thy gift, and let thy hymne be this." The second part, an offertory hymn, follows. In addition to these more traditional hymns relating to public offices in the Church, there are many of a more private character which may, like "Sunday," have had musical settings. Among them are those dominated by musical imagery and those using sound effects for structural purposes. "Dooms-day" is an instance of the first, "Deniall" of the second. But it would not be reasonable to expect all Herbert's hymns and song texts to refer to music. A still larger group of poems are suitable for musical setting on account of their stanza forms, which, as noted in Chapter 2, look as if musical considerations helped shape them. Without further evidence, however, there is no way to draw a definitive line between poems Herbert set or intended to set to music and those he did not.

Another class of sacred songs in "The Church" is closer to the psalm genre than the hymn. According to Walton, Herbert preached to his congregation in support of the Anglican practice of daily psalm recitation.[1] A verse from "Antiphon (I)" is suggestive:

> The church with psalms must shout,
> No doore can keep them out:
> But above all, the heart
> Must bear the longest part.

Prose psalms were set and sung in cathedral services, metrical psalms were sung in Scottish and English churches as well as privately or in conventicles. Herbert, increasingly governed by his sense of Church tradition as embodied in the prayerbook, may have come to have some doubts about this form. Seven metrical psalms, printed as his by Playford, but called doubtful by Hutchinson, may have been products of his youth. They exhibit the difficulties of the genre but are not so bad as some critics imply. If they are his, Herbert chose to omit them from *The Temple*. He did include one metrical psalm, perhaps not only because it met his poetical standards but in order to give this important genre representation.

Martz, who notes a possible influence of the Sidneian psalms on Herbert, remarks that the psalms were the Church's "prime model for meditation." [2] They were also its prime model for song. Set in the common meter, Herbert's "The 23d Psalme" asks to be sung to one of the old tunes:

> The God of love my shepherd is,
>   And he that doth me feed:
> While he is mine, and I am his,
>   What can I want or need?

He leads me to the tender grasse,
  Where I both feed and rest;
Then to the streams that gently passe:
  In both I have the best.

          .   .   .

Surely thy sweet and wondrous love
  Shall measure all my dayes;
And as it never shall remove,
  So neither shall my praise.

This is one of the finest examples in English of a genre that, without its music, suffers almost insuperable handicaps. Herbert, if anyone, had the talent to produce a whole psalter to this high standard; but we may be grateful to have *The Temple* instead.

Martz finds that "hundreds of phrases from the Psalms, especially in the Coverdale (Prayer-Book) version, echo throughout the *Temple*." [3] That the prayerbook version should predominate is not surprising, knowing the place it had in Herbert's daily devotions. "Providence," Martz points out, is modeled on such psalms as 104, which according to the Authorized Version is "A meditation upon the mighty power and wonderful providence of God." But the psalms were thought of as David's songs of praise as well and are full of musical imagery. "Providence," written in simple four-line stanzas, certainly sounds as if it belongs to the metrical psalm genre, a free version rather than a translation. This is especially evident in the opening:

O Sacred Providence, who from end to end
Strongly and sweetly movest, shall I write,
And not of thee, through whom my fingers bend
To hold my quill? shall they not do thee right?

Of all the creatures both in sea and land
Onely to Man thou hast made known thy wayes,
And put the penne alone into his hand,
And made him Secretarie of thy praise.

Beasts fain would sing; birds dittie to their notes;
Trees would be tuning on their native lute
To thy renown: but all their hands and throats
Are brought to Man, while they are lame and mute.

Man is the worlds high Priest: he doth present
The sacrifice for all; while they below
Unto the service mutter an assent,
Such as springs use that fall, and windes that blow.

He that to praise and laud thee doth refrain,
Doth not refrain unto himself alone,
But robs a thousand that would praise thee fain,
And doth commit a world of sinne in one.

Not only is man the creatures' secretary and priest, he is also
their voice to sing the universal hymn of nature, otherwise
dumb. There are many similar examples elsewhere in "The
Church" of the influence of metrical psalmody. The popular
penitential psalms, for example, are almost surely a major influence on Herbert's frequent groans of sorrow and affliction.
    While several settings for Herbert's poems by other com-
posers survive, his own music has vanished entirely. If the
"many *divine Hymns* and *Anthems*" that Walton claimed Herbert
set to music are equivalent in part at least to poems now in *The
Temple,* what happened to the settings? Possibly Herbert kept
his musical versions separate. The 1633 edition was probably
set up by the printers either from a surviving manuscript in the
Bodleian (MS. Tanner 307) that was copied by the Little Gidding community from a lost original bequeathed to Nicholas
Ferrar, or else from that lost original itself. Ferrar might have
omitted musical notations that were in the original on account
of costs or difficulties in printing. But that is unlikely, both
because of Ferrar's fondness for hymns and musical devotions
and because he states in his preface to *The Temple* that "The
world therefore shall receive it in that naked simplicitie, with
which he left it, without any addition either of support or or-
nament, more then is included in it self." Ferrar has in mind an

absence of additions or glosses, but his phrasing seems to rule out significant subtractions as well.

Probably Herbert himself left out the music, as other poets usually did when they printed their poems. Although *The Temple* includes many hymns, anthems, and sacred songs, it is not fundamentally a musical collection. Music, or vocal prayer, is an important weapon in its devotional armory, but it is nevertheless only one of many. Some poems might be sung, others spoken; still others appeal more to the eye than the ear or are primarily directed inward to the mind. The variety of devotional and poetic forms in *The Temple* is astonishing and is one of its most characteristic features. As Martz notes, there are specimens of the sonnet, the pattern poem, the anagram, the acrostic, the ring, the wreath, the riddle, the charm, the animal fable, the narrative allegory, the psalm translation, the echo-song, the emblem poem, the posie, and still others. "A total reading of the *Temple* leaves one with the impression that the writer has taken special pains to include at least one example of every kind of short poem popular in his day, along with at least one example of every kind of devotional practice." [4]

That is a significant insight, although because of his particular concerns Martz does not trace out all its implications. It is evident from reading *The Temple* that Herbert was familiar with a number of devotional methods congenial to him, and that he turned now to one, now to another, or sometimes combined several in one poem. Among the more important of these devotional methods are vocal prayer and song, of which we have seen several subgroups; meditation, which also (as Martz shows) includes many forms, moods, and techniques; and (related to meditation) a species of devotion reliant on visual forms: shaped poems, icons, emblems, analogous to using a crucifix, statue, or stained-glass window for devotional purposes. To these major types may be added one more. There is a brief flash of poetry in *The Temple* which (I believe) is based on contemplation or true mystical prayer.

We shall look more closely into Herbert's use of vocal prayer, meditation, emblem, and contemplation, but instead of continuing to take them up one at a time, it is worthwhile to attempt to see them not only as they occur in individual poems but as they are woven together in "The Church" as a whole. To confront the entire work is to face difficult problems on account of the sheer quantity of poems, but something can be learned from a representative sample. With Herbert one may suggest rather than complete. Many critics have noticed a number of distinct sequences in "The Church." We shall choose for our sample one of the longest and tightest of these groups: the ten poems of the opening sequence.[5]

3. Varieties of Devotion: A Sequence

At the entrance to "The Church," set off by printer's ornaments and differentiated by the absence of ¶ before the title, is "The Altar." This poem is an emblematic meditation in the *schola cordis* tradition, except that the accompanying picture is replaced by the shape of the poem itself. The central conceit is a parallel between stone altar and living heart. As a meditation it appeals to both reason and will: understanding leads to compunction and thence to assent. But what the poem says is different from how it is shaped. Herbert speaks of a "broken" altar, "Made of a heart, and cemented with teares." Out of these unpromising materials, God is to form the ultimate shape or "frame" of the altar. But the poem's shape on the page does not share in this temporal process of building fragments into a whole. Instead, the altar stands finished, perfect and symmetrical. The sacrifice is accepted and the altar sanctified. The implied assumption is that, although the reader of *The Temple* is sinful like all men, he has (with the poet) undergone the first stages of regeneration: is purified or "groneth to be so."

Each time a user opens the pages of "The Church," he is reminded of this transformation: what he was and what God has made him. Without needing to reread the poem, he sees an emblematic altar on which to rededicate himself. Such is the basic function of religious emblems: to focus the mind, to recall in a moment a meditation that may have taken some time and labor. So Harington explains the engravings in his translation of *Orlando Furioso:* "The use of the picture is evident, which is, that (having read over the booke) you may reade it (as it were againe) in the very picture." [6] The picture first works with and assists the text and then sums it up.

After the dedicatory altar, in effect the Church's frontis-piece, stands "The Sacrifice" at the entry of "The Church" proper. It is the longest and most complex of the devotions. Rosemond Tuve samples some of the many strands of tradition that contribute to it.[7] Basically these are of three sorts: liturgical ritual, vocal and musical; iconography, in book illuminations and stained-glass windows; meditation, liturgical and private. Reflecting these sources, the devotional method of "The Sac-rifice" is also complex. The dominant mode, however, is vocal. The poem is a ritual monologue, Christ's lament to sinful man. Its main liturgical source is "the Improperia or Reproaches of Christ which in the Roman Use are recited on Good Friday." [8] Like Donne, Herbert evidently was attracted to a Catholic form no longer employed by the Anglican Church but that could, with care, be adapted to its spirit. As Donne's "A Litanie" is generically a litany, though recited in the chapels of his friends' hearts rather than in church, so "The Sacrifice" belongs to the vocal and ritual genre of the Good-Friday Reproaches. During their long development, the Reproaches had been variously set to music, from plainsong to polyphony, but this music had not been heard in England for a century, so it is doubtful that Herbert thought of the poem as a musical text. It is a spoken, priestly monologue.

Although "The Sacrifice" is primarily vocal in mode, it is filled with images from the biblical tradition that had long been used as food for meditation.

> Arise, arise, they come. Look how they runne!
> Alas! what haste they make to be undone!
> How with their lanterns do they seek the sunne!
>   Was ever grief like mine?

In stanzas like this one hears a lamenting voice in a dramatic situation. Christ speaks and the reader, responsible for his agony, listens. At the same time there are vivid pictures and a series of compressed theological paradoxes on which to meditate. Several methods of devotion are combined, vocal and meditative. The speaking voice is inseparable from the scene and the scene is inseparable from its theological implications. Hearing, vision, and understanding have simultaneous employment.

Following "The Sacrifice" is a more private poem, "The Thanksgiving," which tries to digest Christ's long lament. The poet addresses Christ in a dramatic, spoken response—or attempted response. How can he answer such suffering and grief? Can he turn it into poetry or joyful song?

> Shall I then sing, skipping thy dolefull storie,
>   And side with thy triumphant glorie?
> Shall thy strokes be my stroking? thorns, my flower?
>   Thy rod, my posie? crosse, my bower?

To transform Christ's passion into soothing art seems blasphemous. Yet, after making a series of resolutions, that is just what the poet resolves to do:

> My musick shall finde thee, and ev'ry string
>   Shall have his attribute to sing;
> That all together may accord in thee,
>   And prove one God, one harmonie.

But these are two musical moments in an unmusical poem, spoken mostly in a halting voice and ending on a note of failure.

> O my deare Saviour, Victorie!
> Then for thy passion—I will do for that—
>   Alas, my God, I know not what.

The formal, rhythmic lament of Christ, semi-liturgical in mode, effectively contrasts with the poet's sincere, informal, but stammering response. Stylistically and devotionally, it is the difference between priestly chant and private speech.

The following poem, "The Reprisall," is closely linked to its predecessor as part of the poet's response to "The Sacrifice." It was entitled "The Second Thanks-giving" in the Williams Manuscript. Yet a reader is immediately struck by its difference of form and rhythm. It is the song Herbert promised to attempt: severe and chastened, but a song nonetheless. It finds a solution to the question that defeated him: there is no solution, yet that very admission of failure is the solution.

> I have consider'd it, and finde
> There is no dealing with thy mighty passion:
> For though I die for thee, I am behinde;
>   My sinnes deserve the condemnation.
>   .   .   .
> Yet by confession will I come
> Into thy conquest: though I can do nought
> Against thee, in thee I will overcome
>   The man, who once against thee fought.

Unlike the previous poem, the stanzas are appropriate for a song text and the lines suggest not stumbling speech but somber music.

The poet's response to Christ continues in "The Agonie." The poem turns from speech and song to formal meditation. It is a brilliant example of both composition of place and composition by similitude. Two terms, sin and love, are made real to the imagination and feelings by Herbert's adaption of traditional meditative methods:

> Who would know Sinne, let him repair
> Unto Mount Olivet; there shall he see
> A man so wrung with pains, that all his hair,
>   His skinne, his garments bloudie be.
> Sinne is that presse and vice, which forceth pain
> To hunt his cruell food through ev'ry vein.

> Who knows not Love, let him assay
> And taste that juice, which on the crosse a pike
> Did set abroach; then let him say
>   If ever he did taste the like.
> Love is that liquour sweet and most divine,
> Which my God feels as bloud; but I, as wine.

Behind the poem lie centuries of typological interpretation, of Israel as the vineyard of God, and Christ as the vine and the bunch of grapes.[9] What makes "The Agonie" so striking is that, though one might expect Herbert to define "sin" and "love" by two opposite images, he employs essentially only one. This deepens his investigation of paradoxical connections between these theological realities and the related connections between the suffering Christ and the poet or reader. Because of their sins, they have participated in causing Christ's agony. But the same sins brought about the opportunity for Christ's act of love and make it more admirable because it is so thoroughly undeserved. The meditation involves a twofold movement. First the reader is carried to Olivet and Gethsemane by composition of place. Then the events he witnesses there are brought back home to him, in the church, by means of the eucharistic transformation. Blood becomes wine, sacrifice sacrament. Thus meditation on the passion becomes meditation on receiving communion. The private returns to the liturgical.

"The Sinner" turns further inward. This sonnet is an examination of conscience, which turns from sin in general to the state of this individual sinner. At the same time it is a petition, in which the poet addresses Christ:

> Yet Lord restore thine image, heare my call:
>   And though my hard heart scarce to thee can grone,
>   Remember that thou once didst write in stone.

The imagery echoes "The Altar" and is further echoed in the poems that follow.[10]

The permutations on Christ's sacrifice and man's response conclude with "Good Friday." In it, Herbert returns to the liturgical mode: it is the first of the holy-day hymns. Like others in the series it is in two parts. Both look like hymn texts but are visual as well as aural. The first, in fact, is a shaped poem, its five stanzas forming crosses: [11]

> O my chief good,
> How shall I measure out thy bloud?
> How shall I count what thee befell,
>   And each grief tell?

In a poem concerned with counting, the five stanzas may have numerical significance (the five wounds, the five sorrowful mysteries), but one hesitates to draw conclusions without more specific evidence. The second part (in three stanzas close to Long Measure but without overt reference to the Trinity) is a petitionary hymn that plays another variation on divine writings in the heart:

> Since bloud is fittest, Lord, to write
> Thy sorrows in, and bloudie fight;
> My heart hath store, write there, where in
> One box doth lie both ink and sinne:
>
> That when sinne spies so many foes,
> Thy whips, thy nails, thy wounds, thy woes,
> All come to lodge there, sinne may say,
> *No room for me,* and flie away.
>
> Sinne being gone, oh fill the place,
> And keep possession with thy grace;
> Lest sinne take courage and return,
> And all the writings blot or burn.

The poem refers to the parable of the garnished house (Mat. xii. 43–45) and to some traditional emblems of the passion, whips, nails, wounds, woes. These are objects of meditation, and the poem has an obvious relation to meditative emblem books such as Hugo's *Pia Desideria* or Harvey's *Schola Cordis*. In form and method the poem is an emblematic hymn.

"Redemption," one of Herbert's finest poems, has attracted so much commentary not much more need be said. It is a sonnet, like "The Sinner," and answers that poem's problems. Typology, notably a contrast between the Old-Testament God writing laws on stone and the New-Testament God putting his spirit into the living heart, has been a constant theme in poems up to this point. In "Redemption," the two testaments are the central concern. By composition by similitude, Herbert presents God as a landlord, man as his tenant, and the testaments as two leases. The Old Covenant requires a price fallen man is unable to pay. At the same time, using composition of place, Herbert puts the reader into a variety of allegorical places and simultaneously moves Christ into the reader's own world of deeds and rents, theaters and gardens:

> Having been tenant long to a rich Lord,
>   Not thriving, I resolved to be bold,
>   And make a suit unto him, to afford
> A new small-rented lease, and cancell th' old.
> In heaven at his manour I him sought:
>   They told me there, that he was lately gone
>   About some land, which he had dearly bought
> Long since on earth, to take possession.
> I straight return'd, and knowing his great birth,
>   Sought him accordingly in great resorts;
>   In cities, theatres, gardens, parks, and courts:
> At length I heard a ragged noise and mirth
>   Of theeves and murderers: there I him espied,
>   Who straight, *Your suit is granted,* said, and died.

The poem ends with one of Herbert's brilliant understatements: it is by dying that Christ purchases the "new small-rented lease."

"Sepulchre," a Holy Saturday poem that falls between the Crucifixion and the Resurrection, is the most extensive of the sequence's many comparisons between man's heart and stone. It also movingly develops the related theme of the questionable fitness of man's heart as a dwelling-place for Christ. The tomb is quieter and more peaceful.

> O Blessed bodie! Whither art thou thrown?
> No lodging for thee, but a cold hard stone?
> So many hearts on earth, and yet not one
>   Receive thee? . . .
> Where our hard hearts have took up stones to brain thee,
> And missing this, most falsly did arraigne thee;
> Onely these stones in quiet entertain thee,
>   And order.

Appropriate to its place in the cycle of divine mysteries, "Sepulchre" reaches a low point of desolation and pessimism about man's sinful condition. Yet however great man's sin, and its greatness is shown by what it does to Christ, nothing can impede Christ's love.

> And as of old the Law by heav'nly art
> Was writ in stone; so thou, which also art
> The letter of the word, find'st no fit heart
>   To hold thee.
> Yet do we still persist as we began,
> And so should perish, but that nothing can,
> Though it be cold, hard, foul, from loving man
>   Withhold thee.

After Holy Saturday comes Easter. Into the bleak mood established by the sequence, which has proposed various grounds for theological hope but has failed, in spite of attempts in various modes, to turn thorns into flowers, bursts the hymn "Easter." Its musical harmonies and unalloyed joy shine in contrast with what precedes it. Herbert could not be contented by the prospect of his own redemption when that rested on Christ's passion and death. But there is another counterbalance to that "mighty passion" with which he could not deal: Christ's Resurrection, which truly cancels sorrow. Coming to the hymn on Easter from the Good Friday poems and "Sepulchre," one also sees new meaning in its joyous opening phrase: "Rise *heart;* thy Lord is risen."

The holy-week sequence closes with "Easter-wings," the best of Herbert's shaped poems. It may have been the printer's idea to turn it vertically on the page, a doubtful artificiality. For the shape is not merely extrinsic or visually significant. The basic movement is heard and felt if the poem is read aloud. Indeed, only then does the visual pattern take on full meaning. The contraction and expansion of line lengths corresponds to an analogous psychological and spiritual contraction and expansion. Summing up the history of man, as race and individual, the poem also sums up the events and emotions of the sequence it concludes. Through sorrow and suffering it reaches joy, arriving at Easter by way of Good Friday and drawing the whole story into perspective:

> Lord, who createdst man in wealth and store,
>   Though foolishly he lost the same,
>   Decaying more and more,
>   Till he became
>   Most poore:
>   With thee
>   O let me rise
>   As larks, harmoniously,
>   And sing this day thy victories:
> Then shall the fall further the flight in me.

In addition to contraction-expansion (famine and feast, sorrow and joy), there is a downward-upward motion in each stanza: man's fall, Christ's rising. While it is primarily a visual poem, sound plays so large a part in it that it would not be difficult to treat it as a song text, which indeed the last lines almost call for: "O let me rise / As larks, harmoniously, / And sing this day thy victories." Like "The Altar," "Easter-wings" has a visual function too: a reader who has once made the poem his own can relive the experience in a moment merely by seeing it on the page.

After the opening sequence of "The Church" other sequences follow. There are two transitional poems on baptism, a sonnet and a hymn. Then a new sequence starts with "Nature," a poem concerning man's bondage to original sin. An obvious progression follows: "Sinne (I)," "Affliction (I)," "Repentance," "Faith," "Prayer (I)," and "The H. Communion." The sinner's progress may be read in the titles. Having got this far, he celebrates communion by singing "Antiphon (I)," which is followed by two sonnets on "Love." "The Temper (I)" ushers in a new progression or perhaps a further stage in the same sequence. "The Church" is not organized on a single or simple principle. It is partly liturgical and sacramental, partly based on the Christian year, partly on the pattern of man's fall, redemption, and ultimate salvation, partly on the concomitant separation and reunion of God and man, and partly on the vicissitudes of life or of the soul in devotion. What most characterizes *The Temple* is unity in diversity, a vital balance between the one and the many, which (men assumed) was also the basic organizational principle of the universe as God constructed it.

The variety in *The Temple* is greater than a brief analysis can show. What the opening sequence reveals, nevertheless, is that this variety is both poetic and devotional. The poems are linked by broad organizational principles: Holy Week, man's fall and rise, his varied participation in Christ's passion and resurrection. They are also linked by continuity with variation in images and themes, most notably, the stone and the heart. Themes and moods are further varied by shifts in the poems' devotional procedures, from pure meditation to pure song but usually combining several modes in the same poem. Another poet might have gathered his sonnets, hymns, meditations, poems on love or affliction, communion verses, into distinct groups. Had Herbert meant to do so, there should be evidence of it even in early drafts. We do not know whether *The Temple* as we have it is finished and ready for publication. On balance, the evidence suggests that it is. In any event, the experience of reading it or using it as a devotional aid confirms the rightness of his presumed decision. The order is most effective as it stands.

4. Contemplative Desolation

According to Martz, the "plateau" of the spiritual struggle in *The Temple* is marked by a group of four poems, "The Search," "Grief," "The Crosse," and "The Flower." Joseph Summers agrees on the close connection between "The Crosse" and "The Flower." [12] The last and most remarkable of these poems Martz calls "a poem of summation, of spiritual achievement," while Arnold Stein praises it as "one of the greatest lyrics in the language." [13] In this group of poems, Herbert pierces deeper into the spiritual life than anywhere else in *The Temple*. He seems, in fact, to enter for a time the paths of mystical prayer. Conditions in the Anglican Church in the seventeenth century militated against the sustained practice of contemplation by its orthodox members. Mysticism was deeply mistrusted. Herbert's friend Nicholas Ferrar confronted constant suspicions about the practices of his "Arminian Nunnery" at Little Gidding. The monastic institutions that sheltered contemplatives had been abolished. Baker's disciple Serenus Cressy complains of Anglicans:

> Their avarice having swallowed all the revenewes which nourished men in a solitary life of meditation and contemplation, they both want such effectual helps thereto, and dare not for feare of being censured as halfe-Catholiques commend or practise the meanes proper and conducting to it, insomuch as the very name of Contemplation is unknow'n among them, I meane in the mysticall sense.[14]

Doubtless some Anglicans practiced contemplation, but they had no institutional framework to "nourish" it and usually no friends to confide their experiences to.

Yet either Herbert underwent a genuine mystical experi-

ence or he decided to borrow, at a climax in *The Temple,* traditional language and modes of devotion that mystics used to
express themselves. At the least, he employed a mode reminiscent of contemplation to convey some deep religious experience.

The first clue is in the opening lines of "The Search":

> Whither, O, whither art thou fled,
>   My Lord, my Love?
> My searches are my daily bread;
>   Yet never prove.

The poet's situation is that of the beloved abandoned by her
lover. The source of a long mystical tradition on this theme, as
one might expect, is the Song of Solomon:

> By night on my bed I sought him whom my soul loveth: I
> sought him, but I found him not. I will rise now, and go
> about the city in the streets, and in the broad ways I will
> seek him whom my soul loveth: I sought him, but I found
> him not. The watchmen that go about the city found me: to
> whom I said, Saw ye him whom my soul loveth? (iii.1–3)

This passage came to be read as an expression of the soul's
spiritual desolation or sense of abandonment at certain stages
of the mystical way. One instance of the tradition is the poem
"Canciones entre el alma y el Esposo" by St. John of the Cross.
In the opening lines the Bride (the soul) addresses a lament to
the divine Spouse:

> Where can your hiding be,
> Beloved, that you left me thus to moan
> While like the stag you flee
> Leaving the wound with me?
> I followed calling loud, but you had flown.[15]

The soul, wounded with love, is abandoned by her beloved. She
is in one of what St. John calls the "dark nights of the soul."

Mystics explain this desolation and feeling of abandonment, commonly experienced in the mystical way, as a trial, a means God uses to strengthen and purify the soul's love and to purge that love from dependence on the senses or on merely emotional consolations. If the soul persists in spite of spiritual dryness, it is rewarded by a renewal of God's presence.

Another source of this traditional theme is the psalms. The speaker in Psalm 88 cries: "Lord, why casteth thou off my soul? why hidest thou thy face from me?" He is echoed in the eighth stanza of "The Search":

> Where is my God? what hidden place
>   Conceals thee still?
> What covert dare eclipse thy face?
>   Is it thy will?

Herbert echoes the psalms, an important locus of the legal image of God as man's advocate or defense counsel, in two other stanzas:

> Since then my grief must be as large,
>   As is thy space,
> Thy distance from me; see my charge,
>   Lord, see my case.

> O take these barres, these lengths away;
>   Turn, and restore me:
> Be not Almightie, let me say,
>   Against, but for me.

The verse style strikingly resembles the metrical psalms. The poem combines vocal techniques from metrical psalmody with imagery connected with mystical prayer. Such a combination has precedents. Sung or recited, the psalms were long used for meditation; a parallel tradition used them (especially 119) as food for contemplation and a means of expressing contemplative experience.

"The Search" clearly implies that it must be God's will that his face is hidden. No cloud or covert would dare conceal the

Creator from his creature. The situation is entirely different from that in several earlier poems in "The Church," when Herbert fled the religious life and God pursued. "The Search" ends without the speaker attaining his goal, yet a final paradox promises its future attainment. The greater his present affliction, the greater his future joy; the further the distance from God, the closer their union when they reunite. If their separation is by definition infinite, their union will be infinite too:

> When thou dost turn, and wilt be neare;
> > What edge so keen,
> What point so piercing can appeare
> > To come between?
>
> For as thy absence doth excell
> > All distance known:
> So doth thy nearenesse bear the bell,
> > Making two one.

On this note the poem ends. The ultimate goal of the mystical life is union between the soul and God, "Making two one." That promise is held forth here, but not yet. For the present, the search fails.

The next poem in the sequence is "Grief." It starts like a Shakespearean sonnet but goes on too long by an extra quatrain. Its conventional form is further disturbed by enjambments and wild invocations, flamboyantly metaphysical, for tears sufficient to express the poet's sorrow. His "grief hath need of all the watry things, / That nature hath produc'd." Such exaggeration is unusual in Herbert save in such poems as "The Collar," in which he allows a posturing persona to express a wrongful impatience in order to show it rebuked and controlled in the conclusion. Donne uses the technique in "Holy Sonnet 5." But "Grief" is different from "The Collar." It is one of a very few poems in *The Temple* whose dissonance is not finally resolved. Martz suggests as sources Job, Jeremiah, the Psalms, and "the Southwellian literature of tears."[16] But the Magdalene poems are foreign to Herbert's spirit. More than ordinary grounds would be necessary for such displays: a last rhymed couplet that excludes "measure, tune, and time" and a broken, extra-metrical nineteenth half-line that closes the poem without even a semblance of order: "Alas, my God!" Only one grief is great enough to justify such an exhibition from Herbert's orderly pen: his continued sense of absolute desolation arising from the loss of God's presence, after being so wounded by love that nothing else can satisfy him.

Prayers, sighs, groans, and tears having failed to break down the barrier, Herbert turns to a never-failing source of inspiration in "The Crosse." Here is an emblem that can instantly revive old devotions, an object for familiar meditations. But, as documented by Sartre and Beckett, familiar objects may become suddenly unrecognizable in moments of spiritual crisis or alienation from what seemed real and dependable:

> What is this strange and uncouth thing?
> To make me sigh, and seek, and faint, and die,
> Untill I had some place, where I might sing,
>   And serve thee; and not onely I,
> But all my wealth and familie might combine
> To set thy honour up, as our designe.
>
> And then when after much delay,
> Much wrastling, many a combate, this deare end,
> So much desir'd, is giv'n, to take away
>   My power to serve thee; to unbend
> All my abilities, my designes confound,
> And lay my threatnings bleeding on the ground.
>   .   .   .
> To have my aim, and yet to be
> Further from it then when I bent my bow;
> To make my hopes my torture, and the fee
>   Of all my woes another wo,
> Is in the midst of delicates to need,
> And ev'n in Paradise to be a weed.

The poem belongs to Herbert's much-discussed struggle to come to terms with his vocation. Having denied the promise of his birth and the pleasures of the world, he finds, as in the better-known "Affliction (I)," that God in turn has deprived him of any pleasure in the religious life. He has sacrificed much and been rewarded with nothing. As a priest, he lives "in the midst of delicates," yet without communion with God is no more than a weed in Paradise.

In the last stanza Herbert ends his anatomy of suffering and turns to prayer:

> Ah my deare Father, ease my smart!
> These contrarieties crush me: these crosse actions
> Doe winde a rope about, and cut my heart:
>   And yet since these thy contradictions
> Are properly a crosse felt by thy Sonne,
> With but foure words, my words, *Thy will be done.*

What more vivid image for his state could be imagined than "winde a rope about, and cut my heart"? The ending echoes the Lord's Prayer, but a closer source is Christ's acceptance of the passion in Gethsemane. It is an *imitatio Christi.* If Herbert can call these "my words," it is because suffering draws him into unity with his Savior. Up to this point the poem seemed to demonstrate the poet's inability to use the cross for devotional purposes. The last stanza unexpectedly turns his experience into a kind of passion and crucifixion. What seemed to be distraction from prayer, digression from the point, incapacity to meditate on the crucifix, is transformed by the act of acceptance into a successful exercise in devotion. His inability to pray becomes his prayer.

5. Contemplation: "The Flower"

Contemplative or mystical prayer is defined by two essential characteristics. It is a kind of prayer that involves, in some sense, a direct approach of the soul to God, leading eventually to union; and it is a kind of prayer that is radically passive. The active agent is not the soul but God. There are other differences from ordinary prayer. Vocal prayer, song, meditation all

involve, indeed necessitate, sense imagery and engagement of
the emotions. Thus they are basically similar to poetry, which
Milton calls simple, sensuous, and passionate. Sensuous immediacy, dramatic engagement, and strong emotion make
Donne's "Holy Sonnets" or Herbert's "The Agonie" good
poetry as well as effective meditation. The poetry of meditation
has another important quality, which is that it is most effective
when it describes a present action or an ongoing process: a
dramatic scene being participated in, emotions being felt, logic
being worked out. Except for "The Extasie," with its narrative
frame, nearly all Donne's poems, secular and religious, describe
actions and thought processes presently occurring. Or more
accurately, they give that illusion. In a meditative poem, the
reader follows the poet through a re-creation of the process of
meditation.

Unlike meditation, prayer of the will or contemplation
cannot be described in sensible or emotional terms. Contemplation is imageless and, as all mystics agree, impossible to describe
discursively.[17] Over the centuries, mystics developed whole systems of terminology to talk about their experiences, but their
terms are metaphorical and indirect, pointing toward contemplation from outside. They recollect an experience rather than
evoke or recreate it. A meditative poem may coexist with the act
of meditation and assist it; a contemplative poem cannot.
Poetry like that of Crashaw or Vaughan, as we shall see, may
point toward or reflect mystical experience but cannot imitate
the experience itself. A poem like St. John of the Cross's "En
una noche oscura," together with its explanatory treatise, *The
Ascent of Mount Carmel,* suggests obscurely what contemplation
is like and may serve as a guide; but it is not itself contemplative. No more so is the Song of Solomon, although (whatever its
original meaning) it is the great source of contemplative imagery.

In a meditative poem, everything works to achieve an effect
of dramatic immediacy:

This is my playes last scene, here heavens appoint
My pilgrimages last mile; and my race

Idly, yet quickly runne, hath this last pace,
My spans last inch, my minutes latest point,
And gluttonous death, will instantly unjoynt
My body, and soule.

The illusion of immediacy is gained by poetic means, of which
the Metaphysical Poets were great masters. Donne's sonnet is a
poem rather than a meditative prayer, yet it achieves the effect
of putting a willing reader into a state of meditation. It gives
him at least an illusion of going through the meditative process.
A religious reader might profit, an agnostic reader experience
for a moment what meditation might be like. The subject of this
particular meditation, of course, is death: what it is like to die,
to experience the last terrified minutes of life in a state of un-
readiness. The purpose is to evoke the moment with its
thoughts and emotions, then move with the weight of these
emotions toward a resolution of the predicament so vividly presented: to live well (by grace) and thus in future to die not
resisting in terror but with peaceful acceptance.

Donne's sonnets are built so as to imitate or evoke in the
reader the meditative process. Mystical or contemplative states
cannot be so evoked. The difference is clearly seen in the poem
that concludes Herbert's contemplative sequence: "The
Flower." In it, Herbert describes events in his interior life that
resemble mystical experience. He uses a combination of image
systems that are central to the traditional language of mystics.
One is the interior garden or growing plant of the soul, watered
by the rain of God's grace or blasted by the heats and frosts of
spiritual desolation. The most familiar locus is St. Teresa's *Life,*
but the tradition goes back at least to the Song of Solomon.[18]
The other main traditional image is man as a "sunflower," directing his soul toward God as a flower follows the course of the
sun. It is a favorite image of Vaughan's.[19]

After the bleak desolations of "The Search," "Grief," and
"The Crosse," the opening of "The Flower" gives the reader a
sense of freshness and relief:

How fresh, O Lord, how sweet and clean
Are thy returns! ev'n as the flowers in spring;

To which, besides their own demean,
The late-past frosts tributes of pleasure bring.
   Grief melts away
   Like snow in May,
 As if there were no such cold thing.

Who would have thought my shrivel'd heart
Could have recover'd greennesse? It was gone
   Quite under ground; as flowers depart
To see their mother-root, when they have blown;
   Where they together
   All the hard weather,
Dead to the world, keep house unknown.

These are thy wonders, Lord of power,
Killing and quickning, bringing down to hell
   And up to heaven in an houre;
Making a chiming of a passing-bell.
   We say amisse,
   This or that is:
Thy word is all, if we could spell.

O that I once past changing were,
Fast in thy Paradise, where no flower can wither!
   Many a spring I shoot up fair,
Offring at heav'n, growing and groning thither:
   Nor doth my flower
   Want a spring-showre,
My sinnes and I joining together.

But while I grow in a straight line,
Still upwards bent, as if heav'n were mine own,
   Thy anger comes, and I decline:
What frost to that? what pole is not the zone,
   Where all things burn,
   When thou dost turn,
And the least frown of thine is shown?

And now in age I bud again,
After so many deaths I live and write;
  I once more smell the dew and rain,
And relish versing: O my onely light,
      It cannot be
      That I am he
  On whom thy tempests fell all night.

These are thy wonders, Lord of love,
To make us see we are but flowers that glide:
  Which when we once can finde and prove,
Thou hast a garden for us, where to bide.
      Who would be more,
      Swelling through store,
  Forfeit their Paradise by their pride.

The weed in Paradise is transformed potentially into a flower in Paradise. Yet springtime does not last in a world whose only constant rule is change. More winters and frosts may be expected. The flower, as in several other Herbert poems, is a symbol of evanescence: its root is ever in its grave. God has a Paradise where his flowers live and bloom forever, and experiences such as the poem describes suggest what that Paradise is like. But life has taught Herbert the lesson that paradise will only be found, except for momentary anticipations, in the next world. To seek to have it now is to risk losing all. On that terrible note the poem ends.

"The Flower" devotes proportionately more time to winter and change than to spring. In its ending it resembles *The Pilgrim's Progress,* whose long, triumphant conclusion is abruptly qualified by a postscript reminding us that hell has doorways that may open fast by the gates of heaven. Yet critics rightly read the poem as a brilliant expression of joy. Stein suggests one reason this may be so. He notes that the poem moves from "the lyrical immediacy of the moment" in its first stanza back to "the history before the moment" in its body.[20] In fact, the manipulation of time is more complicated than that. Through skillful control of time, Herbert gives the poem its emphasis and, in addition, conveys what is essentially a timeless contemplative experience in time's common language. His handling of his materials, as poet and devotional writer, is nearer to Wordsworth than to Donne.

The poem begins in the present: "How fresh, O Lord, how sweet and clean / Are thy returns." From this vantage it refers only briefly to the past: the "late-past frosts" that now serve to water the flowers as they melt. The second stanza moves back into history, to the time when his "shrivel'd heart" went underground to escape the winter. The third stanza generalizes, commenting on the swiftness of these changes: "These are thy wonders, Lord of power." The fourth longs for a time past change, "Fast in thy Paradise, where no flower can wither." Often the poet seems to approach this state, described in the historical present tense: "Many a spring I shoot up fair, / Offring at heav'n." The fifth stanza, however, still using the historical present, reveals that his progress is illusory: "But while I grow in a straight line . . . / Thy anger comes, and I decline." The sixth stanza, the climax of the poem, seems to return finally to the simple present of the poem's opening:

> And now in age I bud again,
> After so many deaths I live and write;
> I once more smell the dew and rain,
> And relish versing: O my onely light,
>   It cannot be
>   That I am he
> On whom thy tempests fell all night.

He is reborn, a new man. It is as if God's tempests fell on someone else at a time now firmly moved into the completed past.

But is the sixth stanza set in the simple present, as its verbs and its intense, sensuous immediacy suggest? One would say so if the poem ended here, but it does not. A further twist is given by Stanza 7. This last stanza is sometimes treated as an anti-climactic moral tacked onto the poem. But it is much more. It represents a necessary return to present time as the world knows it. In it, we hear a voice addressing the Lord of love. It is the same voice we heard a while earlier addressing the Lord of power, and it speaks from approximately the same point in time. This speaker is the poet, back in time present, now recollecting rebirths as well as afflictions and thus completing the lesson of change. The "now" in which he buds again has receded. The only true stability, he insists, lies in the promised future: that garden where man will one day "bide." Already, the "present" moment of rebirth has faded into the past and become one with the spiritual frosts and deaths of earlier experience. According to tradition, eternity is properly spoken of in the present tense. It is the everlasting now, the great "I am." Once out of eternity, however, the soul looks back on its eternal but momentary experience and sees something whose essence is irrecoverable: past and gone. Thus three distinct kinds of present tense are employed in "The Flower": historical present, eternal present, and simple present. Such complexity helps recapture and indirectly convey something of Herbert's spiritual experience.

The devotional mode of "The Flower" is not typical of Herbert's poetry as a whole. Yet as one acquaints himself with *The Temple* he becomes aware that no single devotional method is typical. The variety of mood, technique, genre, and devotional mode is extraordinary. There is something for everyone, food for nearly any spiritual state or inclination. Even the most seemingly trivial poem contributes to the whole. Yet, in spite of this variety, Herbert is constantly in control of his material. Outbursts, exaggerations, dissonances have their purposes. He is equally adept at psalm or hymn, petition, celebration, or complaint, song or speech, meditation or contemplation. Yet this variety is so well ordered that he never seems to leave the *via media*, to violate Anglican propriety or spiritual and poetic simplicity. One reason is that Herbert represents the varieties of devotion in reasonable proportions. *The Temple*'s devotional mixture corresponds to a full, typical spiritual life, which is seldom pure vocal prayer, song, meditation, or contemplation, but a combination of them all. In breadth of devotion and truth to experience, Herbert is unsurpassed.

Notes

1. Izaak Walton, *The Lives* (London: Oxford University Press, 1927), p. 296.
2. Louis Martz, *The Poetry of Meditation* (New Haven: Yale University Press, 1962), p. 279.
3. Martz, p. 279.
4. Martz, pp. 280–281.
5. The unity of *The Temple,* subject of several recent dissertations, is discussed by Martz, pp. 291–294. He includes the two poems on baptism in the first sequence and posits a greater difference than I between it and the remaining poems.
6. Cited by Rosemary Freeman, *English Emblem Books* (London: Chatto & Windus, 1948), p. 15. On visual poetry see also Dick Higgins, *George Herbert's Pattern Poems: In Their Tradition* (West Glover, Vermont: Unpublished Editions, 1977).
7. Tuve, *A Reading of George Herbert* (Chicago: University of Chicago Press, 1952), pp. 19–99.
8. Freeman, *English Emblem Books,* pp. 160–161.
9. See Tuve, pp. 112–137.
10. See Martz, p. 294.
11. This idea (first called to my attention by a review of his *The Editor as Critic and the Critic as Editor*) J. Max Patrick considers at least a "possibility" (letter of January 1977 in response to a query).
12. Martz, p. 309; Summers, *George Herbert: His Religion and Art* (London: Chatto & Windus, 1954), p. 188.
13. Martz, p. 311; Stein, *George Herbert's Lyrics* (Baltimore: Johns Hopkins Press, 1968), p. 196. See also A. L. Clements, "Theme, Tone, and Tradition in George Herbert's Poetry," *ELR,* 3 (1973), 264–283, which touches briefly on these poems as a sequence embodying the "alternations" of mystical experience.
14. Cressy, *Exmologesis* (Paris, 1647), p. 641.
15. *The Poems of St. John of the Cross,* trans. Roy Campbell (New York: Pantheon Books, 1953), pp. 14–15.
16. Martz, p. 310.
17. See St. John of the Cross, *The Complete Works,* ed. E. Allison Peers (Westminster: Newman Press, 1964), I, 105.
18. *The Complete Works of St Teresa of Jesus,* ed. E. Allison Peers, 3 vols. (London: Sheed & Ward, 1944–1946); see also Stanley Stewart, *The Enclosed Garden* (Madison: University of Wisconsin Press, 1966).
19. See R. A. Durr, *On the Mystical Poetry of Henry Vaughan* (Cambridge: Harvard University Press, 1962). An alternative terminology might describe "The Flower" as about gaining and losing grace; but the action is unlike typical Puritan conversion experiences and still deserves, on account of God's active role, to be called extraordinary or mystical.
20. Stein, p. 197.

5.

Richard Crashaw: Sensible Affection

1. Baroque Aesthetics

Critics have not treated Crashaw's poetry kindly. It is commonplace to accuse him of bad taste and extravagance. He is incapable of enforcing a structure on his poems. He pursues images for their own sake. He cannot write strong, simple poetry. He is un-English. He is too passionate or he is too cold and calculating. In a revaluation for *Scrutiny*, John Peter finds him indulging in the "suspicious habits" of Shelley and Swinburne.[1] Robert M. Adams speaks of his "grotesque metaphor," finds a typical image "slightly nauseating," and asserts that Crashaw's must be a God who views man as "a joke in slightly bad taste."[2] Austin Warren, usually sympathetic to Crashaw's thinking, finds his "sanguinary metaphors . . . repugnant to normal taste."[3] Mario Praz defends Crashaw against these squeamish reactions by arguing that he only did what dozens of Italians and Neolatinists were equally guilty of. "Neither religion nor love is actually at the back of such a glitter of conceits, but only indulgence in a self-congratulatory and self-complacent play of wit."[4] It is an odd defense.

Crashaw's poetic style may be partly understood in terms of two aesthetics that flowered in Europe during the seventeenth century: Mannerism and Baroque. The painting,

116

sculpture, architecture, and music of the period share, so far as differing media may, characteristics common in Crashaw's poetry. Bernini's statue of St. Teresa in ecstasy and his Baldacchino in St. Peter's have become standard illustrations of Crashaw's spirit. "The baroque style is exuberant, rhetorical, sensual, grandiose. The repose and symmetry of Renaissance art have yielded to agitation, aspiration, ambition, an intense striving to transcend the limits of each genre." [5] Equally relevant to Crashaw's poetry are certain qualities of Mannerist art: "A mode which stresses shock value, distortion, illogicality, disturbance, and . . . outrage to the 'conventional sense of decorum.' " [6]

Seventeenth-century artists were fond of relating one medium to another. Crashaw reputedly was a skilled painter and musician. But, having named such general resemblances, one can go only so much further in drawing specific conclusions. Architecture is architecture, music is music, poetry is poetry. The problems and opportunities of each medium are different, and the techniques developed in one medium are not always transferable to another. Mannerist and Baroque are useful terms generally, but as soon as one begins to consider specific painters, musicians, or works of art, they begin to break down as such terms tend to do. Is the Baroque musician Bach more agitated than the Renaissance sculptor Michelangelo? Are Poussin's landscapes more unbalanced than Petrarch's poetry? One need only begin asking such questions to realize the limitations of such sweeping categories.

Moreover, Crashaw's style is not the product of aesthetic considerations alone. Poetic style in a committed seventeenth-century religious poet cannot be divorced from devotional method. Attempts have been made in recent years to relate Crashaw to various devotional figures or schools: to St. Teresa, St. John of the Cross, Joannes Mauburnus, St. Ignatius, and St. Francis de Sales.[7] But while there are echoes of Ignatian, Salesian, and Spanish mystical influences in Crashaw's poetry, sometimes confirmed by his translations or references, attempts to link him with single authorities or methods are unconvincing. Like Donne and Herbert, he was a highly educated man, widely read in the literature of theology and devotion. His father, an anti-Catholic polemicist, assembled a large devotional library in the course of his work. As a fellow of Peterhouse, the stronghold of Laudianism, and as a friend of Nicholas Ferrar, another famous collector of continental devotional books, Crashaw had almost unlimited access to the religious treatises of his time. He was not likely to restrict himself, in life or poetry, to a single master or method. No major seventeenth-century devotional poet did.

2. Vocal Devotions and Hymns

Liturgy and vocal prayer played an important part in the Laudian revival at Peterhouse. Cosin, the Master, put a marble altar in the new college chapel and adorned it with candlesticks and an incense pot. There were a crucifix, a roof of angels, and stained-glass windows. The Puritan Prynne complained of "Popish ceremonies" and noted that "the common report was that none might approach the altar in Peterhouse but in sandals." [8] More seriously, Cosin revived the primer or manual of vocal prayer, which fell out of use under Henry VIII. His *A Collection of Private Devotions* (1627) is an office book, consisting mainly of prayers for the canonical hours, with penitential psalms, a litany, prayers for the King and Queen, and similar observances. The Puritans immediately recognized the significance of such a devotional manual from so authoritative a source and attacked it violently. There is no doubt that Crashaw was much exposed to the rituals of vocal prayer and divine song, both in his college and at Little Gidding, where he was a frequent visitor.

A close relationship between Crashaw's poetry and the liturgical environment of Peterhouse is suggested by two accounts of his life. David Lloyd reports that Crashaw habitually wrote his poems in the small church where he was curate: "making his Verses not in his Study at St. *Peters-house,* but in his Devotions, wherein he spent many a night, at St. *Maries* Church; warbling his Hymns for St. *Ambroses* his Saints, under

Tertullians Roof of Angels." Anthony Wood repeats the story, adding that Crashaw nested in this church like a "swallow near the House of God," and that "like a primitive Saint he offer'd more prayers in the night, than others usually offer in the day." [9]

Crashaw has been called, with Herbert and Vaughan, the most musical of the Metaphysical Poets. His best-known poem in this respect is "Musicks Duell," which achieves remarkable effects. A dozen of his hymns are almost equally musical. He wrote a number of hymns on the liturgical year, including the famous hymn on the Nativity. There are hymns for the New Year, Epiphany, and Easter, and for two recent additions to the Roman calendar: the Holy Name of Jesus and the Assumption.[10] In 1648 a series of translations of traditional Latin hymns appeared as well: *Vexilla Regis, Sancta Maria Dolorum, Adoro Te, Lauda Sion Salvatorem, Dies Irae,* and *O Gloriosa Domina.* All but two of these translations, made while Crashaw was still an Anglican, look like texts for musical setting. Crashaw also wrote two metrical psalms, 23 and 137.

Crashaw's translations of the psalms and the Latin hymns are very free. *"Sancta Maria Dolorum"* is subtitled "A Patheticall descant upon the devout Plainsong of *Stabat Mater Dolorosa."* Warren remarks that "the same rubric might have done service for all of the group." [11] The hymns are descants, poetic elaborations on an original "plainsong" text, analogous to recent developments in sacred music. They are also pathetical: like the music of the *seconda pratica,* they play deliberately on the hearer's affections. If one approaches these hymns expecting to find the letter or even the spirit of the originals he will be disappointed. They are as far from their sources as Palestrina is from Gregorian. Yet in their way they are very good. Crashaw's *Dies Irae* is typical. Instead of a spare and sonorous clangor, one finds something much warmer:

> Ah then, poor soul, what wilt thou say?
> And to what Patron chuse to pray?
> When starres themselves shall stagger; and
> The most firm foot no more then stand.

But thou giv'st leave (dread Lord) that we
Take shelter from thy self, in thee;
And with the wings of thine own dove
Fly to thy scepter of soft love.

Dear, remember in that Day
Who was the cause thou cams't this way.
Thy sheep was stray'd; And thou wouldst be
Even lost thy self in seeking me.

In this hymn on the terrors of Judgment Day, Crashaw characteristically dwells more on love than fear, and Christ in Majesty becomes the Good Shepherd.

Crashaw's purest exercise in vocal devotion is "The Office of the Holy Cross." This free translation in prose and verse, made from a medieval Latin book of hours or a Marian primer, consists of introductory versicles and responses, a hymn, an antiphon, more versicles, and a collect for each of the canonical hours from Matins to Compline. Its theme is the Passion and Crucifixion. After he became a Catholic priest, Crashaw would have recited daily offices from the breviary, but he probably used a book of hours while still at Peterhouse. Cosin's adaption was published in 1627, Crashaw's in 1648. The first version omits a prayer for the dead restored in 1652, suggesting that Crashaw hoped these devotions could be used by Anglicans and that perhaps they were written when he was still an Anglican himself.

Crashaw's feast-day hymns, his most original exercises in vocal devotion, have with one exception been neglected. Yet they are among his most characteristic works. The three hymns of 1646, on the Nativity, the Circumcision (later "New Year's Day"), and Easter, are the least innovative technically. They employ regular stanzas like the hymns of Donne and Herbert. The hymns on the Epiphany and the Holy Name are different. The first, marked for three solo parts and a chorus, resembles *dramma per musica* or sacred oratorio. Other analogies are the classical hymns, Greek and Latin, which influenced Monteverdi, Schütz, and other contemporary composers. A real set piece, the Epiphany hymn would be at its best performed in church with full chorus and orchestra.

The central image in the Epiphany hymn is Christ as the true light, appearing at night to signal the first motion toward the dawning of eternal day.[12] The sun is put to shame and pagan darkness dispelled. Physical light is no match for spiritual light:

> (1.) His superficiall Beames sun-burn't our skin;
>   (2.) But left within
> (3.) The night and winter still of death and sin.
> (*Cho.*) Thy softer yet more certaine *Darts*
> Spare our eyes, but peirce our *Harts.*

One part of the hymn is sometimes cited as evidence that Crashaw was a mystic. The paradox of light in darkness (as in Vaughan's "The Night") leads Crashaw to Dionysius the Areopagite:

> (2.) By the oblique ambush of this close night
>   Couch't in that conscious shade
> The right-eye'd Areopagite
> Shall with a vigorous guesse invade
> And catche thy quick reflex; and sharply see
>   On this dark Ground
>   To descant *Thee.*
> (3.) O prize of the rich *Spirit!* with what feirce chase
>   Of his strong soul, shall he
>   Leap at thy lofty *Face,*
> And seize the swift Flash, in rebound
> From this obsequious cloud;
>   Once call'd a sun.

This is brilliant, evocative poetry; but by suggesting that God can be caught by leaps of violent effort it contradicts the observations of most mystics, who insist on passivity. There is a chain of musical references in the passage, however, that is essentially vocal, and that a musical setting would bring out more clearly:

the "quick reflex," the "dark Ground" against which the soloist plays "descant," the "feirce chase" and "rebound."

"To the Name Above Every Name, the Name of Jesus: A Hymn" is not marked for parts. It is a first-person singular devotion that constantly stresses an I-thou relationship with God. Unlike Donne, Crashaw is unrestricted by the thirty-nine articles and begins by addressing the Saints. In the first part of the hymn, song and music are continually evoked. From the Saints, the singer turns to Nature:

> Goe, *Soul,* out of thy Self, and seek for More.
>   Goe and request
> Great *Nature* for the *Key* of her huge Chest
> Of Heavns, the self involving Sett of Sphears
> (Which dull mortality more Feeles then heares)
>   Then rouse the nest
> Of nimble *Art,* and traverse round
> The Aiery Shop of soul-appeasing Sound:
> And beat a summons in the Same
>   All-soveraign Name. . . .
> Shall we dare This, my Soul? we'l doe't and bring
> No Other note for't, but the Name we sing
>   Wake *Lute* and *Harp*
>   And every sweet-lipp't Thing
>   That talkes with tunefull string;
> Start into life, And leap with me
> Into a hasty Fitt-tun'd Harmony.
>   Nor must you think it much
>   T'obey my bolder touch;
> I have Authority in *Love's* name to take you
> And to the worke of Love this morning wake you
>   Wake; In the Name
> Of *Him* who never sleeps, All Things that Are,
>   Or, What's the same,
>   Are Musicall;
>   Answer my Call
>   And come along;
> Help me to meditate mine Immortall Song.

Crashaw first invokes the music of the spheres, symbolizing universal harmony. We know from Milton's Nativity poem that man's fall broke this music so "dull mortality" no longer hears it in this world, though in devotion it may "feel" it. Art's role is to answer Nature's music. Then Nature is reinvoked as Crashaw calls on "All Things that Are" to sing the praises of the Name. At this moment, all things that are equals all things that are musical. The created world is filled with harmony answering the divine music, and no part is incapable of song.

Much of the effect of this hymn depends on the skillful building of musical effects over a large number of lines. The music continues, interweaving Art and Nature, Heaven and Earth, until it reaches a crescendo of "All-imbracing *Song*." The hymn is long, and to get a better idea of its full effect interested readers should consult the whole text.

Music is not the only sensuous means by which the hymn supports devotion. As in the Epiphany hymn, much use is made of light imagery. Taste and touch are frequently evoked. "Lo how the thirsty Lands / Gasp for thy Golden Showres!" Toward the end an increasing appeal is made to the sense of smell.

> *Sweet Name,* in Thy each Syllable
> A Thousand Blest *Arabias* dwell;
> A Thousand Hills of Frankincense;
> Mountains of myrhh, and Beds of spices.

The senses are not just appealed to, they are overloaded: of which, more later. The full power of Crashaw's technique is unstopped in the climax when the Name appears:

> Lo, where Aloft it comes! It comes, Among
> The Conduct of Adoring *Spirits,* that throng
> Like diligent Bees, And swarm about it.
>   O they are wise;
> And know what *Sweetes* are suck't from out it.
>   It is the Hive,
>   By which they thrive,
> Where All their Hoard of Hony lyes.

Lo where it comes, upon The snowy *Dove's*
Soft Back; And brings a Bosom big with Loves.
Welcome to our dark world, Thou
    Womb of Day!

Few of Donne's or Herbert's hymns are pure vocal devotions. Some are, others are meditative, emblematic, mystical. "To the Name Above Every Name" is influenced musically by recitative theories and methods, which are reflected in its irregular lines and unabashed emotions. Devotionally, it is an affective hymn, which appeals as directly as possible to the senses and feelings. Like the Name it evokes, it is a "universal *Synod* of All sweets."

3. *Affective Meditation*

Few poems in the Crashaw canon pursue an Ignatian type of meditation such as one finds in Donne or to a lesser extent in Herbert or Vaughan. Indeed, relatively few of his important poems are meditative at all. Crashaw's favorite forms are the epigram and the hymn, with the verse epistle a distant third. Some of the epigrams are meditative. For example, "On the wounds of our crucified Lord" is a meditation on the crucifixion:

O these wakefull wounds of thine!
    Are they Mouthes? or are they eyes?
Be they Mouthes, or be they eyne,
    Each bleeding part some one supplies.

Lo! a mouth, whose full-bloom'd lips
    At too deare a rate are roses.
Lo! a blood-shot eye! that weepes
    And many a cruell teare discloses.

O thou that on this foot hast laid
    Many a kisse, and many a Teare,
Now thou shal't have all repaid,
    Whatsoe're thy charges were.

This foot hath got a Mouth and lippes,
   To pay the sweet summe of thy kisses:
To pay thy Teares, an Eye that weeps
   In stead of Teares such Gems as this is.

The difference onely this appeares,
   (Nor can the change offend)
The debt is paid in *Ruby*-Teares,
   Which thou in Pearles did'st lend.

The first stanza addresses the crucified Christ, the second has no specific address, and the remainder address Mary Magdalene. The poem has several of the qualities one expects of meditation. It is based on biblical texts. First is the story of the woman, traditionally Mary Magdalene, who poured a box of ointment on Jesus' head, washed his feet with her tears, wiped them with her hair, and kissed them. The disciples complained she had wasted a great deal of money on the ointment that should have been spent on the poor, but Jesus told them "she did it for my burial." Second is the parable of the pearl of great price. Third are passages that place Mary Magdalene at the Crucifixion. Expanding on these passages was the tradition that took her as the prime symbol of profane love converted to sacred. The biblical passages, with the theology of the atonement, explain the thread of business imagery that some critics find inappropriate.

The poem, although intellectually rigorous, does not have an Ignatian structure. It appeals to the senses and constructs the imagined scene entirely differently. A rough analogy is to cinematic technique. An Ignatian exercise begins by taking in the whole scene—the two armies, the Crucifixion—with a middle- or long-distance shot. It may then move in for close-ups. We watch the Holy Family and then run up to kiss the baby. In Crashaw's poem, however, we begin with close-ups, both as to viewpoint and emotional involvement. The focus is closely on the wounds from the beginning; there is no attempt to see the Crucifixion as a whole. Only part way through the poem do we realize that Mary Magdalene is present, and even then we never turn from the wounds to look at her. This kind of technique leads critics to complain that they cannot visualize Crashaw's poems properly. It has even led some of them to argue that Crashaw's imagery is purely intellectual rather than sensory, surely a counsel of desperation.[13] This is a highly sensory poem and Crashaw is a highly sensory poet. It is idle to argue how clearly one pictures the scene or the wounds when it makes one's eyes ache and body squirm to read the poem. These and similar effects are not the extraneous by-products of Crashaw's poetry: they are at the center of what he is doing.

The Ignatian meditation employs intellect in a rigorous investigation, closely assisted by imagination, which gives sensible body to the intellect's discoveries and motivates the will toward a proper resolution. The intellectual content of Crashaw's poem is not connected in the same way with the imaginative content. The affections and the will are not manipulated by the poem's intellectual structure so much as aroused by direct evocation through the senses. Crashaw's method is more affective than the traditional Ignatian method. One might link the poem with the broad seventeenth-century movement of "devout humanism," of which St. Francis de Sales was a leading exponent. Popular devotions centering on the wounds of Christ, his Sacred Heart, the Seven Sorrows of Mary, the tears of the Magdalene, and similar topics were enjoying a tremendous vogue everywhere in Catholic Europe. These devotions involved more emotion and less intellect than traditional meditation. The emphasis shifted from discipline to intensity and even abandonment. Frequently devotions of this kind departed from meditation altogether, because they involved strong feelings accompanied by no intellectual effort whatever. One might call such a poem as "On the wounds of our crucified Lord" a Salesian meditation, but only as a convenient label, not an indication of a specific debt to St. Francis or his school. Marc Bertonasco points out that the characteristic emotional forms of devotion in the seventeenth century were by no means monopolized by the Catholic Counter-Reformation. Northern Baroque art can be more extreme than that of the south. Similar intense devotional phenomena are common in the lives and poetry of Englishmen, including respectable Puritans.[14] For this reason, "affective meditation" is the best term to describe this kind of poetry.

One influence on Crashaw's technique may have been Mannerism. The expression of feelings unfettered by rational constraint is often made possible in his poetry by means of a novel perspective or viewpoint. "Our Lord in his Circumcision to his Father" is another case in point. The poem's effect depends on its viewpoint: not Crashaw meditating on the circumcised Christ, but Christ addressing the Father and overheard by the reader.

> To thee these first fruits of my growing death
> (For what else is my life?) lo I bequeath.
> Tast this, and as thou lik'st this lesser flood
> Expect a Sea, my heart shall make it good.
> Thy wrath that wades heere now, e're long shall swim
> The flood-gate shall be set wide ope for him.
> Then let him drinke, and drinke, and doe his worst,
> To drowne the wantonnesse of his wild thirst.

Not even Jonathan Edwards could put the stark and terrible implications of redemption theology more vividly. Infinite wrath for sin and infinite love, infinite justice reconciled with infinite mercy: these are constant themes of seventeenth-century poetry, yet nowhere portrayed with such compressed power or so thoroughly realized through the senses and emotions.

Crashaw approached the theme of Christ's crucifixion again and again, always from some fresh viewpoint or unusual vantage. The subject of one of the few epigrams reprinted in his last collection is summed up by its title: "Upon the Body of our Bl. Lord, Naked and Bloody":

> They'have left thee naked, *Lord,* O that they had!
> This garment too I would they had deny'd.

> Thee with thy self they have too richly clad;
> Opening the purple wardrobe in thy side.

O never could there be garment too good
For thee to wear, But this, of thine own Blood.

Crashaw extends the traditional themes and paradoxes in this
meditation. The robe of blood is suggested by the purple robe
the soldiers mocked Christ in, and it in turn suggests a wardrobe because his side is opened to take it out. Since all men must
be clothed in Christ's blood to be saved, a wardrobe full of robes
is necessary. Crashaw's intellect and metaphysical wit transform
the conventional material. Again the reader's senses are deeply
affected, less his eyes or outward senses than the internal sense
that responds to violations of the body's integrity.

In their handling of sense and emotion, Crashaw's poems
represent an extreme. They lie at the boundary of the meditative mode. As Austin Warren points out, contrary to the opinion and perhaps the wish of many critics, Crashaw did not
discipline or intellectualize this emotional exuberance in his
latest or best poetry. If anything, as he perfected his craft,
writing new poems and polishing old ones from one edition to
the next, he gave the senses and emotions freer reign. He did
not move up a Platonic ladder from sense to spirit. Instead, he
added the most notorious stanzas to "The Weeper" and composed the hymn on the Holy Name. There are a number of
meditative epigrams among the earlier work, but the meditative
mode has very nearly been abandoned by the time *Carmen Deo
Nostro* was published. Crashaw was moving increasingly toward
a different devotional form: a form that paradoxically reaches
further down into the senses and higher up into the spirit.

4. Sensible Devotion

When a soul reaches the contemplative stages of prayer it
abandons meditation and discursive methods as long as this
prayer lasts. According to Francis de Sales, meditation is a
method of seeking and contemplation is what is sought. "Praier
is named meditation, till such time as it have produced the
home of devotion, and then it is converted into contemplation."
"The desire we have to obtain divine love, makes us meditate,

but love obtained, makes us contemplate." Contemplation is a mystical prayer in which the soul is said to enter a "dark cloud of unknowing" or divine darkness. St. Francis writes: "Knowledge having produced holy love, Love doth not staie within the compasse of knowledge which is in the understanding, but goes forward, and passeth far beyond it." I quote from St. Francis's contemplative work, *A Treatise on the Love of God,* which was translated by Miles Car (Douai, 1630), the editor of *Carmen Deo Nostro* and a close friend of Crashaw's in Paris.[15]

The seventeenth century also saw widespread movement away from emphasis on rational devotion in the lower stages of mental prayer. In his meditative treatise, the *Introduction to the Devout Life,* St. Francis stresses intellect far less than St. Ignatius. He advocates simplicity of method and warns Philothea against "searching out curious inventions." [16] His follower, Jean Pierre Camus, Bishop of Belley, in another book translated by Car, puts the matter more strongly. Ignatian meditation is too complicated and confusing, he urges, save for the intellectually inclined. For many "it is easier to Contemplate, then to meditate; and that more doe contemplate, (though they reflect not of it) then do meditate." Camus does not use "contemplate" strictly but refers to a "kind of simple contemplation in simple soules, which forerunns meditation." [17] His terminology is confusing but reflects his experience of actual devotional practices as a confessor and spiritual adviser.

Camus was not alone. Augustine Baker and his followers often voice similar arguments, usually impelled by their disapproval of forced imposition of Ignatian methods on those for whom they were unsuited. Baker was impressed by Fr. Balthazar Alvarez, the Spanish Jesuit who became St. Teresa's spiritual adviser. As recounted by Luis de Puente in his Life of Alvarez, after sixteen years of fruitless persistence in Ignatian meditation, he abandoned discursive prayer and met with immediate success. He wrote a long relation of his experience to the head of his order.[18] Baker, who had similar experiences and suffered similar resistance to his methods while he was spiritual adviser to the Benedictine nuns of Cambrai, retells the story in *Sancta Sophia* (III.i.7).

Experience led Baker to propose a third form of elementary prayer in addition to vocal and meditative. He called it "sensible affection" or "sensible devotion." Like Camus, Baker was impelled by practical exigencies to describe a kind of prayer for which he found no precise terminology in the literature. It is possible to suggest his source for the term. During his discussion he refers in passing to "Harphius," who is Heinrich Herpf, the German mystic. Baker once translated Herpf's *Scala Perfectionis* into English. A passage describing the fourth rung on the ladder to perfection may be his source for the term "sensible devotion":

> On the Fourth Staffe are they which not only by corporall exercises . . . but also by spirituall: as by mentall praiers, gronings, compassions, and godly desires, doe serve God according to inward man. But yet these have not utterly denyed themselves: for in theyr exercises, they seeke not so much the pleasure of Almightie God, as theyr owne sensible devotion.[19]

Like Francis de Sales and others, Herpf speaks negatively of sensible devotion: it is not to be used but risen above. Yet it occurs on the fourth rung. A perfectionist, willing to stop at nothing short of contemplation, might deprecate it, yet those not yet risen so far might find it useful.

Baker's was the dilemma of those, impelled by experience, who are forced to adapt an old term to a new meaning. A considerable part of his discussion of sensible devotion treats the term like his predecessors. It is often characterized by physical manifestations: "drawing *teares* from the eyes, procuring *heate* and *reddnes in the face, springing motions in the heart.*" It may involve "a too *gluttonous delectation in sensible sweetnesses.*" There are dangers in this kind of prayer. "Inward *sweetnesses* formerly felt will be turned into *sadnes, dejection* and *stupidity.*" Sweetness may give place to *"Anguishes, scrupulosities, pusilanimity,* and perhaps even *desperation."* Therefore one should remain in sensible devotion as briefly as possible, rising above it and making it "an instrument to fortify and establish the solide true love and esteeme of God in the superiour soule." [20] Baker echoes established views. One recognizes, in the tears, the burning heart, the *"gluttonous delectation in sensible sweetnesses,"* some of the qualities of Crashaw's poetry, but the attitude toward these phenomena is not very helpful. One is reminded of critics who are anxious that Crashaw should rise above these manifestations and their insistence, against the evidence, that he did so.

But Baker did not always speak of sensible devotion negatively. Elsewhere in *Sancta Sophia* he recognizes that for many people this is the most appropriate and natural kind of prayer, even the only form of which they are capable. For example, he writes that meditation on the Passion is one of the most useful forms of devotion, but that many find alternative methods more efficacious:

> Soules are not to be discouraged if they find in themselves a disability to meditate on it: Whether this disability proceede from some naturall temper of the Internall senses, or from abundance of affections in the Heart . . . they doe not need curiously to search Motives from the unde[r]-standing and Discourse. . . . Neither are the persons driven to the paines and expence of time in finding out Reasons and Motives to raise their affections to our Lord, but immediatly and without more a doe suffer the Affections to flow.[21]

Such a personality is reflected in Crashaw's poetry. There is no lack of intellectual activity in his poems, yet the affections seem to flow spontaneously, to require no promptings from reason or discursive imagination.

Baker speaks positively of sensible devotion in another passage:

> And as for the exercise of *sensible Affections,* it belongs only to such soules as in their naturall temper are more tender and affectionate; whose love expresses it selfe with great *liquefaction* in sensible nature, so that they are easily moved to *teares,* and doe feele *warmth* and quick motions about the *heart.* . . .

> Such *tender soules* as these, having withall a naturall good *propension to seeke God in their Interiour,* can easily exercise their affections to God in and by their corporall nature, without troubling themselves with seeking reasons and motives for it. Yea in a short time they come to have a kind of disgust in inventing or considering motives represented by the understanding. . . .
>
> The principall care that such soules ought to have is, to endeavour to rayse this their love out of sensitive nature to the Superiour spirituall will.[22]

Nothing is said about progressing from sensible affections to meditation and thence to contemplation. Instead, the affections are raised from the senses to the will (according to St. Thomas the seat of love), and from this prayer of pure will the soul may progress to true contemplative prayer. Intellectual methods are unnecessary at any stage along the way.

I have not found anyone other than Baker who treats sensible devotion in quite these terms, as a separate and legitimate form of prayer and an alternative to meditation. Yet anyone who reads the religious literature of the period, English and Continental, Protestant and Catholic, is likely to find that Baker puts a name to a genuine, widespread phenomenon. Much of the religious poetry in the period reflects sensible devotion, including some Jesuit poetry. The twin poles of art and devotion were alike marked by probing intellection and passionate sensation. In Crashaw, intellectual though he was, sensation predominates and gives the devotion in his poetry its chief driving force.

We need not ask whether Crashaw wept during his midnight devotions in Little St. Mary's loft or felt burning sensations around his heart. But his poetry reflects an interest in such manifestations. Just as a reader of Donne's "Holy Sonnets" tastes what it is like to make an Ignatian meditation, a reader of Crashaw's poems is introduced to the experience of sensible affections. The author of the Preface of *Steps to the Temple* (1646) tells us that Crashaw's poems "shal lift thee Reader, some yards above the ground. . . . So maist thou take a Poem hence, and tune thy soule by it, into a heavenly pitch; and thus refined and borne up upon the wings of meditation, in these Poems thou maist talke freely of God, and of that other state." The writer nicely describes the kind of effect Crashaw's poems are meant to produce, except that "meditation" is the wrong word. He finds nothing eccentric in Crashaw's devotional procedures, which were common at the time, but falls back on a catchall term for lack of a better.

5. Sensible Devotion: "The Weeper"

"Sainte Mary Magdalene, or The Weeper" is the most often abused of Crashaw's poems. Whenever a critic wants a horrible example to condemn him by, he need look no further than its "walking baths" and "compendious oceans." One reason for this lack of sympathy is that "The Weeper" belongs to a devotional mode the existence of which has not previously been recognized. It is an extreme example of affective or sensible devotion. A reader expecting to find the methods and structure typical of meditation is bound to be disappointed. Even if his expectations are not explicit, he may have been conditioned by the meditative methods of other Metaphysical Poets. The result is much the same as if one approached a pastoral elegy expecting an epic. Critics, not always recognizing the nature of the difficulty, may throw the blame not on their criteria but on the poem.

Crashaw is often treated this way. Equally often, critics admit that the expected criteria do not apply, yet explain this by taking refuge in assertions that Crashaw was a foreigner, or was indulging in sterile imitations of Marino and Francis Remond. The effort to understand Crashaw becomes an effort to make allowances for him. It is useful to trace a poem to its analogues and sources, and "The Weeper" belongs to an extensive literature about Mary Magdalene and her tears, but this does not necessarily explain the poem. Other seventeenth-century poems reveal similar echoes and debts. Eventually one returns from the analogues to the poem in order to come to terms with it.

The ultimate authority on which "The Weeper" is based is

the Bible. The story of the woman who poured ointment on Christ's head is given in all four gospels, but only Luke mentions her tears. This is the text on which Crashaw's poem plays its descant:

> Behold, a woman in the city, which was a sinner, when she knew that Jesus sat at meat in the Pharisee's house, brought an alabaster box of ointment, And stood at his feet behind him weeping, and began to wash his feet with tears, and did wipe them with the hairs of her head, and kissed his feet, and anointed them with the ointment. . . . And he turned to the woman, and said unto Simon, Seest thou this woman? I entered into thine house, thou gavest me no water for my feet: but she hath washed my feet with tears, and wiped them with the hairs of her head. Thou gavest me no kiss: but this woman since the time I came in hath not ceased to kiss my feet. . . . Wherefore I say unto thee, Her sins, which are many, are forgiven; for she loved much: but to whom little is forgiven, the same loveth little. And he said unto her, Thy sins are forgiven . . . Thy faith hath saved thee; go in peace. (Luke vii.37–50)

If one were to compose a meditation on this episode, the first thing would be to construct the scene, beginning with the Pharisee's house, the entry of the woman, and so on. Crashaw's poem works differently. It is another example of wrenched viewpoint, more extreme than those considered earlier. In the affective meditation on the Crucifixion, we only realize part way through that Mary Magdalene is present. In "The Weeper," we only realize that the present scene is the Pharisee's house of Luke when we reach the last two lines, spoken by the tears: "Crown'd Heads are toyes. We goe to meet / A worthy object, our lord's *Feet.*" In a long poem these final lines are all that remain of composition of place. The rest of the poem lies in another framework. Crashaw's approach is so oblique (of course he owes much to the tradition), and the meditative framework is so miniscule, that "The Weeper" cannot be called an affective meditation. Rather it is an almost pure affective devotion.

Is a poem a devotion when it is addressed primarily to Mary Magdalene and her tears rather than God? In St. Luke's gospel the story is treated as an illustration of repentance and forgiveness. It is also concerned with approaching Christ, winning from him the accolade: "Thy faith hath saved thee." In other words, it is an instance of successful devotion. Throughout the poem, the tears of Mary are directed toward Christ, though their goal is not explicitly revealed until the last couplet. As is frequently the case in Crashaw's most successful devotional poems, he approaches God indirectly, through the medium of a woman. Teresa and Mary Magdalene are the most significant of his intermediaries; other instances are the epistle to the Countess of Denbigh, the hymns and meditations to the Virgin, the lament of Alexias, and the ode on a Prayerbook. In "The Weeper," Mary Magdalene is an Everyman or Everywoman; she is the soul in search of God.

According to Augustine Baker, two of the commonest symptoms of sensible devotion are a fiery, expansive sensation in the heart and plentiful tears. As the summary epigraph suggests, Crashaw's poem involves both:

Loe where a *Wounded Heart* with Bleeding *Eyes* conspire.
Is she a *Flaming* Fountain, or a Weeping fire!

Baker writes that there are two kinds of sensible devotion, a lower and a higher. There are those working their way up the first steps of devotion, seeking to redirect their sensible affections toward higher things, and there are those who have reached the highest stages of mystical prayer, in whom spiritual abundance "over-flowes . . . into *Inferiour sensitive nature.*" [23] Imperfect souls who find themselves weeping excessively should try to suppress their tears or they may suffer undesirable consequences. But "the case is otherwise in *Perfect soules,* when God by an extraordinary Grace bestowes on them *the Gift of teares:* (as to *S. Arsenius,* who is said to have flowed almost continually with them:) For in this case they doe *begin from the Spirit.* . . . And such teares flow (*tanquam pluvia in vellus*) *like a shower of raine into a fleece of wooll,* without the least disturbance and bitternes in inferiour nature." [24]

Critics often remark that the tears in "The Weeper" are scarcely sorrowful. If anything, one seems meant to derive spiritual pleasure from them. Their remote origin is Mary's repentance for her former sins. It is a "given" that Mary Magdalene is a repentant sinner, but nothing is seen of her sins in Crashaw's poem, which is not penitential. Rather, the Magdalene's tears are primarily the overflow of her devotions. They are the physical manifestations of her spiritual love, which is too intense to be contained.

This is a paradox: a "sweet Contest; of woes / With loves." But it is not quite so eccentric or Baroque as it first seems. It is "the wit of love," but it is more than sublimated Petrarchanism. In *The Act of Creation,* Arthur Koestler argues persuasively that tears—weeping rather than crying—are manifestations of self-transcendence:

> Listening to Mozart, watching a great actor's performance, being in love or some other state of grace, may cause a welling up of happy emotions which moisten the eye or overflow in tears. Compassion and bereavement may have the same physical effect. The emotions of this class, whether joyous or sad, include sympathy, identification, pity, admiration, awe, and wonder. The common denominator of these heterogeneous emotions is a feeling of participation, identification, or belonging; in other words, the self is experienced as being a *part of a larger whole,* a higher unity—which may be Nature, God, Mankind, Universal Order. . . . I propose to call the common element in these emotions the *participatory* or *self-transcending* tendencies. This is not meant in a mystical sense (though mysticism certainly belongs to this class of emotion); the term is merely intended to convey that in these emotional states the need is felt to behave *as a part* of some real or imaginary entity which transcends, as it were, the boundaries of the individual self.[25]

Koestler's analysis of weeping strikes me as extraordinarily perceptive. Nearly all the emotions he mentions are relevant to

Crashaw's poem: sorrow, compassion, sympathy, identification, pity, admiration, awe, wonder. These terms apply both to Mary's feelings toward her Savior and Crashaw's (or the reader's) directed through her toward the same end. The goal is to transcend the self by participating in something larger: here God and the love of God.

Mary Magdalene does not weep in Crashaw's poem in order to work up her affections or stir them to greater heights. Just the opposite: she weeps involuntarily; she reveals the body's autonomic efforts to relieve itself of excessive emotion. Her love is so intense and its object so high that relief is unattainable. Weeping becomes perpetual and extensive as "oceans." What is true of her may also be true of the poet. "The Weeper," sometimes characterized as an effort to whip up emotions artificially, even frigidly, may rather be an attempt to order strong emotions already felt by means of art's cathartic rituals. "The Weeper" works least successfully with readers who come to it cold. Like Shelley's greatest lyrics it addresses chiefly those who supply their own emotions before they begin the first lines. As a minimum, there must be some willingness to surrender to an initially high level of feeling.

The purpose of an Ignatian meditation is to arouse the affections, to search for good motivations; the purpose of an affective poem is to channel affections or even to purge and reduce them. In a meditation, one employs "masculine" intellect, takes the initiative, acts; in an affective devotion one assumes an attitude of "feminine" receptivity, allows oneself to be guided, and is acted upon. "Masculine expression" is a term that the seventeenth century used to describe Donne's poetry. Modern critics find the metaphor apt, while they frequently apply the term "feminine" to Crashaw. It is usually implied that masculine is better than feminine. But in the realm of devotion, beyond a certain stage, it is traditional to refer to God as the Lover and the soul as the Beloved. It is a question whether critics who call Crashaw feminine are (as they think) responding to his style or whether they are responding unwittingly to his passive devotional stance. To some extent it is the reader of a Crashaw poem who is asked to play a feminine role, a role that many resent. Since the time of Eliot and Leavis, the other sort of poetry has been preferred, which invites a reader to play an active, even an assertive or egotistical, part. To resign oneself, to become involved in something larger than oneself, to give in to a state of self-effacement or transcendance, is to go counter to the tenets of much modern academic criticism concerning the proper relation of the reader and the work of art. Poetry that manipulates me or tries to hypnotize me, that deprives me of the opportunity to check each stage of the way with a nod of assenting reason is, according to this view, bad. Certainly there are dangers in poetry of this kind, but to extend such a critical insight to the point of dogma (or worse, unconscious axiom) is to put oneself in blinkers.

Martz entitles a recent article "The Action of the Self: Devotional Poetry in the Seventeenth Century." As the title suggests, he equates devotional with active poetry. " 'Devotion,' then, is an active, creative state of mind, a 'poetical' condition, we might say, in which the mind works at high intensity." The article concludes that this high level of mental activity could not be kept up in England for more than a few decades: "The inner tensions of the time could not for long be tempered to the spirit of devotion. John Milton found that he could not complete his poem on the Passion." [26] Milton, however, was surely one of the century's great devotional poets. Martz's description may be valid, but it equates one form of devotion with devotion itself. The accomplishment of the seventeenth-century devotional poets was far wider and more varied than this suggests.

The logical structure of "The Weeper" is revealed by its final couplet: tears in pursuit of Christ's feet or, more generally, human devotion directed toward the divine object who initially inspired it. Within this general structure, the poem moves by the logic of affection and the dream-logic of association rather than intellectual analysis. As in all Crashaw's poems, intellect and theology play their parts, but their parts are different from what they would be in a meditative poem.

Let us examine three typical passages. The first five stanzas form an affective sequence:

I.

Hail, sister springs!
Parents of sylver-footed rills!
Ever bubling things!
Thawing crystall! snowy hills,
Still spending, never spent! I mean
Thy fair eyes, sweet *Magdalene!*

II.

Heavens thy fair eyes be;
Heavens of ever-falling starres.
'Tis seed-time still with thee
And starres thou sow'st, whose harvest dares
Promise the earth to counter shine
Whatever makes heavn's forhead fine.

III.

But we'are deceived all.
Starres indeed they are too true;
For they but seem to fall,
As Heavn's other spangles doe.
It is not for our earth and us
To shine in Things so pretious.

IV.

Upwards thou dost weep.
Heavn's bosome drinks the gentle stream.
Where th'milky rivers creep,
Thine floates above; and is the cream.
Waters above th' Heavns, what they be
We'are taught best by thy *Teares* and thee.

V.

Every morn from hence
A brisk Cherub somthing sippes
Whose sacred influence

Addes sweetnes to his sweetest Lippes.
Then to his musick. And his song
Tasts of this Breakfast all day long.

These verses have been called frigid and overly conceited,
exhibitions of ingenuity rather than passion. But the basic
conceit—tears which rise rather than fall—embodies a
psychological commonplace: the upward motion of prayer.
King Claudius complains in Hamlet: "My words fly up, my
thoughts remain below; / Words without thoughts never to
Heaven go." Vaughan, in "The Morning-watch," notes the
paradox of his early prayer vigil: "O let me climbe / When I lye
down!" In *Paradise Lost,* the repentant prayers of Adam and
Eve rise from the Garden of Eden:

To Heav'n thir prayers
Flew up, nor missd the way . . .
then clad
With incense, where the Golden Altar fum'd,
By thir great Intercessor, came in sight
Before the Fathers Throne.

(XI.14–20)

Milton, following his theological beliefs, allows only one
"Intercessor" to receive the prayers and present them to the
Father. Crashaw, as a Roman Catholic (and earlier an extreme
Laudian), allows a cherub to mediate, breakfasting on the tears
and converting them into the song forever sung about the di-
vine throne. Here too God is ultimately the recipient.

Other aspects of the imagery are also natural enough. The
tears are like stars. They resemble seeds because they promise a
harvest: devotion leading to salvation (as in Luke) and saintly
example leading to spiritual progeny (as in the Hymn to Saint
Teresa). The tears are like cream because they nourish. That
this cream returns to heaven's bosom has seemed odd, but it
follows the logic of devotion, since the bosom is the source of
the affections now returning to their origin. St. Bernard and
Francis de Sales (in the *Treatise on the Love of God*) frequently use

the image of the soul as a suckling child receiving divine nourishment. Thus although the opening sequence incorporates a profusion of images and metamorphoses, the passage is emotionally consistent and its associative transformations lead in the same direction.

The following stanzas are also emotionally consistent. Crashaw returns from heaven to earth through the red evening weeping for the dying sun (VI). "Sorrow," a word akin to Milton's "Melancholy," will from now on manifest itself in Nature not in dew or balsam (VII–IX) but in the Magdalene's tears.

X.

Yet let the poore drops weep
(Weeping is the ease of woe)
Softly let them creep,
Sad that they are vanquish't so.
They, though to others no releife,
Balsom maybe, for their own greife.

Tears are the balsam, the healing medicine, of grief and the easers of woe. Devotion is the balsam of sin, of the fallen human condition. Both lead to salvation, that is, healing.

XI.

Such the maiden gemme
By the purpling vine put on,
Peeps from her parent stemme
And blushes at the bridegroome sun.
This watry Blossom of thy eyn,
Ripe, will make the richer wine.

XII.

When some new bright Guest
Takes up among the starres a room,
And Heavn will make a feast,
Angels with crystall violls come
And draw from these full eyes of thine
Their master's Water: their own Wine.

From the weeping dew-laden primrose and the "balsom-sweating bough," Crashaw moves insensibly back into the spiritual realm. Mary's tears are like the flowers or grapes just appearing on the branches of a grape vine. Two traditional metaphors are compressed. First is Christ's parable: "I am the vine, ye are the branches: He that abideth in me, and I in him, the same bringeth forth much fruit" (John xv.5). Second are two metaphors: Christ as the sun (Malachi iv.2) and as the bridegroom (Song of Solomon). Growing from the grapevine, under the life-giving influence of this sun, the flower becomes a fruit and then is further transformed into wine. A simultaneous metaphor referring to the miracle of the wedding feast at Cana transforms the watery tears into wine. The poem moves once more toward heaven and God, with echoes of communion, divine inebriation, and the wedding feast of the soul with her Savior.

In the following stanzas Crashaw returns to the natural world. Mary's silver tears are more precious than the waters of golden Tagus (XIII). Their harvest is more lovely than May's growth after April showers (XIV). Their fountain waters the garden of spiritual beauty in her face (XV). The opposites sorrow and love feed on each other in a "sweet Contest" of mutual nourishment (XVI). The power of love mixes fire with flood and reconciles them (XVII). These celebrations of the spiritual over the natural lead into the poem's best-known stanzas:

XVIII.

Twas his well-pointed dart
That digg'd these wells, and drest this Vine;
And taught the wounded *Heart*
The way into these weeping Eyn.
Vain loves avant! bold hands forbear!
The lamb hath dipp't his white foot here.

XIX.

And now where're he strayes,
Among the Galilean mountaines,

Or more unwellcome wayes,
He's follow'd by two faithfull fountaines;
Two walking baths; two weeping motions;
Portable, and compendious oceans.

XX.

O Thou, thy lord's fair store!
In thy so rich and rare expenses,
Even when he show'd most poor,
He might provoke the wealth of Princes.
What Prince's wanton'st pride e're could
Wash with Sylver, wipe with Gold.

XXI.

Who is that King, but he
Who calls't his Crown to be call'd thine,
That thus can boast to be
Waited on by a wandring mine,
A voluntary mint, that strowes
Warm sylver shoures where're he goes!

These stanzas are among the latest additions to the poem. Christ's dart, which "digg'd these wells, and drest this Vine" (both images with complex biblical sources), owes something to Cupid's arrows in secular love poetry, but its primary source is presumably St. Teresa's dart and perhaps St. John of the Cross's "wounds of love." [27] What this stanza makes clear is that the source of the tears is Christ, who dug the wells, and that Mary plays a passive role. Her tears go to meet his feet, but it was he who, as *Agnus Dei,* first dipped his white foot in her tears or heart's blood.

These stanzas (perhaps all some critics have read) have given rise to the misconception that "The Weeper" describes a peripatetic Magdalene, perpetually following Christ about the Palestinian landscape. But Crashaw refers to the future. "Now" in Stanza XIX means "from this time forward." After this moment of conversion and forgiveness, Mary will follow Christ wherever he goes, literally and devotionally, until he reaches the "unwellcome ways" of the crucifixion. There she will weep tears at his death. But at the close of Stanza XX we are reminded of the present scene: Christ is washed with silver, wiped with gold, referring to Luke's account. Not until the last two lines, however, is the scene definitely set. The reference to washing and drying Christ's feet seems at this point only another timeless image. Crashaw is not interested in setting the scene here; indeed a reader who tried to picture a specific scene while reading the poem would find that the effort conflicted with Crashaw's use of imagery following an affective devotional pattern.

In "A Valediction: Of Weeping," Donne carries the imagery of the lover's tears to remarkable lengths:

> On a round ball
> A workeman that hath copies by, can lay
> An Europe, Afrique, and an Asia,
> And quickly made that, which was nothing, *All*,
>   So doth each teare,
>   Which thee doth weare,
> A globe, yea world by that impression grow,
> Till thy teares mixt with mine doe overflow
> This world, by waters sent from thee, my heaven dissolved so.

If these images are wild and sweeping, a reader is unlikely to object, because they appropriately evoke the extremities of a lover's feelings. So with the Magdalene's walking baths and compendious oceans. Should "good taste," that is, restraint, be demanded of an image that embodies extreme intensity of feeling? We do not require it of Donne. Significantly, Keats, who was also concerned with the intensities of feeling and sensation, vies with Crashaw for the honor of being England's poet of bad taste. How often we make excuses for them. Crashaw is handicapped by his surrender to a foreign religion, Keats by his ineradicable Cockney heritage! No wonder they went astray. Donne at least is comfortably intellectual.

The imagery of Mary as a storehouse of wealth, a walking mint, is suggested by the Apostles' complaint that she wasted money on the ointment. After Christ rebukes them, Judas, their treasurer, leaves to carry out his betrayal. He objects to Christ's priorities. But as Crashaw suggests, the most precious thing Mary gave Christ was not the ointment but the tears of love. If he is to be King, it is appropriate he should have a mint to coin money—a chief prerogative of kingship. Since his kingdom is not of this world, his money is not of this world either. "Even when he show'd most poor, / He might provoke the wealth of Princes." This is an ingenious series of conceits: washing with silver, wiping with gold, owning a portable mint strewing warm showers of silver tears. Yet it is also perfectly simple and straightforward, part of the poem's argument that spiritual cream, flowers, wine, fire, silver are better than their physical counterparts. The conceits raise material objects and sensations above themselves. Heavenly sorrow and love embody themselves in the physical and draw it up to heaven. Through her affections the soul is invited to share in the heavenly banquet. This is the poem's goal; but Crashaw keeps firmly in touch with the physical world of objects and senses until the end. At the poem's climax, angels do not breakfast on Mary's tears and change them into song, nor are they served at the induction feast of a new saint into heaven. Instead, in a return to the literal scene, they fall toward the solid feet of Jesus, the divine intermediary and Word made flesh.

6. Sensible Devotion: The Teresa Poems

Crashaw was the most sensuous of the Metaphysical Poets. Yet we are told by his good friend Thomas Car that he was totally unconcerned with gratifying his senses:

> No care
> Had he of earthly trashe. What might suffice
> To fitt his soule to heavenly exercise,
> Sufficed him. . . .

What he might eate or weare he tooke no thought.
His needfull foode he rather found then sought.
He seekes no downes, no sheetes, his bed's still made.
If he can find a chaire or stoole, he's layd,
When day peepes in, he quitts his restlesse rest.
And still, poore soule, before he's up he's dres't.[28]

Sensible devotion risks that instead of physical love becoming spiritual, the opposite may occur. There were many instances of this happening, among Anabaptists, Ranters, Familists, and the later Jansenists. But Crashaw avoided the danger. In the post-Freudian era, we sometimes speak of sublimation and unconscious sexual urges as if sex were unknown before Freud. Poets in the seventeenth century were aware of long traditions that used religious imagery to speak of secular love and secular imagery to speak of religious. Critics rightly perceive a good deal of sensual imagery in Crashaw's religious poetry. For the most part, however, it is used by an artist aware of what he is doing. And sex is only one of the colors in Crashaw's palette of sensations and emotions. It need not be ignored, but neither should it be overemphasized.

In an essay on Crashaw, Martz cites a passage from Southwell's prose treatise on Mary Magdalene's funeral tears: "Passions I allow, and loves I approve, onely I would wishe that men would alter their subject and better their intent." [29] Such is Crashaw's method in his devotional poetry: to baptize the passions and desires of natural man by redirecting them. The method is seen in the great poems on St. Teresa. "A Hymn to the Name and Honor of the Admirable Sainte Teresa," the earliest of these works, is a model of poetry based on affective methods of prayer. It opens to the point: "Love, thou art Absolute sole lord / Of *Life* and *Death.*" The theme and motivating force of the poem is love; he will "prove" this opening statement by an example. The poem resembles Herbert's "The Agonie," which defines "love" and "sin." But while Herbert's method is meditation on the Passion, Crashaw's is affective evocation of love through kaleidoscopic scenes and images.

The hymn begins with Teresa's determination, as a child, to suffer martyrdom among the Moors:

She never undertook to know
What death with love should have to doe;
Nor has she e're yet understood
Why to show love, she should shed blood
Yet though she cannot tell you why,
She can *Love,* and she can *Dy.* . . .
Be love but there; let poor six yeares
Be pos'd with the maturest Feares
Man trembles at, you straight shall find
Love knowes no nonage, nor the *Mind.*

Again and again in this and the following passages Crashaw
emphasizes that love, not understanding, is the key to Teresa's
spirituality. She does not understand her action; she cannot tell
why; yet "She can *Love,* and she can *Dy.*" She needs neither
adult strength nor an adult mind. Love is sufficient: it has its
own kind of non-rational knowledge.

Teresa's love comes from outside. It is not an active search,
though it inspires to action, but a passive suffering.

Love touch't her *Heart,* and lo it beates
High, and burnes with such brave heates;
Such thirsts to dy, as dares drink up,
A thousand cold deaths in one cup.

But the pressure of divine love has another end in view for her:
not death among the Moors, but mystical death through its own
increasing intensity:

Thou art love's victime; and must dy
A death more mysticall and high.
Into love's armes thou shalt let fall
A still-surviving funerall.
His is the *Dart* must make the *Death*
Whose stroke shall tast thy hallow'd breath;
A Dart thrice dip't in that rich flame
Which writes thy spouse's radiant Name
Upon the roof of Heav'n.

Crashaw portrays this mystical passion and death by the fiery dart of God's seraph as a process both of intensification and spiritualization (but not intellectualization) of sensory experience and emotions:

> O how oft shalt thou complain
> Of a sweet and subtle *Pain*.
> Of intolerable *Joyes;*
> Of a *Death,* in which who dyes
> Loves his death, and dyes again.
> And would for ever so be slain.
> And lives, and dyes; and knowes not why
> To live, But that he thus may never leave to *Dy.*

The mature St. Teresa, like the six-year-old child, still "knowes not why." Nor does she care to know. Not active intellectual search but passive suffering of the pains and joys of love is her method, and Crashaw's method as well.

In the conclusion, St. Teresa is taken up into heaven, where she will inspire through love thousands of followers to join her as a crowned throng of souls. They are taught to gain heaven not by intellectual means but by the example of her life and love. Crashaw employs the image of a kindling flame rising and becoming a brilliant light, his favorite metaphor for passion becoming spiritual ecstasy:

> put on (hee'l say) put on
> (My rosy love) That thy rich zone
> Sparkling with the sacred flames
> Of thousand soules, whose happy names
> Heav'n keeps upon thy score. (Thy bright
> Life brought them first to kisse the light
> That kindled them to starrs.) and so
> Thou with the *Lamb,* thy lord, shalt goe;
> And whereso'ere he setts his white
> Stepps, walk with *Him* those wayes of light
> Which who in death would live to see,
> Must learn in life to dy like thee.

The disciples of St. Teresa, like the saint, learn to follow the affective way to heaven.

Crashaw's "Apologie for the Fore-going Hymne" does not express regret that he wrote it while "yet among the protestantes," as the subtitle has it. Rather it is a defense and advocacy of St. Teresa against the anti-Spanish sentiments of his English audience. Its main purpose is to assert that true devotion knows no boundaries:

> O 'tis not spanish, but 'tis heav'n she speaks!
> 'Tis heav'n that lyes in ambush there, and breaks
> From thence into the wondring reader's brest;
> Who feels his warm *Heart* hatch'd into a nest
> Of little *Eagles* and young loves, whose high
> Flights scorn the lazy dust, and things that dy.

Crashaw makes a clear statement about how devotional writings work on the reader. They touch not his mind but his heart, and persuade him not with argument but ambushes of love. They do not convey ideas but give life, hatching out little eagles which one day (according to common belief) will fly up and gaze into the sun itself. Crashaw speaks of Teresa's writings, but might be speaking of his own.

"The Flaming Heart" belongs to the genre of poems that comment on a picture, in this case, of St. Teresa and the seraph with the flaming dart. It is uncertain whether Crashaw had a particular work in mind or refers to the sum of paintings on this popular subject. The subtitle asks us to visualize a picture of Teresa "as she is usually expressed." One might expect an emblematic meditation to follow. At first, this is so, but as the poem progresses it leaves meditation behind for another mode of devotion.

The first part develops a paradox. The seraph plays the active part in the picture, St. Teresa the passive. Yet St. Teresa has had a remarkable impact on the world. Shouldn't the painter have given her the dart instead? She is the source of love's contagion. "Give then the dart to her who gives the flame." Although the poem does not go into historical detail,

Crashaw presumably was motivated by the paradox that a cloistered, contemplative nun founded a whole chain of monasteries and influenced devotion all over Europe. Can this properly be called a passive life? Of course, Crashaw knows that the seraph held the dart, that the picture cannot really be changed. The paradox must be accepted:

> Leave *Her* alone *The Flaming Heart.*
>   Leave her that; and thou shalt leave her
> Not one loose shaft but love's whole quiver.
> For in love's feild was never found
> A nobler weapon then a *Wound.*
> Love's passives are his activ'st part.
> The wounded is the wounding heart.
> O *Heart!* the æquall poise of lov'es both parts
> Bigge alike with wounds and darts.
> Live in these conquering leaves; live all the same;
> And walk through all tongues one triumphant *Flame*
> Live here, great *Heart;* and love and dy and kill;
> And bleed and wound; and yeild and conquer still.

"Love's passives are his activ'st part": love does not convey itself like force or logic. After the initial failure to find a rational method to account for the paradox or bring it into line with reason, Crashaw abandons the attempt. In the first part of the poem he has been described as working many "arid variations" on the roles of saint and seraph.[30] There are grounds for this criticism. But the first part is a preparation for the second. It leads to a realization that love is not accountable to logic: the precise point at which the verse takes fire. Like Vaughan's "Regeneration," "The Flaming Heart" shifts from meditation to another devotional mode in mid-course.[31] But Vaughan, though he abandoned meditation in several poems, wrote excellent meditative poetry when he chose to. Crashaw is so constituted that only sensible or affective devotion arouses his gifts.

Many critics agree that the last part of "The Flaming Heart" is the best poetry Crashaw wrote. Yet they may have difficulty with its structure. Martz writes: "The Baroque

method of building, we might say, moves from the concrete to
the abstract, moves from the picture before the poet's eyes to
the 'draughts of intellectuall day.' The Baroque tries, by the
multiplication of sensory impressions, to exhaust the sensory
and to suggest the presence of the spiritual. It does not analyze
the image in Donne's manner, but rather it piles image upon
image, in a way that sometimes defies and destroys the basic
principles of poetical architecture." [32] It is not so much the
architecture of the poem that breaks down, however, as the
abortive attempt to analyze or rationalize devotion. Logic
breaks down; the poem is firmer than ever. While Crashaw
moves away from the Donnean analysis of a single scene, he
does not move from the concrete to the abstract, either from
the first part of the poem to the second or within the second.
Although it may exhaust the reader's sensory capacity, the
poem continues to intensify emphasis on sense experience to
the last. What we have is not the decay of meditation but a shift
to another method that relies on sensory intensification:

> O thou undanted daughter of desires!
> By all thy dowr of *Lights* and *Fires;*
> By all the eagle in thee, all the dove;
> By all thy lives and deaths of love;
> By thy larg draughts of intellectual day,
> And by thy thirsts of love more large then they;
> By all thy brim-fill'd Bowles of feirce desire
> By thy last Morning's draught of liquid fire; ·
> By the full kingdome of that finall kisse
> That seiz'd thy parting Soul, and seal'd thee his;
> By all the heav'ns thou hast in him
> (Fair sister of the *Seraphim!*
> By all of *Him* we have in *Thee;*
> Leave nothing of my *Self* in me.
> Let me so read thy life, that I
> Unto all life of mine may dy.

There is nothing unintellectual or slack about this. But the
poem does not end with a rational emphasis on "draughts of

intellectual day." From this early image it moves in sequence through bowls of fierce desire, draughts of liquid fire, and expiration in a "final kiss" that seizes the departing soul. The culmination of the sequence and Crashaw's concluding prayer is not intellectual illumination but death by ecstasy.

Unlike Donne's meditative sonnets, this is a poetry that makes no attempt (after the beginning) to form a distinct scene or dramatic situation. It follows no structure of rational analysis. Its images are felt rather than concretely imagined. Yet a structure is clearly evident: the progress and intensification of feelings and senses. What this poetry attempts—successfully, to judge from most readers' reactions—is to catch hold of the emotions and point them in the desired direction, and thus to hatch eagles in the reader's heart. Like meditation, affective prayer cannot be learned simply by reading a few poems. Moreover, for such poems to have the effect Crashaw intended, the reader must be willing to believe or suspend disbelief; willing, in addition, to let himself be seized and guided, which implies a degree of trust. Yet as Donne's poems suggest to any but the most unsympathetic reader what it feels like to pray meditatively, Crashaw's suggest what it is like to pray affectively.

7. Crashaw and Mysticism

A question remains: Is Crashaw a mystical poet? Certainly some of his poems concern the mysticism of others. Mary Magdalene, as he portrays her, may be a saint observed in contemplation. He has read St. Teresa and effectively translated into poetry what she stands for. At the end of "The Flaming Heart," the speaker prays for his own annihilation and mystical death; these might be the words of a mystic or they might be the plea of someone who longs to be a mystic. The Teresa poems have a full measure of one of mysticism's basic characteristics, passivity. But passivity also characterizes affective poetry. Likewise, affective rapture may look like mystical rapture, and the affective release of self in empathy with another might be mistaken for mystical union. As Baker points out, tears and an ardent heart may be the signs of a low level of affective prayer or they may overflow from the highest forms of contemplation. It is easier to distinguish the meditative from the contemplative mode, because one is active and the other passive, one discursive and the other simple, one imaginative and the other imageless. But the pathway that runs upward through sensible affection to contemplation, though it begins lower down the scale of faculties than meditation, appears—at least to an outsider—more continuous.

The problem is well illustrated by Crashaw's poem advising a young lady concerning prayer and presumably reflecting his own devotional methods. Warren considers it Crashaw's most definitely mystical poem and A. F. Allison links it with St. Teresa's *Interior Castle*.[33] "Prayer. An Ode, which was Praefixed to a little Prayer-book given to a young Gentle-woman" begins affectively. The prayerbook is to work through the Lady's senses on her heart. Provided that her hands and eyes be pure, the prayers will make their way directly from the "ignoble sheets" of the printed page into her heart with no intermediary stages: "Hold but this book before your heart / Let prayer alone to play his part." She is not instructed how to meditate or order her prayers; instead, she is simply to let prayer act on her. Her only task is to refrain from sin or worldly distraction.

If her heart leaves its chaste abode to "gadde abroad," it may miss its opportunity.

> Doubtlesse some other heart
>   Will gett the start
> Mean while, and stepping in before
> Will take possession of that sacred store
> Of hidden sweets and holy joyes.

So far, the poem is essentially affective. The feminine heart in its devotions tastes the sweets, flowers, and embraces of divinity. But at this point, sensible affection seems to rise up into contemplative prayer:

Words which are not heard with *Eares*
(Those tumultuous shops of noise)
Effectuall wispers, whose still voice
The soul it selfe more feeles then heares;
Amorous languishments; luminous trances;
Sights which are not seen with eyes;
Spirituall and soul-peircing glances
Whose pure and subtil lightning flyes
Home to the heart, and setts the house on fire
And melts it down in sweet desire
    Yet does not stay
To ask the windows leave to passe that way;
Delicious *Deaths;* soft exalations
Of soul; dear and divine annihilations.

Crashaw still uses sensory language, but he seems to have crossed a line into mysticism, because the images cease to be even remotely descriptive and become entirely metaphoric. They are, paradoxically, too extremely sensory to remain the language of literal or even exaggerated sensation.

The "she" of whom the last part of the poem speaks is no longer the young lady but any heart or soul whom the divine Bridegroom finds home when he arrives. Perhaps it may be the poet's. Crashaw does not indicate whether he speaks from experience or the insights of reading.

O happy and thrice happy she
    Selected dove
    Who ere she be,
    Whose early love
    With winged vowes
Makes hast to meet her morning spouse
And close with his immortall kisses.
Happy indeed, who never misses
To improve that pretious hour,
    And every day
    Seize her sweet prey

All fresh and fragrant as he rises
Dropping with a baulmy Showr
A delicious dew of spices;
O let the blissfull heart hold fast
Her heavnly arm-full, she shall tast
At once ten thousand paradises;
  She shall have power
  To rifle and deflour
The rich and roseall spring of those rare sweets
Which with a swelling bosome there she meets
  Boundles and infinite
  Bottomles treasures
Of pure inebriating pleasures.
Happy proof! she shal discover
  What joy, what blisse,
How many Heav'ns at once it is
To have her *God* become her *Lover.*

There are many parallels to this passage in the writings of Saints Bernard, Teresa, John of the Cross, Francis de Sales, or Catherine of Siena. The root source of the imagery is the Song of Solomon, as read and interpreted by many generations of mystics. Because it is imageless and ineffable, mystical experience cannot be directly reproduced, so that one cannot speak of mystical poetry in quite the same sense as meditative poetry. It would seem reasonable, however, to use the term to describe poetry that flows from, reflects, or attempts to describe mystical experience, whether the poet's or another's. And while this poetry cannot directly transcribe the experience, it should, in one way or another, try to convey the experience as well as it can. Most mystics appear to find affective imagery a useful tool in this effort.

"Prayer" was first printed in 1646, and an early manuscript version names the author as "R. Crashaw / Coll. Petren:"— which suggests that Crashaw wrote the poem while he was still a Fellow of Peterhouse. That would mean that, if "Prayer" is a mystical poem, Crashaw reached the contemplative levels of prayer or deeply understood them early in his poetic career. One may argue that the poem reflects only Crashaw's affective prayer and readings in mysticism. The language of the final section is, like the rest, relentlessly sensuous, filled with scents and tastes and "inebriating pleasures." Yet these are, in their intensity, characteristic metaphors of mystical experience. Crashaw himself says "many a mystick thing" occurs in the divine embrace for which "dull mortality" knows no "name." One has the impression, reading such works as "Prayer" and the Teresa poems, that Crashaw knew mystical experience at first hand, but there is no certain proof. What is evident is that, however far he progressed toward the mystical states he so keenly desired, sensible affection was the means he took toward his goal.

8. Taste

A problem often touched on in this chapter but perhaps not exorcised is the question of Crashaw's taste. Taste is relevant to Crashaw in at least three ways. First are questions of aesthetic taste. When Crashaw speaks of walking baths and compendious oceans, he violates our sense of poetic proprieties. Not much can be said on this score. Taste is taste, and there is no proving where the lines should be drawn or whether they should be drawn at all. These are, at least, memorable conceits, emotionally relevant to the poem.

Taste may also be a matter less of aesthetics than emotions. "Walking baths" may be described as grotesque. That is not true of all Crashaw's offending images. Another kind of bad taste involves excessive emotion or what appears to many to be inappropriate evocation of senses and feelings in the wrong context. A good example is found in "A Hymne of the Nativity," otherwise one of Crashaw's more universally admired works. A stanza printed in 1646 and 1648 but omitted in 1652, whether by Crashaw or Car, describes Mary nursing the infant Jesus:

Shee sings thy Teares asleepe, and dips
    Her Kisses in thy weeping Eye,

Shee spreads the red leaves of thy Lips,
   That in their Buds yet blushing lye.
Shee 'gainst those Mother-Diamonds tryes
The points of her young Eagles Eyes.

The "excess" here is different in kind from the offending stanzas of "The Weeper." Crashaw introduces sensations and intimate feelings that seem inappropriate to some readers. In this case, one can make a more positive response. Modern man is embarrassed by the idea of a nursing baby. That is his eccentricity. The subject is less unmentionable than a few years ago and perhaps taste may shift back. Jesus nursing at Mary's breast, revealing his humanity and his loving relationship with his mother, was a favorite subject of Medieval, Renaissance, and Baroque painters and illustrators. It was an image often evoked in the sermons of serious moralists, Catholic and Puritan, and by saints from Bernard to Francis de Sales. One might be embarrassed to find such a picture embarrassing. As elsewhere, Crashaw puts human feelings to work in the service of devotion. He is a writer who by his daring can embarrass, offend, or provoke uneasy laughter. Some of that is due more to our cultural heritage of "Anglo-Saxon" reserve than to his excess. Not, perhaps, all, for Crashaw is one of our poets of embarrassment. He often writes of blushing cherubs, modesty, and shame. Critics usually consider embarrassment the one impermissible emotion in art or literature; but it may be that this very human and in many ways desirable emotion is a legitimate weapon in Crashaw's affective armory.[34]

The last form of bad taste I want to consider is bad taste in devotion. One can scarcely begin to look at devotional practices in the seventeenth century without finding manifestations of affective devotion. Yet little was written on the subject by devotional theorists, except for their frequent warnings to beware of the senses and the lower affections. One might apply the senses in meditation, but should keep them under a tight leash of rationality. Crashaw's modern critics often sound similar. The fact is that, in the twentieth century as the seventeenth, affective devotion is not for everyone, either to practice or to respond to in poetry. Donne's devotional poems are accessible to most readers. Herbert appeals to an even wider audience, because his devotional methods are so varied. Crashaw's range is narrower: vocal, musical, affective, possibly contemplative. Yet one thing that makes up for this relative narrowness of range is (considering only the major devotional poets) that most of Crashaw's poetry covers ground the others leave untouched. That may mean that if one likes Donne, Herbert, and Vaughan, he will not like Crashaw. It also means that acquaintance with Crashaw results in a new range of experience.

Personally, I find more strain in adjusting to Crashaw than to any other major seventeenth-century poet, religious or secular. Our situation is like Samuel Johnson's when he looked back on Cowley and the strange tribe of Metaphysicals. Revolutions in taste have brought us to the point where we wonder not at Johnson's interest in these poets but at his reservations. What was for him a brilliant putting aside of prejudices is for us a matter of course. But we have not acclimated ourselves to Crashaw as well as to his fellows, and for the moment his poetry is less easily accessible. That is all the more reason to read him.

Notes

1. Peter, "Crashaw and 'The Weeper,' " *Scrutiny,* 19 (1953), 269.
2. Adams, "Taste and Bad Taste in Metaphysical Poetry: Richard Crashaw and Dylan Thomas," *Hudson Review,* 8 (1955), 64, 66–67.
3. Warren, *Richard Crashaw: A Study in Baroque Sensibility* (Ann Arbor: University of Michigan Press, 1957), p. 88.
4. Praz, *The Flaming Heart* (New York: Doubleday, 1958), p. 226.
5. Warren, p. 65.
6. Lee A. Jacobus, "Richard Crashaw as a Mannerist," *Bucknell Review,* 18 (1970), 79.
7. See A. F. Allison, "Crashaw and St. François de Sales," *RES,* 24 (1948), 295–302; Louis L. Martz, *The Poetry of Meditation* (New Haven: Yale University Press, 1962), pp. 331–352; Anthony Raspa, "Crashaw and the Jesuit Poetic," *UTQ,* 36 (1966), 37–54; James B. Anderson, "Richard Crashaw, St. Teresa, and St. John of the Cross," *Discourse,* 10 (1967), 421–428.
8. William Prynne, *Canterburies Doome* (London, 1646), p. 73, cited by Warren, pp. 33–34.

9. See Martin, pp. 416–418.

10. See A. R. Cirillo, "Crashaw's 'Epiphanie Hymn': The Dawn of Christian Time," *SP*, 67 (1970), 67–88; Francis X. Weiser, S.J., *Handbook of Christian Feasts and Customs* (New York: Harcourt, Brace, 1958), p. 138.

11. Warren, p. 153.

12. Cirillo, "Crashaw's 'Epiphanie Hymn.' "

13. Praz, *The Flaming Heart;* Marc Bertonasco, *Crashaw and the Baroque* (University: University of Alabama Press, 1971).

14. Bertonasco, pp. 48–55; on Salesian meditation, see Bertonasco and A. F. Allison, "Crashaw and St. François de Sales."

15. The first two quotations, p. 329 (VI.iii.2); the third, p. 332 (VI.iv.1). Miles Car or Carre is also known as Thomas Carre and Miles Pinckney.

16. Cited by Martz, *The Poetry of Meditation*, p. 30.

17. Camus, *A Spirituall Combat*, trans. Thomas Carre (Douai, 1632), pp. 222–235; cited by Martz, pp. 56–57.

18. See *The Life of Father Balthazar Alvarez*, by F. Louis du Pont [Luis de Puente], 2 vols. (London: Thomas Richardson and Son, 1868), I, 141–154.

19. Henrie Herpe, *The Ladder of Perfection* in *Nine Rocks to be Avoided*, gathered by T. H. D. (Douai, 1600), sig. B8ᵛ.

20. Baker, *Sancta Sophia* (Douai: John Patte and Thomas Fievet, 1657), II, 45–48 (III.i.5.8–12).

21. Baker, *Sancta Sophia*, II, 124–125 (III.ii.5.8).

22. Baker, *Sancta Sophia*, II, 139–140 (III.iii.1.6–9).

23. Baker, *Sancta Sophia*, II, 44 (III.i.5.6).

24. Baker, *Sancta Sophia*, II, 49 (III.i.5.15.).

25. Koestler (London: Pan Books, 1975), p. 54.

26. Martz, in *Metaphysical Poetry*, ed. Malcolm Bradbury and David Palmer, Stratford-Upon-Avon Studies 11 (London: Edward Arnold, 1970), pp. 101–121; 103, 121.

27. See the excellent brief discussion in Warren, pp. 143–146.

28. Car, "Crashaw: The Anagram," Martin, pp. 233–234.

29. Martz, *The Wit of Love* (Notre Dame: University of Notre Dame Press, 1969), p. 141.

30. Warren, p. 141.

31. See Chapter VI below.

32. Martz, *The Wit of Love,* p. 131.

33. Warren, p. 187; Allison, "Some Influences on Crashaw's Poem 'On a Prayer Booke Sent to Mrs. M. R.,' " *RES*, 23 (1947), 34–42.

34. For opening my eyes I am indebted to Christopher Ricks, *Keats and Embarrassment* (Oxford: The Clarendon Press, 1974).

6.

Henry Vaughan: Journey to Light

1. Background

Henry Vaughan is a more varied and artful poet than many critics recognize. Unlike Donne, his secular poetry has received little attention, while his religious verse suffers from narrow expectations. Those poems that do not fit certain "restrictive criteria" tend to be ignored or dismissed as failures of inspiration.[1] The chief arguments among critics of the religious poems are whether Vaughan is a mystic, a hermeticist, or a meditative poet. Any of the possible cases may be proved by selection from the evidence; in some ways or in some poems all are true. Some of Vaughan's best poems are mystical but not all of them. Some use conventional meditative techniques but others do not. Many reflect his interest in alchemy and occult philosophy but never to the exclusion of the main currents of Christian orthodoxy and practical religious experience. What is needed is a broader approach that does not try to force the poems into a predetermined mold.

According to the preface to *Silex Scintillans* (1655), the true end of poetry is not to show the author's wit or increase his fame but to benefit his readers. The greatest benefits flow not from *"idle words"* or *"lascivious fictions"* or even from superficial religious verse, but only from sacred poetry based on truth and stemming from "true, practick piety." Its purpose is to *"turn many to righteousness"* and give "nourishment or help to *devotion.*" Conversion is a desired end, and Vaughan calls himself a convert of Herbert. But conversion implies many things, from pagans abruptly seeing the light to Christians making steady progress over the years. Spectacular conversions are accidental results of religious poetry, which has the staple purpose of *nourishing devotion* in the well disposed. Vaughan might hope his poems could cooperate with grace and convert unbelievers, but as a poet he could not plan on such results. What he could do is employ poetic and devotional methods so as to give readers appropriate materials for spiritual use. He hopes the poetry will be "as useful now in the *publick,* as it hath been to me in *private.*" Vaughan himself has used his poetry devotionally and hopes his readers will do likewise.

There is no use entangling ourselves in the question of Vaughan's conversion. But it may be said that, though the devotional poems were products of a conversion experience of some kind, whether sudden or gradual, they were also the means of furthering and consolidating that experience. The process was two way. There is no obvious falling-off in inspiration or fervor between the two parts of *Silex Scintillans.* We can only speculate about the initial stages of Vaughan's conversion and the influence of such particular events as his enforced retirement to Wales, the Civil War, the king's execution, the death of his younger brother, and the death of his wife. Whatever their onset, the spiritual experiences reflected in *Silex Scintillans*— especially the unique mystical poems—did not end after a single flash but must have lasted some time. It should be added that we know nothing about these mystical experiences but what is reflected in the poems. Vaughan's puzzling and fluctuating attitudes toward publishing his secular verse are not necessarily related to these experiences and cannot be used to date them. Probably during his last years Vaughan's spiritual life receded from the mystical heights, but the evidence does not allow certainty.

Regrettably we know much less about Vaughan than

Donne or Herbert. Yet we have one tantalizing reflection of his devotional practices during the key years. His treatise on devotion, *The Mount of Olives,* appeared in 1652. On its title page is a motto from Luke: "Watch ye therefore, and pray always." This advice, familiar from his poems, sums up the work. It is not a detailed exposition of method but consists mainly of the prayers themselves. Like the primers or such later works as Edmund Bunny's popular *Booke of Christian Exercise,* the reader is given a series of specific prayers for regular use throughout the day. There are prayers for waking, rising, going on a journey, going to church, receiving Communion, and returning home. There are prayers for sunset, evening, and going to bed. To bring prayer further into daily life there are brief ejaculations for such moments as hearing a clock strike or occasions of anger and sorrow.

Vaughan does not say how the reader is to use these prayers. There are a few substantial meditations, notably the preparation for Holy Communion. From time to time he advises the reader to meditate on a text or other subject, but he does not always seem to use the term strictly. For the most part, the prayers are not primarily meditative. They make no substantial use of the method's characteristic structures or detailed techniques. Instead, they seem meant to be read aloud (or to oneself) like the collects in a prayerbook.

The devotional practices outlined in *The Mount of Olives* do not exclude Vaughan's using additional methods himself. According to the Preface, he wrote the book to comfort readers, presumably beginners in prayer, who were bewildered by the turmoil and harmful religious advice emerging from the Civil War. He attacks the authors of devotional manuals, presumably Puritans, who "assume to themselves the glorious stile of Saints" and boast "frequent *Extasies,* and raptures to the third heaven." This is not a repudiation of mysticism but a polemic against false prophets. Mystics regularly warn their readers against pseudo-mysticism and extravagances masquerading as spirituality. The atmosphere of wild enthusiasm among the sects in the 1650s sufficiently accounts for the book's sober emphasis on the basics of prayer. Vaughan promises his audience "sound directions and wholsome words." He rises no higher up the ladder than "Meditations before we come to the Lords Table."

As author of a prose manual of prayer, Vaughan chose to acquaint his readers only with those elements of his devotional experience that were safest and most basic. But as a poet he rose to greater heights. This may explain why, although Vaughan often committed himself to the poetic principles of clarity and perspicuity, he left much in *Silex Scintillans* that would puzzle ordinary readers.[2] In the 1655 Preface, he regrets that readers may find some passages *"remote."* If so, they must be satisfied, for it would not "conduce much" to their "greater *advantage"* to explain them. It is implied that those who understand these passages will profit; others are better left ignorant. Vaughan had ample precedent for this procedure in his readings among both mystical and occult authors. But the hermeticism in *Silex Scintillans* is not the kind forbidden to the vulgar. Vaughan draws only on 'the public part of alchemical language . . . fundamentals that practically everybody was aware of." [3] More probably he is referring to the mystical element in his poems. Most mystics agree that a little knowledge of mysticism is dangerous, especially in enthusiastic times.

From *The Mount of Olives* and various prefaces, one may conclude that Vaughan valued vocal prayer highly as a devotional form and probably practiced it extensively himself. But meditation and higher forms are not ruled out. The main point of the prose manual, confirmed by the poetry, is that prayer should be continual, practiced at all times of the day. Like Ferrar, Vaughan also commends rising at night to pray. If this is not possible, he insists that everyone at least rise before the sun every morning. One passage throws further light on his practices and his interest in vocal prayer:

> In the *Primitive* Church . . . the *Saints* of God used to rise at midnight to praise the *Rock of their salvation* with *Hymns and Spiritual Songs.* In the same manner shouldst thou do now, and Contemplate the *Order* of the Stars, and how they all in their several stations praise their Creator. When all the world is asleep, thou shouldst watch.[4]

Vaughan would not have given readers this advice had he not practiced it himself.

2. Psalms and Hymns

Continual devotion, such as Vaughan advocates in *The Mount of Olives,* implies the use of various devotional methods. Not even St. John of the Cross spent all his time in contemplation, not even Ignatius meditated every hour of the day. As one might expect, Vaughan made considerable use in his devotional poetry of vocal prayer and song. There are three metrical psalms, all praises of nature. One is in the common meter, one in 5, 5, 5, 3, and one in tetrameter couplets that (with one enjambment) divide into quatrains. Vaughan can be very good at this demanding genre. A description of the natural cycle in "Psalme 104" typifies the rest; it would be equally effective as a spoken poem or a text for singing:

> To the wilde goats the high hills serve for folds,
>   The rocks give Conies a retyring place:
> Above them the cool Moon her known course holds,
>   And the Sun runs his race.
>
> Thou makest darkness, and then comes the night;
>   In whose thick shades and silence each wilde beast
> Creeps forth, and pinch'd for food, with scent and sight
>   Hunts in an eager quest.
>
> The Lyons whelps impatient of delay
>   Roar in the covert of the woods, and seek
> Their meat from thee, who doest appoint the prey
>   And feed'st them all the week.
>
> This past, the Sun shines on the earth, and they
>   Retire into their dens; Man goes abroad
> Unto his work, and at the close of day
>   Returns home with his load.

If he wanted to sing these praises, Vaughan had no need to seek a composer, for numerous popular psalm tunes were waiting to be used.

Vaughan is often admired for his "gift of song," but the implications have not been followed up.[5] He not only had a gift for musical phrasing, he also wrote a number of secular love songs and hymns. No musical settings from his own time survive, but many of his poems were adapted for hymnbooks in the eighteenth and nineteenth centuries, and many are eminently suitable as musical texts. He called the Preface to *Silex Scintillans* the "Preface to the following Hymns," and in it hopes, like "holy *Herbert*," to write "A true *Hymn*." At the back of the 1655 edition is a table of "all the Hymns or Sacred Poems in these two Books." Only two poems are specifically entitled hymns, for Easter and Ascension. But there are other poems on the Church's principal feasts that also look like hymn texts. Vaughan may have been following Herbert's example, but both poets were working in the Anglican tradition. As the Civil War progressed and singing of holy-day hymns was outlawed by the Puritans, the practice took on deeper meaning for royalists like Vaughan. He followed Herbert's example and chose not to gather these hymns together but scattered them through both books. Yet all but "Palm-Sunday" are in the order of the yearly sequence.

Like several of Herbert's holy-day poems, "Palm-Sunday" has a meditative introduction followed by a hymn. Using standard techniques, Vaughan joins in imagination the festive throng that welcomes Jesus to Jerusalem. At the same time he anticipates the hymn by employing the vocal as well as the meditative mode:

> Hark! how the children shril and high
> > *Hosanna* cry,
> Their joys provoke the distant skie,
> Where thrones and Seraphins reply,
> And their own Angels shine and sing
> > In a bright ring:
> > Such yong, sweet mirth
> > Makes heaven and earth
> Joyn in a joyful Symphony.

The appeal is primarily aural. As is often the case in Vaughan's holy-day poems, the hymn that follows, in Long Measure, is more personal and inward:

> I'le get me up before the Sun,
> I'le cut me boughs off many a tree,
> And all alone full early run
> To gather flowers to wellcome thee.

The hymns, usually outbursts of affection, take the place of the resolution and colloquy that traditionally follow meditative prayer. But with Vaughan meditation and resolution are permeated with music.

Vaughan wrote a number of Passion poems appropriate to Good Friday, but none have that title. There are two for Easter. "Easter-day" consists of two intricate, eight-line stanzas. It is similar to a madrigal text which, because of complications and repetitions in the music, seldom had more than two or three stanzas.

> Thou, whose sad heart, and weeping head lyes low,
>   Whose Cloudy brest cold damps invade,
> Who never feel'st the Sun, nor smooth'st thy brow,
>   But sitt'st oppressed in the shade,
>   Awake, awake,
> And in his Resurrection partake,
>   Who on this day (that thou might'st rise as he,)
>   Rose up, and cancell'd two deaths due to thee.

> Awake, awake; and, like the Sun, disperse
>   All mists that would usurp this day;
> Where are thy Palmes, thy branches, and thy verse?
>   *Hosanna!* heark; why doest thou stay?
>   Arise, arise,
> And with his healing bloud anoint thine Eys,
>   Thy inward Eys; his bloud will cure thy mind,
>   Whose spittle only could restore the blind.

The poem is not systematic or analytic, like meditation, but impressionistic. Its chief concern is not intellect but feeling. Like many seventeenth-century songs, it embodies two broadly contrasting emotions, developed at length. Bruce Pattison points out that song, unlike poetry that one reads, cannot easily adjust to quick shifts of feeling. A poem can achieve an emotional change with one word, but music usually needs a phrase to accomplish the same effect.[6] "Easter-day" is the kind of text a composer would look for when seeking to unite the affects of music and poetry. Vaughan's familiar contrasts—cold and warm, dark and light, down and up, sad and joyous—could be underlined by such favorite devices as falling and rising tunes, especially on the trumpeted phrases "Awake, awake" and "Arise, arise."

"Easter Hymn," in spite of its title, is not printed in stanzas but, like "Psalm 65," in tetrameter couplets. It has two paragraphs, of twelve lines and six; perhaps it should be divided into three six-line stanzas, giving it the same form as several song texts by Jonson and Campion. This Easter hymn surprisingly addresses death, but in a tone to suit the occasion:

> Death, and darkness get you packing,
> Nothing now to man is lacking,
> All your triumphs now are ended,
> And what *Adam* marr'd, is mended;
> Graves are beds now for the weary,
> Death a nap, to wake more merry.

This is a long way from Donne's introspective meditations on death in the "Holy Sonnets" or from "Death be not proud." It is not a bad poem, but its poetic and devotional modes are entirely different.

For Ascension Day, Vaughan again provides an introductory poem followed by a hymn. The first of these, "Ascension-day," mostly in pentameter couplets, is a set piece of Ignatian devotion. Vaughan puts himself into the Palestinian landscape, follows his Savior from the sepulcher to the heavens, and concludes with a prayer for the Second Coming, when Christ will once again appear upon the clouds. The orderly progression of couplets and meditation is interrupted, however, by a brief burst of song:

> I soar and rise
> Up to the skies,
>   Leaving the world their day,
> And in my flight,
> For the true light
>   Go seeking all the way.

It is as though Vaughan cannot remain in the silence and discipline of mental prayer but must stop to vent his emotions aloud before continuing.

As one might expect of a meditative poem, "Ascension-day" is primarily concerned with the imaginative reconstruction of Christ's Ascension. In contrast, "Ascension-Hymn," the finest of his works in this genre, turns to the personal implications of that event. Vaughan uses an image system common in many of the other poems, picturing ascension as a journey from earth to heaven, body to spirit, and darkness to light. The central image is the purification of man's dust and clay by Christ, the divine refiner and fuller. The emotional tenor is effectively underlined by expanding stanzas. As with Herbert's shaped poems, they are more than patterns on the page; their chief effect is aural rather than visual. We have no music, but can easily imagine the kind of rising effect a contemporary composer would have given this hymn:

> Man of old
> Within the line
> Of *Eden* could
> Like the Sun shine
> All naked, innocent and bright,
> And intimate with Heav'n, as light;

> But since he
> That brightness soil'd,
> His garments be

All dark and spoil'd,
And here are left as nothing worth,
Till the Refiners fire breaks forth.

Then comes he!
Whose mighty light
Made his cloathes be
Like Heav'n, all bright;
The Fuller, whose pure blood did flow
To make stain'd man more white then snow.

Hee alone
And none else can
Bring bone to bone
And rebuild man,
And by his all subduing might
Make clay ascend more quick then light.

Vaughan employs a double image based on Malachi, iii.2: "But who may abide the day of his coming? and who shall stand when he appeareth? for he is like a refiner's fire, and like fullers' soap." The refiner purifies gold and silver by fire; the fuller uses clay to whiten cloth. Vaughan evokes both processes at once, and refers to other biblical motifs as well: the Transfiguration, the wedding garment, Ezekiel's dry bones, the washing of robes in the blood of the Lamb (Rev. vii.14). It is a brilliant synthesis, yet in Vaughan's hands it appears unforced and effortless—as a hymn should.

In "White Sunday," a celebration of Pentecost in Long Measure, Vaughan once more employs his favorite imagery of light shining into darkness and transforming sinful man. Like "The World" and several other poems, it begins with eternal light, descends into the world of time, and rises back to eternity. The pattern of image and emotion are seen in miniature in the first stanza:

Wellcome white day! a thousand Suns,
Though seen at once, were black to thee;
For after their light, darkness comes,
But thine shines to eternity.

After briefly describing the first Pentecost, Vaughan turns from past to present, to the situation he deplored in *The Mount of Olives:* men of darkness have arisen who claim to possess the light. He recalls the biblical prophecy that the last times shall be *"the worst."* Wolves prevail over sheep and shepherd. Most terrible, if things have come to the prophesied worst, there will be no recovery: it is "A State, that no redress admits." The Apostles touched by tongues of flame have degenerated to evildoers boasting the Lord's candle "shines upon their heads." One hope remains: if the terrible events in England are signs of the last days, Judgment is at hand. The conclusion is colored by this apocalyptic expectation:

> As thou long since wert pleas'd to buy
> Our drown'd estate, taking the Curse
> Upon thy self, so to destroy
> The knots we tyed upon thy purse,
>
> So let thy grace now make the way
> Even for thy love; for by that means
> We, who are nothing but foul clay,
> Shal be fine gold, which thou didst cleanse.
>
> O come! refine us with thy fire!
> Refine us! we are at a loss.
> Let not thy stars for *Balaams* hire
> Dissolve into the common dross!

Man's "drown'd estate" recalls the flood as well as original sin, refining fire suggests Judgment Day as well as Pentecost.

Vaughan appropriately celebrates "Trinity-Sunday" with a poem consisting of three three-line stanzas. The hymn is as intricate as Herbert's, but not one of Vaughan's best. "Christs Nativity," a much better work, is divided into two parts, in effect two poems. Like the twin poems for the other feasts, the first has elements of meditation. Vaughan vacillates between two traditional techniques for composition of place: putting oneself into the imagined scene and imagining the events taking place within one's heart. Unlike "Ascension-day," the first Christmas poem is also in the mode of a hymn. The imagery plays upon several senses, but is dominated by the aural effect of joyful music, while the verse form is suitable for musical setting:

> Awake, glad heart! get up, and Sing,
> It is the Birth-day of thy King,
>> Awake! awake!
>> The Sun doth shake
> Light from his locks, and all the way
> Breathing Perfumes, doth spice the day.
>
> Awak, awak! heark, how th' *wood* rings,
> *Winds* whisper, and the busie *springs*
>> A Consort make;
>> Awake! awake!
> Man is their high-priest, and should rise
> To offer up the sacrifice.
>
> I would I were some *Bird,* or Star,
> Flutt'ring in woods, or lifted far
>> Above this *Inne*
>> And Rode of sin!
> Then either Star, or *Bird,* should be
> Shining, or singing still to thee.
>
> I would I had in my best part
> Fit Roomes for thee! or that my heart
>> Were so clean as
>> Thy manger was!
> But I am all filth, and obscene,
> Yet, if thou wilt, thou canst make clean.

When Vaughan wishes he could put himself into the scene at Bethlehem by becoming a bird or a star, we have a perfect instance of how poetry can combine the techniques of meditation and song: shining and singing.

The second Christmas poem asks why Vaughan's contemporaries do not lift up their voices to celebrate the nativity. Although the lines are run together, they divide into four stanzas in Common Meter. At the end is a tetrameter couplet, set apart from the rest by its different rhythm and indentation.[8]

> How kind is heav'n to man! If here
>   One sinner doth amend
> Straight there is Joy, and ev'ry sphere
>   In musick doth Contend;
> And shall we then no voices lift?
>   Are mercy, and salvation
> Not worth our thanks? Is life a gift
>   Of no more acceptation?
> Shal he that did come down from thence,
>   And here for us was slain,
> Shal he be now cast off? no sense
>   Of all his woes remain?
> Can neither Love, nor suff'rings bind?
>   Are we all stone, and Earth?
> Neither his bloudy passions mind,
>   Nor one day blesse his birth?
>   Alas, my God! Thy birth now here
>   Must not be numbred in the year.

If one sinner repents, the spheres of heaven contend in musical part-song and counterpoint. Should not man reciprocate? "And shall we then no voices lift?" The long series of persistent questions castigates man for his coldness to God in the face of what He has done for him. Are we too insensate to lift up our voices in thanks for Christ's Passion or birth? Then Good Friday and Christmas no longer have a place in the calendar.

The poem attacks those Puritans who believed the old feasts should not be observed. On 23 December 1644, Parliament forbade special observation of Christmas or Good Friday.[9] Feelings ran high in some quarters that the feast days were remnants of Roman Catholicism that should be rooted out of the Reformed Church. Earlier, Anglicans celebrated the feast days according to the prayerbook calendar with special music and hymns. The meaning of Vaughan's poem is that, by abolishing hymn singing on these special days, man no longer sends up thanks. Christmas is no longer part of the year and Christ is repaid with ingratitude. In *Primitive Holiness* (1654), Vaughan says of those who abolished the feast days: "They will not allow him two daies in the year, who made the dayes and the nights. But it is much to be feared, that he who hath appointed their daies here, will allow them for it long nights." [10]

Part of the effect of Vaughan's second Christmas poem resides in its form. It is in the usually vocal mode of Common Meter. Vaughan and Herbert both wrote psalms in this measure, which was not uniquely Puritan, but one wonders if Vaughan's choice of it for this particular poem and subject is not an additional challenge to the Puritans. If it is not a song text, it is a reminder of the sung psalms. One could imagine it sung to "Canterbury" or some tune used for Sternhold and Hopkins; but the ultimate twist is the concluding tetrameter couplet. If the body might be sung like a metrical psalm, in defiance of Parliament and Puritans, the last couplet is a subtle commemoration of the moment that the singing had to stop. It will not fit the tune. It cannot be sung, only spoken.

The most characteristic form taken by Vaughan's secular poetry is the rhymed couplet.[11] Most of the poetry in *Silex Scintillans*, in contrast, is characterized by stanzas of varying complexity. It is reasonable to suppose that in these poems Vaughan, like Donne, Herbert, and Crashaw, was influenced by musical as well as purely literary considerations, whether or not he ever hoped they would be set to music. In addition to the hymns for holy days many other poems can be linked with traditional occasions for hymn-singing and have forms suitable for setting. Some are associated with the cycle of a Christian day, as described in *The Mount of Olives*. Typical are "Midnight," "Dressing," and "The Evening-watch." Other occasions are marked by such poems as "Son-dayes," "Church-Service," and "The Holy Communion." "Buriall" also looks like a hymn. As with Herbert, it is hard to draw precise lines between hymns, poems affected by music, and non-musical poems. Still, vocal devotion and sacred song are clearly important elements in *Silex Scintillans*.

3. Music and the Dynamic Style

Although only some of Vaughan's poems are hymns, metrical psalms, or song texts, nearly all are musical in at least some sense. They are less visually oriented than Donne's or Herbert's. While Donne typically uses imagery to set a vivid, dramatic scene, even in his hymns (and Crashaw builds affective sequences like a Mannerist painter), Vaughan marshals his images almost like the notes in a piece of music. His difference from Donne particularly is not a weakness, as some critics suggest, but results mainly from difference in devotional methods. "Son-dayes" is one example of how Vaughan works. He employs a technique that Herbert pioneered in "Prayer (I)" but seldom repeated: the pouring out of a flood of images. One cannot stop to meditate on them individually without bringing the poem to a halt. They are like a series of the ejaculations mentioned in *The Mount of Olives,* intended like song to lift the heart rather than exercise the intellect. Sundays are

> The Pulleys unto headlong man; times bower;
> > The narrow way;
> Transplanted Paradise; God's walking houre;
> > The Cool o' th' day;
> The Creatures *Jubile;* Gods parle with dust;
> Heaven here; Man on those hills of Myrrh, and flowres;
> Angels descending; the Returns of Trust;
> A Gleam of glory, after six-days-showres.

Like *The Mount of Olives,* this poem is a devotion little influenced by meditative traditions. A little reorganization using composition of place could make it a meditation, since many of its images are from the Genesis Paradise, but Vaughan chose to write another kind of devotional poem.

If one calls poetry "musical," the term may have several senses. It can refer to lyrical qualities resulting from a poem's being designed for musical setting. It can refer to the effect of imagery involving sound, music, and harmony. Or it can refer to musical qualities in the verse itself, whether or not the poem is technically a song or hymn. The last is difficult to define, yet most readers find some poets and poems more musical than others. Tennyson seems more musical than Browning. While hard to define, this last kind of music is important poetically, especially, as in Vaughan's case, when no accompanying music survives. A book would be needed to examine Vaughan's poems from this perspective, but analysis of some sound effects in two or three poems may suggest how he realizes a mode of vocal devotion by poetic techniques.

"The Morning-watch," one of Vaughan's most-praised poems, evidently is not written for musical setting, because its structure is slightly irregular. The first, second and fourth parts have the same complicated stanza form, but the third rhymes differently and is a line shorter. Though not a hymn, the poem is not meditative nor contemplative. Music is its dominant image and also the dominant effect of the verse's sound. Vaughan borrows a phrase, "Prayer is / The world in tune," from Herbert, who called prayer "A kinde of tune." [12] He also calls prayer "A spirit-voyce, / And vocall joyes," by which man presents the hymn of nature, heard in birdsongs and wind and waterfalls, to the Creator. The poem abounds in musical imagery and specifically speaks of prayer or devotion as a vocal and musical activity.

The music of "The Morning-watch" also resides in its verse. The basic sound effect, introduced with the hymn of creation, is "-ing," which appears and reappears with musical effect. Close variations are also used: *"Hymning," "winds,"* "him," *"Hymnes," "Symphony."* The pattern is especially noticeable from line 9, where it is introduced by Vaughan's exclamation "heark!," to line 18:

> heark! In what Rings,
> And *Hymning Circulations* the quick world
> Awakes, and sings;
> The rising winds,
> And falling springs,
> Birds, beasts, all things
> Adore him in their kinds.

Thus all is hurl'd
In sacred *Hymnes,* and *Order,* The great *Chime*
And *Symphony* of nature.

The italics, all Vaughan's, stress music and harmonious sound.

With the word "Chime" a new sound appears. From this point long *i* echoes through the poem, appearing twelve or sixteen more times, and coming to rest on the poem's last word: "abide." [13] There is still another extensive pattern of sound. The two liquids *r* and *l* run through the poem, often forming intricate combinations. In the first part the pattern *l—r* is set up: "*fl*ow*r*es," "*gl*o*r*y," "*sou*l b*r*eakes," "*A*l*l* the *l*ong hou*r*es," "sti*ll* sh*r*ouds." The frequency of liquids increases in nature's hymn, where the alliterative pattern interweaves with the assonant pattern already mentioned. The sound *l* occurs some 33 times in the poem, *r* 35 times. Sometimes *r* predominates: "And *Spirits* all my Earth! heark! in what Rings"; sometimes *l*: "O let me climbe / When I lye down! The Pious soul by night / Is like a clouded starre." A better sense of the total effect is gained by rereading the poem. The impression made by long-drawn-out patterns of alliteration and assonance, reinforced by imagery and diction, is unquestionably musical. One may stop to analyze it, but it works all the better at an unconscious level. Vaughan, as he evokes the hymning and singing of nature, imitates it. Playing man's priestly role in behalf of the other creatures, like the narrator of Herbert's "Providence," he offers up their song of praise.

Another quality of the poem is only indirectly related to sound: its dynamic forward movement. Partly the movement resides in the imagery: the breaking and budding soul, falling dew, musical circulations, rising winds, falling springs. Lying flat on his bed, the poet is said to "climbe." The stars above the clouds both shine and "move." Everything is "hurl'd / In sacred *Hymnes,* and *Order.*" The word "hurl'd" is often criticized. [14] It is exactly appropriate, however, for what Vaughan is evoking is not a peaceful stasis but a harmony and order that are essentially dynamic, like the old image of the stars and planets in a divine dance. The sense of motion also results from Vaughan's skillful use of run-on lines. Although there are a few full stops at line ends, enjambment is heavy. At the most natural places for a pause, the ends of the sections as determined by the rhyme scheme, the poem invariably plunges on.

Other poems use interwoven sound patterns like "The Morning-watch" and are equally dynamic. There is, for example, an extensive pattern of alliteration, chiefly involving sibilants and liquids, in an often-quoted passage of "The Night":

> Gods silent, searching flight:
> When my Lords head is fill'd with dew, and all
> His locks are wet with the clear drops of night;
> His still, soft call. . . .

Images of flight and search are reinforced by the run-on line at the point of greatest emotional intensity. Even "The Retreat," with its orderly Jonsonian couplets, runs over under pressure of forward movement:

> When yet I had not walkt above
> A mile, or two, from my first love. . . .

> Before I taught my tongue to wound
> My Conscience with a sinfull sound. . . .

> But (ah!) my soul with too much stay
> Is drunk, and staggers in the way.

"The World" is another example of Vaughan's techniques. Its impressive opening, like "The Morning-watch," has an unusual number of *r* and *l* sounds. There is also theme and variation, as in music, achieved by building up and modifying the vowel pattern. The long *i* sound of the first three rhyme words is reinforced by repetition and emphasis, setting up an expectation that is modified in the fourth line by using a slightly different, longer sound in the prominent word "Time." The effect is to emphasize time and stress its difference from eternity:

> I saw Eternity the other night
> Like a great *Ring* of pure and endless light,
>   All calm, as it was bright,
> And round beneath it, Time in hours, days, years
>   Driv'n by the spheres
> Like a vast shadow mov'd. . . .

The difference between eternity and time is further emphasized by opposition between stasis and movement. The first three-and-a-half lines are calm, quiet, controlled, and end-stopped. With the word "Time" a change takes place. The verse becomes dynamic. The strong, regular, monosyllabic rhythm of "hours, days, years," reinforced by progression and expansion in their meaning, moves forward into the next line, which begins with the strong participle "Driv'n." The first lines follow the normal order: subject, object, verb: "I saw eternity." In contrast, the next lines hold the verb in Ciceronian suspension and reinforce the effects of enjambment by periodic structure.[15]

But Vaughan is not a poet to rest happy with the simple opposition of motionless eternity to swift-moving time. The poem proves more subtle. Its body, which describes from an earthly viewpoint various types of worldly men, is unexpectedly static. The obsessed lover is pictured sitting with his emblematic devices about him, poring upon a flower. The statesman exhibits some motion, digging like a mole and clutching his prey, but he moves so slowly one cannot tell if he is moving or not: "He did nor stay, nor go." The miser, like the lover, merely sits, pining away on his heap of rust. The whole midsection is quite different from Vaughan's accustomed style, which may account for the frequent impulse to excise it from anthologies. The three portraits of worldlings are the most extreme examples in *Silex Scintillans* of emblematic style. They are not only influenced by conventional themes and images from the emblem books but also adopt their typically static method. Yet, as Rosemary Freeman points out, the pictorial quality of this part of "The World" is not fully focused; these images "cannot be visualised."[16] They are curiously lifeless, in spite of their satiric energy.

The manner of Vaughan's description contributes to that description and reflects an implied moral judgment. Although the world is a place of time and change, its devotees are mere shadows and dead things. This is all the more evident when Vaughan completes the circle and returns to eternity. The world and the fools who prefer it are "dead and dark." Vitality and dynamic language are reserved for those who rise above these shadows:

> Yet some, who all this while did weep and sing,
> And sing, and weep, soar'd up into the *Ring*,
>   But most would use no wing.
> O fools (said I,) thus to prefer dark night
>   Before true light,
> To live in grots, and caves, and hate the day
>   Because it shews the way,
> The way which from this dead and dark abode
>   Leads up to God,
> A way where you might tread the Sun, and be
>   More bright than he.
> But as I did their madnes so discusse
>   One whisper'd thus,
> *This Ring the Bride-groome did for none provide*
> *But for his bride.*

In his best poems, Vaughan is essentially a dynamic poet. His image of eternity is not stasis but the circling of the stars. On earth it is reflected in falling springs and rising winds, or by the upward growth of plants. He is a poet of "process" and "rapid mutations," as two critics write.[17] In Herbert's poetry, motion is usually a sign of disorder or unrest; few of his poems end in this state. Motion can have this implication for Vaughan too, as for anyone acquainted with the classics, the Elizabethan and Cavalier poets, or the vicissitudes of life. Yet unlike Herbert he is not inevitably repulsed by it. To borrow a familiar metaphor of Donne's, Herbert's poems may be described as well-wrought urns. Most of Vaughan's cannot. His poems do not conform as easily to the favorite modern view of poetry as artifact or object, which may explain why their technique is so seldom admired. Even Simmonds, a defender of Vaughan's formal artistry, concentrates on the earlier, more Jonsonian Vaughan. But his best poems are less like urns than music or planetary dance. They are dynamic, they move through time. Although "The Morning-watch" ends on a note of rest ("both shall in thee abide"), the effect is less like the rounding of an artifact than the resolution of a piece of music. Herbert too is a musical poet. The metaphor of musical closure, borrowed from him, is justly self-applied in several of his lyrics. Nevertheless, there is a difference in degree if not in kind. Vaughan, the poet of eternity, is an artificer whose techniques are deeply rooted in the processes of time.

4. Meditation and Beyond

Vaughan was familiar with basic meditative techniques. Among the vocal prayers in *The Mount of Olives* are meditations of various kinds: for example, under devotions for going on a journey is a meditation by similitude:

> When thou art to go from home, remember that thou art to come forth into the *World,* and to Converse with an Enemy; And what else is the World but a Wildernesse? A darksome, intricate, wood full of *Ambushes* and dangers; A Forrest where spiritual hunters, principalities and powers spread their nets, and compasse it about?

Vaughan favors meditation by biblical analogy:

> Meditate in the way upon the sojournings and travels of the Patriarchs and Prophets, the many weary journeys of *Jesus Christ* in the flesh, the travels of his Apostles by sea and land, with the pilgrimage and peregrinations of many other precious Saints that wandred in Deserts and Mountains, of whom the world was not worthy.

(Martin, pp. 146–47)

Vaughan gives three examples of this kind of meditation, using as models Joseph, Jacob, and Abraham. Thus he shows his familiarity with the method; but prayers like this are distinctly in the minority in his devotional treatise.

There are a variety of meditative poems in *Silex Scintillans*. "Day of Judgement" is the third of a group of meditations on the Last Things, following the opening poem. As in Donne's "Holy Sonnet 4," Vaughan begins with a powerful picture:

> When through the North a fire shall rush
>   And rowle into the East,
> And like a firie torrent brush
>   And sweepe up *South*, and *West*,
>
> When all shall streame, and lighten round
>   And with surprizing flames
> Both stars, and Elements confound
>   And quite blot out their names. . . .

This imaginative exercise sweeps forward through four more stanzas: when, when, when. . . . The main clause of the sentence announces the dreadful conclusion:

> O then it wilbe all too late
>   To say, *What shall I doe?*
> *Repentance* there is out of date
>   And so is *mercy* too.

This leads to the resolution and colloquy:

> Prepare, prepare me then, O God!
>   And let me now begin
> To feele my loving fathers *Rod*
>   Killing the man of sinne!

At the close Vaughan gives the text on which the meditation was based: *"Now the end of all things is at hand, be you therefore sober, and watching in prayer"* (1 Peter iv.7).

This is a traditional meditation on a traditional subject; yet, typically of Vaughan, one must make two qualifications. Unlike most of Donne's set-piece meditations, the poem addresses God throughout, which changes its tone, making it less introspective and lessening the shift from meditation to colloquy. More important, this meditation is more a lyric than a mental prayer. It is in Common Meter. While it uses the techniques and structure of formal meditation, it also partakes of vocal prayer and possibly of song. It is a far cry from an Elizabethan lyric but not unlike the metrical psalms: a grim psalm for a grim time. As Vaughan declares in *Flores Solitudinis* (1654), "I write unto thee out of a land of darkenesse, out of that unfortunate region, where the Inhabitants sit in the shadow of death."

There are other traditional meditative poems in *Silex Scintillans*. "*Isaacs* Marriage" meditates on ideal marriage and its contemporary debasement. "The Incarnation, and Passion" and "The Passion" consider a traditional mystery, while "The Shepheards" meditates on Christmas. In "Repentance," a meditative passage on Christ's suffering is the climax and turning point. "Man" and "The Tempest" are meditations on the creatures. "The Pilgrimage" is a travel meditation like those in *The Mount of Olives*, except that the journey, which is first compared with Jacob's sojourn in the field, proves in turn a metaphor for the passage through life. "The Law, and the Gospel" gives the two dispensations imaginative body by composition of place, with visits to Mount Sinai and Mount Sion; then the mystery is transplanted to the speaker's heart and the historical Sacrifice becomes the Sacrament. "The Palm-tree," "The Timber," and "The Rain-bow" are emblematic meditations on natural objects.

Doubtless I have missed one or two meditative poems, and others contain brief meditative passages. Still, the number of meditative poems in Vaughan is small. There are three or four meditations on the Last Things, a few on Holy Communion, a few on the mysteries of Christ's life, a few on the creatures. In *The Paradise Within*, Martz urges the view that there is another kind of meditation in Vaughan's poetry, which might be called Augustinian, Bonaventuran, or Platonic.[18] He does not discuss this tradition in detail, and it seems to me that what he calls Augustinian meditation, a searching of the wells of memory to recover the experience of communion with God, is more closely related to contemplation than meditation.[19] It is Augustine's effort to recapture an essentially mystical experience. A passage that Martz cites from the *Confessions* has a characteristic mark of mystical experience: passivity of the soul under God's action:

> Thou *calledst,* and criedst unto mee, yea thou even brakest open my *deafenesse.* Thou discoveredst thy beames, and *shynedst* out unto mee, and didst chase away my blindnesse. Thou didst most *fragrantly blow* upon me, and I drew in my *breath* and panted after thee. I *tasted* thee, and now doe *hunger* and *thirst after thee.* Thou didst *touch* mee, and I even *burne* againe to enjoy thy peace.[20]

This is the writing of a man who has had a contemplative experience, marked by complete passivity and even union with God and described in characteristic sensory metaphors. It throws light on Vaughan's poetry, but in terms of contemplation rather than meditation.

Few of Vaughan's meditative poems, as is evident from the foregoing catalog, are among his best work. As Baker and St. Francis argue, not all people find meditation congenial. Vaughan uses the form more effectively than Crashaw, but his devotional and poetic genius lies elsewhere: in vocal prayer and song and, more importantly, in mysticism. Two of his better poems are, in fact, rejections of meditation. They reveal the poet at a critical moment in the spiritual life, leaving the world of objects and images and the corresponding use of discursive and imaginative prayer, to enter upon the imageless world of the *via negativa,* where reason has no place.

"The Search" begins in a traditional meditative vein. Vaughan has spent the night in meditation, searching for God:

> 'Tis now cleare day: I see a Rose
> Bud in the bright East, and disclose
> The Pilgrim-Sunne; all night have I

Spent in a roving Extasie
To find my Saviour; I have been
As far as *Bethlem,* and have seen
His Inne, and Cradle; Being there
I met the *Wise-men,* askt them where
He might be found, or what starre can
Now point him out, grown up a Man?
To *Egypt* hence I fled, ran o're
All her parcht bosome to *Nile's* shore
Her yearly nurse; came back, enquir'd
Amongst the *Doctors,* and desir'd
To see the *Temple,* but was shown
A little dust, and for the Town
A heap of ashes. . . .

Vaughan calls his search an "Extasie" or going-out of the soul. The term has mystical implications but thus far in the poem suggests only a going-out of his meditating imagination, pursuing its way through a landscape it has created from the Bible by composition of place.

Yet Vaughan is always too late. Although he meets and questions the Magi and doctors, the constructions of reason, memory, and imagination can take him only so far. The ancient biblical landscape is, after all, now dust and ashes. The search continues:

Tyr'd here, I come to *Sychar;* thence
To *Jacobs wel,* bequeathed since
Unto his sonnes, (where often they
Into those calme, golden Evenings lay
Watring their flocks, and having spent
Those white days, drove home to the Tent
Their *well-fleec'd* traine;) And here (O fate!)
I sit, where once my Saviour sate;
The angry Spring in bubbles swell'd
Which broke in sighes still, as they fill'd,
And whisper'd, *Jesus had been there*
But *Jacobs children would not heare.*

This is the failure of those under the old dispensation to recognize the Messiah, who brings the new. But failure to find the Messiah is Vaughan's as well as the Jews'.

From his well-loved Old-Testament landscape Vaughan passes into the New Testament:

> Loath hence to part, at last I rise
> But with the fountain in my Eyes,
> And here a fresh search is decreed
> He must be found, where he did bleed;
> I walke the garden, and there see
> *Idæa's* of his Agonie,
> And moving anguishments that set
> His blest face in a bloudy sweat;
> I climb'd the Hill, perus'd the Crosse
> Hung with my gaine, and his great losse,
> Never did tree beare fruit like this,
> *Balsam* of Soules, the bodyes blisse.

This is a traditional meditation on the Passion, but with a difference. Unlike Donne or Herbert in comparable poems, Vaughan makes the scene imaginatively vivid yet at the same time deliberately distances it. He works against the full meditative effect. Instead of a dramatic presentation of Christ's agony, we find *"Idæa's"* of his agony. The central figure is somewhere close behind the description, but still missing. Instead of recreating the action of a meditation for readers to participate in, Vaughan recollects one from the past that was not wholly successful. It succeeds so far as meditation can, but meditation cannot go beyond the mind's inventions. Its landscapes appear and disappear, its figures are there and not there. The poet is striving to reach not an imagined but the real Christ, and meditation goes only part way. Something more is wanted.

The search continues for twenty more lines, taking the poet to the Sepulcher and the Wilderness but no nearer his goal. He could continue on these lines forever. But at this point, the poem turns. The searcher's active devotional pursuit is stopped dead by a voice from without:

But as I urg'd thus, and writ down
What pleasures should my Journey crown,
What silent paths, what shades, and Cells,
Faire, virgin-flowers, and hallow'd *Wells*
I should rove in, and rest my head
Where my deare Lord did often tread,
Sugring all dangers with successe,
Me thought I heard one singing thus;

1.

Leave, leave, thy gadding thoughts;
Who Pores
and spies
Still out of Doores
descries
Within them nought.

2.

The skinne, and shell of things
Though faire,
are not
Thy wish, nor pray'r
but got
By meer Despair
of wings.

3.

To rack old Elements,
or Dust
and say
Sure here he must
needs stay
Is not the way,
nor just.

Search well another world; who studies this,
Travels in Clouds, seeks *Manna*, where none is.

The radical nature of this turn is underlined by the shift in style, from couplets to lyrics, up a level, from speech to song.

At first, the song seems to say that one cannot find God outside the self in Nature. Instead, one should search within.[21] But in the context of the whole poem this reading does not hold, because searching within is precisely what Vaughan has done and is told to abandon. God is not found in external nature, the world of elements and dust that is the "skinne, and shell of things." He is not found by meditating either. "Leave, leave, thy gadding thoughts." The man who journeys after truth in his imagination will never find it. He "Travels in Clouds." The world of his meditation is two removes from reality: it is images of objects, "ideas" of the shell of things. St. John of the Cross explains why imagination is inadequate for the search:

> Imagination cannot fashion or imagine anything whatsoever beyond that which it has experienced through its exterior senses. . . . At most it can only compose likenesses of those things that it has seen or heard or felt. . . . Although a man imagines palaces of pearls and mountains of gold, because he has seen gold and pearls, all this is in truth less than the essence of a little gold or of a single pearl. . . . And since . . . no created things can bear any proportion to the Being of God, it follows that nothing that is imagined in their likeness can serve as a proximate means to union with Him, but, as we say, quite the contrary.[22]

Augustine Baker sums up the concensus of mystical writers when he says that the soul only achieves union with God when it is "ridd of all images . . . without any image and above all images." [23]

What, then, does the voice urge? In brief, to hope for "wings" and "search well another world." Christ cannot be found in this world or in images derived from it, because "no created thing bears any proportion to the Being of God." The other world the poet is to seek is not the world within; it is *another* world, totally divorced from the knowable and imaginable. It is what St. Augustine calls the "region of unlikeness." [24] How authoritative is this voice? Who speaks? It might be God, it might be an angel, it might be the divine spark or *scintilla synteresis*, which lies above reason, will, and memory at the apex of the soul.[25] In the end it comes to the same thing. Angels bear God's messages. In Vaughan the divine spark, like the seed of light in the brain of a crowing cock, has a hidden sympathy with the sun of God's eternal day. The voice speaks from outside and speaks with unquestioned authority. "The Search" is not itself a mystical poem, but it points toward mysticism as the solution to problems posed by the limits of meditation. The search of the title is a search for a means as well as an end, for a method of devotion as well as a Person to whom that method will lead.

A similar search is depicted in another of Vaughan's transitional poems, "Vanity of Spirit."

> Quite spent with thoughts I left my Cell, and lay
> Where a shrill spring tun'd to the early day.
>   I beg'd here long, and gron'd to know
>   Who gave the Clouds so brave a bow,
>   Who bent the spheres, and circled in
>   Corruption with this glorious Ring,
>   What is his name, and how I might
>   Descry some part of his great light.

In this poem the search is carried out not through the Bible but through the creatures. Vaughan describes himself at the beginning of his quest as "Quite spent with thoughts." Presumably, while in his cell, he spent some time pursuing a similar search through regions of his mind. Now, to refresh himself with change, he comes outside to continue the search in a different mode. First, he summons nature; but his meditation on the creatures is in an unusual spirit: rational, scientific, ruthless. Nature is rifled in womb, bosom, and brain, new scientific secrets are learned, but no significant gain is achieved. The method is not so much used as eliminated. From nature, the poet turns to the last of the creatures, himself. Again he enters the inner world, but with a different mental action, examining not images in the mind, but the mind itself:

> Here of this mighty spring, I found some drills,
> With Ecchoes beaten from th' eternall hills;
>   Weake beames, and fires flash'd to my sight,
>   Like a young East, or Moone-shine night,
>   Which shew'd me in a nook cast by
>   A peece of much antiquity,
> With Hyerogliphicks quite dismembred,
> And broken letters scarce remembred.

The poet's activity obeys the philosophical precept: Know thyself. It also resembles the Augustinian inner search. Now Vaughan seems to find something significant: an ancient, discarded "peece," covered with dismembered hieroglyphics and "scarce remembred" broken letters. The imagery still is scientific: the poet is like a Renaissance archaeologist, piecing together fragments of the classical past. His meaning is implicitly Christian, for the defaced "peece" is a relic of Eden, not Rome or Egypt. It is that aspect of man's mind or spirit by virtue of which he is made in the image of God. If the image can be reconstructed, it will offer a clue to the Creator. But, since the mind is defaced by original and actual sin, there is little left to work with and small light to see by.

The poet proceeds to reassemble the fragments of the divine image within himself:

> I tooke them up, and (much Joy'd,) went about
> T' unite those peeces, hoping to find out
>   The mystery; but this neer done,
>   That little light I had was gone:
>   It griev'd me much. At last, said I,
>   *Since in these veyls my Ecclips'd Eye*
>   *May not approach thee, (for at night*
>   *Who can have commerce with the light?)*
>   *I'le disapparell, and to buy*
>   *But one half glaunce, most gladly dye.*

Vaughan was "neer done" when the light went out. He has ransacked all nature and excavated his interior to its depths. Rationality and natural philosophy are checked. The effort to go beyond the "glorious Ring" that encircles the world of "Corruption" or, by plunging within, to go beyond the "veyls" that eclipse the inward spiritual eye from God have failed. The journey ends in darkness.

This failure seems to confirm the poem's bleak title, "Vanity of Spirit." The only remaining way to reach God is through death, the undressing of the soul from its bodily vestments, which veil it from the light. Yet the case may not be hopeless. Vaughan asks, "at night / Who can have commerce with the light?" To paraphrase: Who can communicate directly with God in this life? The answer, though unavailable to the failed methods in this poem, is not necessarily negative. After all, Vaughan tells us in another poem that Nicodemus, when he visited Christ, "Did at mid-night speak with the Sun." A positive answer to both question and search is found in mystical contemplation, a kind of prayer in which the soul works in just those conditions found at the end of the poem. It discards the creatures and their images, disapparels itself, abandons light for darkness, and "gladly" dies. Like "The Search," "Vanity of Spirit" is not a mystical poem but a repudiation of non-mystical methods that points toward mysticism. It takes a negative way and eliminates meditation on the creatures and on the self.

Paradoxically, both these poems use as well as dismiss meditation on their way toward contemplation. Meditation is the method traditionally used to prepare the soul for further advances. In "The Search," meditation in the Ignatian mode on biblical mysteries is the forerunner, by virtue of its successes and its failures, of more advanced methods indicated at the close. In "Vanity of Spirit," meditation on the creatures and the self is less successful, yet its very failure again puts the soul in a position, should it seize the opportunity, to break from its *cul de sac* and go on. At this point the soul becomes more passive. It abandons the busy, active search and accepts the eclipsing darkness imposed on it. It may yet reach its goal, not by finding but by being found.

5. *The Contemplative Way: "Regeneration"*

Vaughan makes no effort to arrange his poems by their order on the ladder of prayer. Hymns, meditations, and contemplations alternate with one another, and give no sense of a soul beginning with lower prayers and progressing upward. There are sequences and interconnections among the poems, but, like Herbert, Vaughan employs devotional variety. "Rules *and* Lessons," in which he mixes spirituality and morality, prayer and preaching, is a miniature of the whole. Exhortations to meditation and examinations of conscience alternate with calls to action and mystical insights. As if to symbolize this variety numerically, the twenty-four stanzas, each sixty syllables, correspond hour by hour and minute by minute with Vaughan's pattern for an ideal Christian day. In the same way *Silex Scintillans* offers by its variety devotional food for a Christian year or life.

Although Vaughan returns often to elementary devotions as *Silex Scintillans* unfolds, the decisive break from meditation to contemplation or ordinary to mystical prayer is at the very start. "Regeneration," like "The Search," begins with a spiritual journey or quest. The poet, realizing that he is a slave to sin and that the pleasures of the world are unreal, steals away to climb the traditional mountain path of the virtuous way:

A Ward, and still in bonds, one day
 I stole abroad,
It was high-spring, and all the way
 Primros'd, and hung with shade;
 Yet, was it frost within,
  And surly winds
Blasted my infant buds, and sinne
 Like Clouds ecclips'd my mind.

2.

Storm'd thus; I straight perceiv'd my spring
 Meere stage, and show,

My walke a monstrous, mountain'd thing
  Rough-cast with Rocks, and snow;
    And as a Pilgrims Eye
      Far from reliefe,
Measures the melancholy skye
    Then drops, and rains for griefe,

3.

So sigh'd I upwards still, at last
    'Twixt steps, and falls
I reach'd the pinacle, where plac'd
    I found a paire of scales,
    I tooke them up and layd
      In th' one late paines,
The other smoake, and pleasures weigh'd
    But prov'd the heavier graines.

The trudging upward journey represents conversion to a virtuous life and spiritual progress. The details are plain enough: the "steps, and falls" of sin and repentance, the upward sighs of prayer, the tears of guilt and affliction. The journey's difficulty is graphically portrayed. Yet when the poet reaches the summit and weighs the great efforts and pains he took getting there, they come to less than the lightest of vanities, pleasure and smoke. He has reached the top and can climb no further, but he has not reached his goal.

    Suddenly there is a turn in the poem. Mysterious voices intervene and the scene and mood change, as active striving gives place to obedience to outward guidance:

4.

With that, some cryed, *Away;* straight I
    Obey'd, and led

Full East, a faire, fresh field could spy
  Some call'd it, *Jacobs Bed;*
  A Virgin-soile, which no
    Rude feet ere trod,
Where (since he stept there,) only go
  Prophets, and friends of God.

According to E. C. Pettet, "The voices at the pinnacle, though they may be angelic, are probably of no particular significance, merely a narrative device." [26] On the contrary, their intervention is absolutely crucial. Whoever speaks—Vaughan is not specific—speaks with authority and is instantly and profitably obeyed. As soon as the voices have spoken, the whole nature of the journey changes, from a mountain-climbing pilgrimage to a sudden flight into another world. Nothing more is said about steps and falls or pains along the way; the transition seems instantaneous. The narrator's activity gives way to passivity. He does not walk but is mysteriously "led" as if on wings. Augustine Baker describes the difference between ordinary prayer and contemplation: "I would compare it to a journey of a thousand miles, that a weak-bodied man had to make on foot; and as if, when he had with much pain and difficulty gone a hundred of those miles, God by his omnipotent power should thereupon carry him and place him in one instant at the end of nine hundred of those miles." [27]

The journey metaphor describes both meditative and contemplative experiences. Precise lines are not easy, but generally a meditative journey is active and shows the evidence of deliberate composition of place. The traveler proceeds by exercising his intellect and imagination. A contemplative journey, to the contrary, is more passive. The traveler uses reason and imagination not to travel but to describe his journey to others after the fact. Contemplation takes place out of time, in the "region of unlikeness" or the "dark cloud of unknowing" where there are no images. After the soul returns, it invents images or borrows them from the tradition to explain where it has been. St. John of the Cross describes such a journey in his poem *"En Una Noche Oscura."* His soul goes forth from her house at night to a meeting with her Beloved in the mystical gardens of Solomon, *"En parte donde nadie parecia,"* in a place where, save for the waiting Christ, no one appears, a region of unlikeness.[28]

The place to which the poet comes is different from such places as the well, lovingly described in "The Search," where Jacob's sons water their flocks on "calme, golden Evenings." He does not describe it as a mental creation but as a place or state to which he is led. When the voices leave him in the field where Jacob saw the angels ascending and descending (traditionally representing communion between God and man), he remains mainly passive, seeing sights and responding to events that happen to him:

5.

Here, I repos'd; but scarse well set,
      A grove descryed
Of stately height, whose branches met
    And mixt on every side;
    I entred, and once in
      (Amaz'd to see't,)
Found all was chang'd, and a new spring
    Did all my senses greet;

6.

The unthrift Sunne shot vitall gold
      A thousand peeces,
And heaven its azure did unfold
    Checqur'd with snowie fleeces,
    The aire was all in spice
      And every bush
A garland wore; Thus fed my Eyes
    But all the Eare lay hush.

One need not read carefully to feel a momentous change in the poem's atmosphere. The place to which the poet has been led is described by a series of bright, archetypal images. There is the enclosed grove from the Song of Solomon and the mystical tradition; there is spring in winter instead of frost, clouds and rain; the air is filled with spices like Solomon's garden; the Godlike alchemic sun shoots down life in prodigal abundance; in the midst is a paradisal fountain.[29]

From the fountain come the waters of life or grace. Pettet aptly cites the Song of Solomon, iv.12: "A garden inclosed is my sister, my spouse; a spring shut up, a fountain sealed." Mystics, untroubled about the sex of lover and beloved, equate the fountain with Christ. In its pool are "divers stones," some round and bright, others ill-shaped and dull. Nearby is another "strange" object:

9.

It was a banke of flowers, where I descried
    (Though 'twas mid-day,)
Some fast asleepe, others broad-eyed
    And taking in the Ray,
    Here musing long, I heard
    A rushing wind
Which still increas'd, but whence it stirr'd
    No where I could not find.

The stones in the pool and the flowers in the sun are images for two kinds of soul, like those, spiritual and earthbound, whom Vaughan describes in "The World." Even amidst the waters of life, some souls are heavier than night and sink to the bottom as if nailed there. Vaughan assumes an Aristotelian-Ptolemaic physics, in which heavy, ignoble things tend by their nature toward the earth's center, while the lightest and noblest strive ever upward toward the heavens. The flowers too are souls, some fast asleep in the very presence of the life-giving noontide sun, others awake and following the source of their spiritual refreshment like sunflowers.[30] Watching while others sleep is a favorite image (and practice) of Vaughan's, related to the biblical parable of the ten virgins (Matthew xxv): some stay awake, expecting the Bridegroom, others foolishly fall asleep and are surprised by his coming.

Some critics suggest that "Regeneration" and "The World"

reveal a concern with the doctrine of predestination.[31] But that is to make Vaughan, a convinced Royalist and High Churchman, too much a Calvinist or Puritan. He touches on the mystery of why some hearts are set on God and others on the world, but his emphasis is not on God's election but man's response. The sun shines on all the flowers alike and all the stones are bathed by the divine fountain. In addition, these poems are not doctrinal analyses or polemics, but devotions.

While watching the flowers, the poet hears a rushing wind, yet, though he examines each leaf and shade, nothing stirs.

> But while I listning sought
>   My mind to ease
> By knowing, where 'twas, or where not,
>   It whisper'd; *Where I please.*
>
> Lord, then said I, *On me one breath,*
> *And let me dye before my death!*

Several biblical passages are echoed. Acts ii.2 describes the descent of the Holy Spirit on Pentecost: "And suddenly there came a sound from heaven as of a rushing mighty wind, and it filled all the house where they were sitting." In John iii.8, Jesus tells Nicodemus: "The wind bloweth where it listeth, and thou hearest the sound thereof, but canst not tell whence it cometh, and whither it goeth: so is every one that is born of the Spirit." The epigraph Vaughan puts at the close is from the Song of Solomon, iv.17: "*Arise O North, and come thou South-wind, and blow upon my garden, that the spices thereof may flow out.*" Explicating one of his poems based on this passage, St. John of the Cross writes:

> By this breeze the soul here denotes the Holy Spirit, Who, as she says, awakens love; for, when this Divine breeze assails the soul, it enkindles it wholly and refreshes it and revives it and awakens the will and upraises the desires which aforetime had fallen and were asleep, to the love of God, in such manner that it may well be said thereof that it awakens the love both of the Spouse and of the Bride.[32]

But one need not seek specific sources. Wind as a metaphor of inbreathing spirit is employed by many mystics and poets.

Vaughan's "Regeneration" ends at much the same place as Crashaw's Teresa poems: with a prayer for mystical death. Moreover, both poets change devotional modes in mid-course, Crashaw moving from meditation to sensible affection and perhaps to contemplation, Vaughan from meditation directly to contemplation. But their paths and poetic styles are different. Crashaw characteristically intensifies sensuous experience while Vaughan escapes the bonds of sense from the beginning, when he perceives them as "meere stage, and show." In a dozen of Vaughan's poems, the soul is a spark of light struggling to free itself from the world's darkness and fly up to the source of light. In a dozen of Crashaw's, it is a flame, burning with intense desires on its way toward what appears an even greater sense-fulfillment in heaven. Because poetry and language have no better tools, Vaughan must, like Crashaw, use sensory imagery; but he employs it differently, from outside the essential experience, striving to describe the ineffable by means of a mystic's indirect language.

6. Mysticism: "The Night"

Vaughan is one of England's few great contemplative poets. This is not to say that all his religious poems are mystical, for he uses other methods throughout both books of *Silex Scintillans*. In the meditative mode, however, his poetry adds relatively little to what Donne and Herbert accomplished. "The Search," perhaps his most effective poem in this genre, repudiates meditation. In the field of vocal or lyric devotion Vaughan was more successful. His brilliant, dynamic control of sound has a part in all his best work, whether or not it is primarily vocal. But it is in those poems that point toward or reflect mystical prayer that Vaughan makes his unique contribution to English religious verse.

Vaughan is often called a nature mystic, and there is something to be said for this view. In his poetry, meditation on the creatures sometimes crosses a line and becomes, in effect, contemplation of the creatures. The boundary is vague yet the distinction between modes is clear. Herbert often uses the creatures meditatively. The rose in "Vertue," which he employs to meditate on death, typifies his best manner:

> Sweet rose, whose hue angrie and brave
> Bids the rash gazer wipe his eye:
> Thy root is ever in its grave,
>   And thou must die.

Vaughan sometimes uses a similar meditative technique: for example, in "The Palm-tree" and "The Timber." But compare these famous lines from "The Retreate":

> . . . on some *gilded Cloud,* or *flowre*
> My gazing soul would dwell an houre,
> And in those weaker glories spy
> Some shadows of eternity.

From time to time, natural objects in Vaughan's poetry become intensely numinous. They are no longer metaphors for meditation but masks of an inbreaking divinity that lies behind nature. Another example is his vision in "The Dawning" of a landscape where the Second Coming may occur at any moment:

> . . . shal these early, fragrant hours
>   Unlock thy bowres?
> And with their blush of light descry
> Thy locks crown'd with eternitie;
> Indeed, it is the only time
> That with thy glory doth best chime,
> All now are stirring, ev'ry field
>   Ful hymns doth yield,
> The whole Creation shakes off night,
> And for thy shadow looks the light,
> Stars now vanish without number,
> Sleepie Planets set, and slumber,
> The pursie Clouds disband, and scatter,
> All expect some sudden matter.

But Vaughan was no Wordsworth. Nature, the creation and reflection of God, plays a large part in his mysticism but by no means an exclusive part. Rather, as R. A. Durr argues, Vaughan's mystical poetry belongs to the central Christian tradition. Sometimes he borrows a term from the occult sciences, but his greatest debt is to his predecessors in the orthodox contemplative way. Some critics think this borrowing of terminology proves he was not himself a mystic, but all mystics borrow language from their predecessors. Their mysticism, if genuine, is experiential and cannot simply be passed on. But their descriptive terminology can. The problem of Vaughan's mysticism is difficult, since we know so little about his life. Most readers find his poems authentic: reflections of his experience and belief in what he wrote about. To be worthwhile, he writes in his Preface, religious poetry must flow from "true, practick piety." Although it cannot be proven, probably Vaughan had a mystical experience or experiences some time in the late 1640s or early 1650s. Since, as an Anglican, he inhabited a milieu hostile to mysticism, he very likely did not develop these experiences as fully as he might otherwise have done.[33] Yet he is England's chief poet of traditional contemplative experience.

Durr argues that Vaughan's poetry is mystical because it uses the "major metaphors" of traditional mysticism. His analyses are acute and his conclusions useful, but this primary assumption is untenable. The three metaphors on which he concentrates, "the growth of the lily," "the dark journey," and "the spiritual espousal," are common in mystical literature but also common outside it. Donne refers to the spiritual espousal in "Batter my heart," and goes on a dark journey in "A Hymne to Christ." Neither is a mystical poem. The image of seed and flower as symbols for death and resurrection are found in hundreds of poems in the period, secular as well as religious. It is significant that Vaughan uses these metaphors, which other mystics used before him, and even more significant that he so often echoes the Song of Solomon. But it is not conclusive.

The two chief marks of mystical prayer are passivity and experience of direct communication with God. Subsidiary marks are an absence of anything that can be grasped by the imagination or reason, a sense of being in another world, and a sense of timelessness. It is popularly supposed that Vaughan, after a period of mystical experience, lost his vision and never again recaptured it. This may or may not be true. One would expect his poetry to be retrospective in any case, to look back on past events with longing and loss, for that is characteristic of mystical poetry. It relates to one of its limitations. A meditative poet can recreate his experience, but a mystical poet cannot— even if it occurred not years but minutes in the past. One finds just such a retrospective technique in many of Vaughan's poems. He constantly evokes something from an earlier time. Sometimes it is from a personal past, as in "They are all gone into the world of light" and "The Retreate." Sometimes he longingly evokes an Old-Testament landscape that no longer exists, as in "The dwelling-place" and "The Search." Sometimes, at the furthest remove of time and mode of being, he craves man's original home in the Garden of Paradise before his fall from grace, as in "Corruption" and "The Palm-tree."

Strictly speaking, contemplative poetry cannot exist in the same sense as meditative poetry does. At most, mystical poems are reflections or emanations of genuine mystical experience. Other kinds of mystical poems are contemplative in the sense that they reflect kinds of prayer that immediately precede mystical prayer, what Baker sometimes calls the "paths of contemplation," which lead into contemplation proper. The prayer that is preliminary to contemplation and leads insensibly into it has been given a number of names: "prayer of loving attention" (John of the Cross), "simple dwelling in the presence of God" (Francis de Sales), "prayer of interior silence" or "acts of will" (Augustine Baker). Poems reflecting this kind of prayer might include anything from Crashaw's powerful, thrusting, affective mode to Vaughan's calm, quiet receptivity. Probably they include the Augustinian inner search, which seeks to recapture contemplative experience but may not in itself be strictly contemplative. Prayer of this kind, and the poems that reflect it, imitates contemplation as well as it can. It tries to be passive, to abandon imagery and active use of reason and imagination, and to hold itself ready for that communion with God that comes only from his initiative. Its motive power is not reason or imagination but love. In poetry it tries to capture the imageless and the ecstasy of union by means of traditional symbols or by intensifying sensory experience until it adumbrates a world above the senses.[34]

It may be argued that a more suitable term to describe experiences of this kind among English Protestants is grace. Catholics as well as Protestants, however, from St. Teresa to George Fox, agree that grace is the necessary underpinning of devotion. There is a family resemblance between the English Quakers, for example, and the Rhineland mystics. The difference between contemplation and other modes of mental prayer is that it is "extraordinary" and they are ordinary. Grace reflects the same two orders. There is the ordinary grace of everyday life and prayer and the extraordinary grace of Puritan conversion experiences or Catholic mysticism. Contemplation, however, seems a more suitable term to apply to Crashaw, a Laudian and Roman Catholic, and Vaughan, a Royalist who spoke slightingly of Puritans who claimed to have inner lights. In any case, contemplation describes a devotional mode and extraordinary grace the gift that underlies that mode.

Vaughan's greatest contemplative poem, perhaps the best evocation of contemplation in English poetry, is "The Night." The poem begins with the midnight visit of Nicodemus to Christ, as described in St. John's gospel. At first, we find a standard meditation on a biblical incident; but there are mystical overtones, especially in the light imagery:

> Through that pure *Virgin-shrine*,
> That sacred vail drawn o'r thy glorious noon
> That men might look and live as Glo-worms shine,
>   And face the Moon:
>   Wise *Nicodemus* saw such light
>   As made him know his God by night.
>
> Most blest believer he!
> Who in that land of darkness and blinde eyes
> Thy long expected healing wings could see,
>   When thou didst rise,
>   And what can never more be done,
>   Did at mid-night speak with the Sun!

The *"Virgin-shrine"* is Christ's body, virginal and born of a virgin, which is the receptacle of his Godhood as well as the veil drawn over the fulness of his glory, permitting men to look on God and live. Two kinds of darkness are evoked: the darkness of those blind to the dawning of the long-promised Messiah, and the darkness that makes light more radiant and visible by setting it off.[35] Just so the veil hides the divine light and allows it to be seen.

The next stanzas develop the contrast between the old dispensation and the new. The first is typified by the sleeping Jews and the dusty, deserted Ark of the Covenant in the Temple.[36] The second is associated with living nature, and more specifically with the Incarnation of God in a new living Ark and Temple: Christ's body.

> O who will tell me, where
> He found thee at that dead and silent hour!
> What hallow'd solitary ground did bear
>   So rare a flower,
> Within whose sacred leafs did lie
> The fulness of the Deity.
>
> No mercy-seat of gold,
> No dead and dusty *Cherub*, nor carv'd stone,
> But his own living works did my Lord hold
>   And lodge alone;
> Where *trees* and *herbs* did watch and peep
> And wonder, while the *Jews* did sleep.

Thus far, the poem might be a meditation on the Incarnation from a novel perspective. But two images foreshadow the mystical stanzas that follow: the Sun at midnight and the reference to Christ's "long expected healing wings." Vaughan remembers the prophecy of Malachi iv.2 about the Messiah's advent: "But unto you that fear my name shall the Sun of righteousness arise with healing in his wings." He also anticipates the mystical images of divine flight at the poem's center.

From this primarily meditative beginning, Vaughan moves

into a more personal, inward world, the other world of contemplative prayer:

> Dear night! this worlds defeat;
> The stop to busie fools; cares check and curb;
> The day of Spirits; my souls calm retreat
>   Which none disturb!
> *Christs* progress, and his prayer time;
> The hours to which high Heaven doth chime.
>
> Gods silent, searching flight:
> When my Lords head is fill'd with dew, and all
> His locks are wet with the clear drops of night;
>   His still, soft call;
> His knocking time; The souls dumb watch,
> When Spirits their fair kinred catch.

The mystical language touched on in the opening meditation grows more specific and insistent. Vaughan draws on the familiar tradition of the Song of Solomon, especially the description of the Beloved awaiting the coming of her Lover: "I sleep, but my heart waketh: it is the voice of my beloved that knocketh, saying, Open to me, my sister, my love, my dove, my undefiled: for my head is filled with dew, and my locks with the drops of the night" (v.2). Traditionally, this figures the soul awaiting God's coming.[37]

In these stanzas, Vaughan evokes the basic contemplative relationship of Lover and Beloved. The locks suggest love, the dew grace. The poem moves insensibly from the historical-material world of the meditating imagination into a spiritual world of mystical contemplation. It is another world, a world of darkness, in which Christ glides like a bird and goes on a kingly progress through his realm. God is the active Searcher and Lover who knocks at the gate of the soul. The soul is passive and expectant, its only activity to hold itself in a "dumb watch." This reverses the usual meditative situation of such poems as "The Search." The tense also changes. Up to this point, the past perfect of completed action was used, and Vaughan even asserted that the experience of Nicodemus, meeting with God at midnight, cannot be repeated. The poem now belies that assertion. What Vaughan describes seems like something presently happening. Grammatically, the two stanzas are an extended apostrophe to Night that have no tense because they lack a main verb. They are in the timeless rather than the simple present, like the equivalent stanza of Herbert's "The Flower."

The next two stanzas enlarge on the mystical experience but reveal a poet no longer presently enjoying it:

> Were all my loud, evil days
> Calm and unhaunted as is thy dark Tent,
> Whose peace but by some *Angels* wing or voice
>   Is seldom rent;
>   Then I in Heaven all the long year
>   Would keep, and never wander here.
>
>   But living where the Sun
> Doth all things wake, and where all mix and tyre
> Themselves and others, I consent and run
>   To ev'ry myre,
>   And by this worlds ill-guiding light,
>   Erre more then I can do by night.

The poem suggests, as vividly as language can, what the soul finds in the "dark cloud of unknowing." One is reminded of Isaiah when the Spirit visits him in the Temple with a coal of fire; but Vaughan's tent is the created universe, roofed by the night sky and filled with sentient beings. Even as the experience is described it slips away, moving into the past and the conditional as the noisy, daylight world assumes the focus of attention and usurps the present tense. One cannot directly imitate such an experience, only recall it. It is described after it has receded and is defined only by metaphors and by contrast with what it is not. Vaughan would prolong it if he could, keeping "in Heaven all the long year" and never returning to wander in the everyday world, where he is caught in the noisy stir of busy fools, himself a busy fool, running from one mire to another.

But only after death can one stay with God "all the long year"; in this world, such timeless moments end.

The last stanza includes several of the poem's most memorable mystical formulations, yet retreats still further from the contemplative center:

> There is in God (some say)
> A deep, but dazling darkness; As men here
> Say it is late and dusky, because they
>   See not all clear;
> O for that night! where I in him
> Might live invisible and dim.

In the parenthetical phrase "some say," Vaughan admits to using the terminology of others. Critics trace the "dazling darkness" to Dionysius the Areopagite, but dozens of mystics in the tradition use the same metaphor. Many critics also take "some say" as a confession that Vaughan did not experience what he writes about. Rather it suggests the difficulty of finding language to express such experience in a poem. It is also, and especially, an appropriate gesture of humble self-effacement, to avoid hubris. Mystics, not seeking worldly fame, often couch their experiences in the third person, as if they happened to someone else. In his Preface, Vaughan gives his chief motive: not to magnify himself but to nourish devotion in others.

Like "Regeneration," "The Night" ends with a prayer that the speaker, who is "here" in the world of men, could plunge back into the experience once more, not for a moment but forever. He asks both a literal death and a mystical one: "O for that night! where I in him / Might live invisible and dim." God seems a deep but dazzling darkness to man because he cannot see reality with true vision. In the world, men say it is dusky not because it is really dark but because weakness in their spiritual vision makes it seem dark. The night for which Vaughan longs, however, is identical with the dawning of eternal day.

206 *Love's Architecture*

Notes

1. James D. Simmonds, *Masques of God: Form and Theme in the Poetry of Henry Vaughan* (Pittsburgh: University of Pittsburgh Press, 1972), p. 15.
2. See Simmonds, pp. 22–41.
3. Alan Rudrum, "The Influence of Alchemy in the Poems of Henry Vaughan," *PQ,* 49 (1970), 470.
4. Martin, p. 143.
5. Joan Bennett, *Five Metaphysical Poets* (Cambridge: Cambridge University Press, 1964), p. 85.
6. See Bruce Pattison, *Music and Poetry of the English Renaissance* (London: Methuen, 1970), pp. 100–105.
7. Cited by Rudrum, p. 474, who speaks misleadingly of an alchemical transformation from clay to gold here.
8. The indentation is unchanged in 1650 and 1655.
9. Martin, p. 738.
10. Martin, p. 379.
11. See Simmonds, pp. 42–52.
12. Martin, p. 734.
13. "Voyce," "joyes," "wind," and "kind" were likely pronounced with long *i;* see Helge Kökeritz, *Shakespeare's Pronunciation* (New Haven: Yale University Press, 1953).
14. Cf. E. C. Pettet, *Of Paradise and Light: A Study of Vaughan's Silex Scintillans* (Cambridge: Cambridge University Press, 1960), p. 125.
15. For more on these lines, see James D. Simmonds, "Vaughan's Masterpiece and Its Critics: 'The World' Revaluated," *SEL,* 2 (1962), 86–88.
16. Freeman, *English Emblem Books* (London: Chatto & Windus, 1948), p. 151. Of the emblematic passages from Vaughan that Freeman cites, this is the only one not involving flow and movement.
17. Rudrum, p. 469; Simmonds, *Masques of God,* p. 42.
18. New Haven: Yale University Press, 1964.
19. On the Augustinian mystical tradition, see Cuthbert Butler, *Western Mysticism* (New York: Harper & Row, 1966).
20. Augustine, *Confessions,* x.27 (London, 1631), cited by Martz, *The Paradise Within,* p. 31.
21. Martz, *The Poetry of Meditation,* p. 90.
22. St. John, *Ascent of Mount Carmel,* II.xii.4, *The Works,* ed. E. Allison Peers (Westminster: Newman, 1964), I, 105.
23. Baker, "Of that Mystic Saying, 'Nothing and Nothing Make Nothing,' " printed as "Father Baker's Tercentenary," *Downside Review,* 59 (1941), pp. 369–370.

24. St. Augustine, *The Confessions,* trans. Edward B. Pusey (New York: Random House, 1949), pp. 133–134.

25. See my *Augustine Baker* (New York: Twayne, 1970), pp. 75–95.

26. Pettet, p. 107.

27. *The Cloud of Unknowing . . . Commentary . . . by Father Augustine Baker,* ed. Justin McCann (Westminister: Newman, 1952), p. 180.

28. *Poems of St. John of the Cross,* ed. Roy Campbell (New York: Pantheon, 1951), p. 10.

29. For light on these images see St. John, St. Teresa, and St. Bernard's sermons on the Song of Solomon; also Stanley Stewart, *The Enclosed Garden* (Madison: University of Wisconsin Press, 1966) and Maud Bodkin, *Archetypal Patterns in Poetry* (London: Oxford University Press, 1934).

30. See R. A. Durr, *On the Mystical Poetry of Henry Vaughan* (Cambridge: Harvard University Press, 1962), pp. 57–58.

31. Pettet, pp. 114–115; Simmonds, "Vaughan's Masterpiece," pp. 82–85, 92–93; Georgia B. Christopher, "In Arcadia, Calvin . . . : A Study of Nature in Henry Vaughan," *SP,* 70 (1973), 408–426.

32. *Spiritual Canticle,* xxvi.3, *Complete Works,* II, 128.

33. On English views of contemplation, see Helen C. White, "Some Continuing Traditions in English Devotional Literature," *PMLA,* 57 (1942), 966–980; Howard Schultz, *Milton and Forbidden Knowledge* (New York: Modern Language Association, 1955).

34. See my *Augustine Baker,* esp. pp. 57–60, 64–67.

35. See S. Sandbank, "Henry Vaughan's Apology for Darkness," *SEL,* 7 (1967), 141–152.

36. See directions for constructing the Ark and Tabernacle (later placed in the Temple) in Exodus xxv ff. The ark, of shittim wood overlaid with gold, contained a "mercy seat of pure gold" with "cherubims of gold" on either side, their wings outstretched. "Carv'd stone" probably refers to the Temple as opposed to Christ's body (Matt. xxvi.61) and the Faithful as temples of the Spirit (1 & 2 Corinthians). The "vail" of Christ's flesh relates to the temple veil, rent at his death, and the "dark Tent" to the Tabernacle that concealed the Ark.

37. Another traditional allegory, of Christ and his Bride the Church, is not relevant to the context.

7.

Robert Herrick: The Religion of Pleasure

1. Epicurean Devotion

Robert Herrick was among the seventeenth century's best poets, but the bulk of his accomplishments, like those of his acknowledged master, Ben Jonson, are secular, not religious. A case can be made that Christianity is not wholly absent from *Hesperides*.[1] Few of those poems, however, could not have been written by a Roman Stoic or Epicurean. Indeed, it is hard to argue even that Herrick was much influenced by Stoicism.[2] On the whole, he was one of Epicurus' own sons. Poem after poem celebrates pleasure and sensuous gratification, whether the object be a beautiful woman, a petticoat, food, wine, a rose, or many another attractive thing. Few poets convey more effectively than Herrick the immediate sensuous apprehension of beauty. In his many poems on time, old age, and death, it is the loss of beauty or youth's power of enjoyment that he mourns.

Herrick's religious poems are seldom discussed, and their relation to the secular poems is sometimes misunderstood. The accomplishment of *Noble Numbers* is clearer if we approach it by way of a brief excursion through *Hesperides*. We shall begin with the scatalogical epigrams, which frequently puzzle the critics.[3] Paradoxically, these ugly poems are the work of a lover of beauty and pleasure. Herrick's chief English predecessor in the genre, Jonson, usually has in view the moral purpose of chastizing vice, as in the splendidly unpleasant "On Gut." Herrick is less concerned with hatred of evil than simple revulsion from ugliness. These lines from "Kisses Loathsome" are typical: "I abhor the slimie kisse, / (Which to me most loathsome is.)" His objection is not moral but aesthetic and sensory.

Even the slightest of Herrick's poems reveal an unusual ability to evoke the sensuous immediacy of objects. He approaches by his vividness a power to shock usually associated with the Metaphysical conceit. "Her Legs" is an instance:

> Fain would I kiss my *Julia's* dainty Leg,
> Which is as white and hair-less as an egge.

Herrick's emphasis is not just on physical beauty and immediacy, it is also on his feelings and reactions to things. Sometimes he investigates sorrow, loathing, guilt, or loss. More often he evokes their happier opposite: pleasure. His praises of pleasure sometimes, as in "A Lyrick to Mirth," do not strike deep philosophical notes:

> Drink, and dance, and pipe, and play;
> Kisse our *Dollies* night and day:
> Crown'd with clusters of the Vine;
> Let us sit, and quaffe our wine.

The famous *carpe-diem* poems belong to a related tradition, though they are more serious in their playfulness. Enjoyment of sensual pleasure is specifically evoked in numerous love poems. One phenomenon is of particular interest: the swooning away through excessive pleasure, as in "To Dianeme":

> Bequeath to me one parting kisse:
> So sup'rabundant joy shall be
> The Executioner of me.

The poem plays on parting as a kind of death, but Herrick typically prefers to die of pleasure.

Epicurus advocated pleasure as the greatest good. But he recognized, and later Christian interpreters emphasized, that there are higher and lower forms of pleasure and that the higher should be preferred. Moderation or suffering may be necessary to gain fuller and more permanent gratification. If one reads all the poems in *Hesperides,* he may conclude that Herrick disliked giving up any pleasure, however slight. Yet some poems are in a more restrained, philosophic vein. "A Country life: To his Brother, M. *Tho: Herrick*" is a traditional encomium of simple country living deriving from Horace. It dismisses the city and court, ambition, riches, and worldly success, in favor of simplicity, moderation, and contentment. The guiding principle is that contentment is achieved by restraint:

> This with that conspires,
> To teach Man to confine desires:
> And know, that Riches have their proper stint,
> In the contented mind, not mint.

So too with other worldly pleasures. One must "coole, not cocker Appetite." The poem concludes with a Stoic apothegm that traditionally rounds off poems in this genre (see Jonson's "To Sir Robert Wroth"):

> Till when, in such assurance live, ye may
> Nor feare, or wish your dying day.

The advice is compatible with Christianity but Stoic in origin. In effect, the whole poem tells the reader: Don't desire too much, even life itself, and you won't be disappointed.

Yet even in this poem sensuous pleasures raise their heads. No sooner has Herrick finished limiting desires than he turns to a brilliant evocation of the beauty and abundance of the countryside.[4] Maren-Sophie Røstvig details how tradition brought Epicureanism into tune with the Horatian poem of retired leisure by applying to pleasure the principle of moderation and

the golden mean.[5] When Herrick arrives at this *topos* shortly
before the poem's conclusion, he gives tradition an unexpected
twist:

> Thus let thy Rurall Sanctuary be
> *Elizium* to thy wife and thee;
> There to disport your selves with golden measure:
> *For seldome use commends the pleasure.*

At first this seems coventional, but is anything moderate
suggested by *Elizium*? The paradox is underlined in the following lines, which marry wild abandon with restraint. Even at this
moment of balance, Herrick's country retreat becomes a very
paradise of pleasure.

English humanists never adapted Epicureanism into their
eclectic form of Christianity with the readiness they extended to
Stoicism or Platonism. When Epicureanism was allowed entry,
it was usually under the rubric of the golden mean. Such assumptions underlie such poems as Jonson's fine Horatian epistle "Inviting a Friend to Supper," or Milton's sonnet to Edward
Lawrence inviting him on a dank "sullen day" to enjoy the
delights of a fire, choice food and wine, music and good company. Jonson and Milton often express sympathy for what may
be called "innocent pleasure," pleasure free of sin, guilt, and
overindulgence. The concept is embodied in "L'Allegro." As
Jonson writes, when the pleasures of his ideal evening are concluded, "we will be, as when / We innocently met." Herrick
delineates similar pleasures in *Hesperides*. The important first
poem, which defines the scope of his poetic universe, promises
that he will sing of "cleanly-*Wantonnesse*." "Twelfe night" describes a pleasant feast like Jonson's and ends with words that
echo the tradition: "Yet part ye from hence, / As free from
offence, / As when ye innocent met here."

The ideal of innocent pleasure in moderation was nearly
the only way Epicureanism could enter English verse on the
side of respectability.[6] Pleasures less limited or controlled were
left to libertines and profligates. But this ideal plainly goes
across the grain of Herrick's temperament, and he observes it

only intermittently. It is not a matter of occasional lapses. Even his poems on flowers, fields, and other innocent objects share an intense feeling that has little to do with philosophical measure. Again and again one encounters a Keatsian intensity of sensuous feeling. Critics are sometimes uncomfortable about this, but it is the very quality that makes Herrick's poetry great. In *"Julia's* Petticoat," he carries aesthetic pleasure to infinity:

> Sometimes away 'two'd wildly fling;
> Then to thy thighs so closely cling,
> That some conceit did melt me downe,
> As Lovers fall into a swoone:
> And all confus'd, I there did lie
> Drown'd in Delights; but co'd not die.
> That Leading Cloud, I follow'd still,
> Hoping t'ave seene of it my fill;
> But ah! I co'd not: sho'd it move
> To Life Eternal, I co'd love.

One notices, in a poem like this, resemblances to Crashaw. Crashaw puts sensation to the service of religion; Herrick returns from religion to sensation. The petticoat is a pillar of cloud leading to the promised land. This might be a piece of wit, skirting the edges of blasphemy like the youthful Donne. Yet the poem foreshadows a more serious theme, which later reappears in Herrick's sacred poetry: the pursuit of pleasure, guided by God, to its uttermost limits—into Heaven itself and "Life Eternal."

Herrick begins *Noble Numbers* with two apologies for his former "unbaptized Rhimes." But it becomes apparent as one reads the religious poems that they are still preoccupied with feelings and pleasure. If Herrick baptized *Noble Numbers,* he also smuggled in Epicurus. This is partly evident from negative examples. An inordinate number of poems are concerned with the twin themes of affliction and chastisement: "No escaping the scourging," "Calling, and correcting," "The Rod," "God has a twofold part," "Persecutions profitable," "Whips," "His Ejaculation to God," "Persecutions purifie," "Sorrowes," "An Ode, or

Psalme, to God," "Correction," "Ease." Similar poems were written by Donne, Herbert, and Jonson, but not in such profusion. Herrick was preoccupied with affliction and, more specifically, pain.

A second group of poems speak of affliction in this life and joy in the next. One title tells the story: "Paine ends in Pleasure." "To his angrie God," "Teares," "Great grief, great glory," "The Staffe and Rod," "God's time must end our trouble"—all describe or pray for conversion of pain to joy. The sentiment is orthodox, but there are a great many of these poems too. Moreover, in several Herrick significantly uses "pleasure" instead of the more traditional "joy" or "bliss" to describe the delights of Heaven. He may be forced to conclude, as one title suggests, that there are "None truly happy here." Yet he sees nothing wrong with pleasure as such, in this world or the next. It is not opposed to God but one of his prime creations:

God suffers not His Saints, and Servants deere,
To have continuall paine, or pleasure here:
But look how night succeeds the day, so He
Gives them by turnes their grief and jollitie.

This poem, "Paine and pleasure," leaves little doubt that though pain may be needed from time to time for man's correction, pleasure is preferable.

One might argue from this evidence that Herrick left his pleasures reluctantly, impelled by pangs of conscience. "When once the sin hath fully acted been, / Then is the horror of the trespasse seen." This argument, which would imply that he never adapted himself successfully to religious poetry, takes a narrow view of what is proper in religious poetry. Herrick is often at his best in *Noble Numbers,* as in *Hesperides,* when his feelings are least balanced or reined in. So far we have spoken mainly of negative cases; as in *Hesperides,* Herrick's verse takes fire not when he turns from pain or ugliness but when he welcomes beauty, life, and pleasure. As Herrick puts it, in "To God," his best emotion is not fear but love:

Come to me God; but do not come
To me, as to the gen'rall Doome,
In power; or come Thou in that state,
When Thou Thy Lawes didst promulgate,
When as the Mountaine quak'd for dread,
And sullen clouds bound up his head.
No, lay thy stately terrours by,
To talke with me familiarly;
For if Thy thunder-claps I heare,
I shall lesse swoone, then die for feare.
Speake thou of love and I'le reply
By way of *Epithalamie,*
Or sing of *mercy,* and I'le suit
To it my Violl and my Lute:
Thus let Thy lips but love distill,
Then come my God, and hap what will.

The poem that most clearly reveals Herrick's love of beauty and pleasure in the service of religion is "The white Island: or place of the Blest." Critics and anthologizers have often been attracted to this poem, one of his best. At the same time, it causes as much protest as admiration. The problem is that Herrick seems to surrender to Epicureanism. According to John Press, "The white island is simply the Earthly Paradise indefinitely prolonged and rendered a shade more edifying by the apparent absence of wine and sex." [7] This remark voices an unspoken assumption of many of Herrick's critics: when he turns to religion, he ought to renounce on the spot all further thought of pleasure. Why this is so is not explained.

In a more sympathetic reading of "The white Island," Roger Rollin writes: "There is . . . a sense of strain in these stanzas" from Herrick's inability "to deny life in the affirmation of afterlife, to renunciate." [8] Rollin asks of Herrick something he could never give as a poet. His way to the afterlife is not renunciation but (like Crashaw's) intensification. The last couplet of *"Julia's* Petticoat" is instructive in this context: "Ah! I co'd not: sho'd it move / to Life Eternal, I co'd love."

What we find in "The white Island" is "minimization of pain and maximization of pleasure" [9] in the service of devotion:

In this world (the *Isle of Dreames*)
While we sit by sorrowes streames,
Teares and terrors are our theames
        Reciting:

But when once from hence we flie,
More and more approaching nigh
Unto young Eternitie
        Uniting:

In that *whiter Island,* where
Things are evermore sincere;
Candor here, and lustre there
        Delighting:

There no monstrous fancies shall
Out of hell an horrour call,
To create (or cause at all)
        Affrighting.

There in calm and cooling sleep
We our eyes shall never steep;
But eternall watch shall keep,
        Attending

Pleasures, such as shall pursue
Me immortaliz'd, and you;
And fresh joyes, as never too
        Have ending.

A major element in the poem's structure is movement of feelings. Although a full stop follows the fourth stanza, the real division is after the third, and there are two upward movements, from sorrow and terror in the first and fourth stanzas to pleasures and joys in the third and last.

Negation is only part of the process that occurs in "The white Island." More important is intensification. Worldly sorrows are left behind but worldly beauty and pleasure are not.

The island of the blest, or Heaven, is described as a *"whiter"* island. The poem is not a journey from darkness into light as in Vaughan (for whom "white" was also emotive) but a journey from light into greater light. For Vaughan the contrast is total: shadows and dust compared to radiant light and everlasting life. For Herrick the matter is different. The world's beauty and pleasure anticipate even greater beauty and pleasure in the afterlife.

Herrick uses language and imagery similar to his secular poems. "The white Island" may be compared with "The Lilly in a Christal," which typifies his fervent response to physical beauty. It is noticeable that "The white Island" directly contradicts traditional metaphors that heaven is calm and cool, *locum refrigerii, lucis, et pacis,* and that death is like falling asleep. With a distinct shock we read, "There in calm and cooling sleep / We our eyes shall *never* steep." The "eternal watch" of the soul in Herrick's heaven is very like the "sleepless Eremite" with "eternal lids apart" of Keats's "Bright Star" sonnet. Both try to intensify life and its pleasures into eternity instead of denying or relinquishing them. Equally revealing is the succession of brilliant adjectives in the third stanza, all with double meanings: physical in their Latin roots, mental or spiritual in their later significations. "Sincere" has a root meaning of pure and clear as well as morally honest. "Candor" means of a dazzling white color as well as fair and impartial. "Lustre" suggests shining brightness as well as spiritual distinction. The effect is not to contrast the physical with the spiritual but to merge them.

When, in the last stanza, Herrick evokes not only the traditional "fresh joyes" of heaven but also "Pleasures" (the word strongly emphasized by its position), he only gives his poem the capstone we might expect. Herrick's Epicureanism, extended to the sacred poems, may be a matter for deprecation or embarrassment; yet he knew what he was doing and did it well. If a dissociation between worldly pleasure and religious joy troubles us when reading him, the flaw may be ours rather than his. There are precedents for Herrick's Christian Epicureanism, his stress not on balance but intensity, his pursuit of pleasure to the throne of God. The strain is rare in English but not wholly unknown. In the case of Crashaw, whose poetry has similar tendencies, the major influences were probably affective devotion and mysticism (whether attained or striven for). In the case of Herrick, although I am unable to trace direct connections, I believe the influence is more philosophical.

The Italian humanists wrote a series of discourses on pleasure, among them three treatises *de Voluptate* by Lorenzo Valla, Marsilio Ficino, and Pico della Mirandola. Traditionally, pleasure was suspect. Ficino writes: "The nature of evil, being insidious, offers itself to us daily under the guise of good, that is, of pleasure, in order to deceive and destroy us miserable people." "If you wish to avoid pain, flee pleasure, the lure of evils; pleasure bought with pain is noxious." [10] Yet, as Edgar Wind notes in his brilliant discussion of the subject, Plotinus, the authority from whom the Neoplatonists derived so many of their ideas, argues that pleasure, not knowledge, is the highest good.[11] Ficino drew back from this doctrine but his unruly disciple Pico did not. Erasmus too was known to have remarked that "if they are Epicureans that live pleasantly, none are more truly Epicureans than those that live holily and religiously." [12] Thomas More, whose credentials as a serious Christian were purchased with his life, made pleasure the ultimate good of his Utopians.[13] Whether More was arguing for or against this view is a matter of interpretation, but within their limits his Utopian philosophers are persuasive. In *The Four Last Things,* More assures penitent sinners that meditating on death and judgment will give them "so great a pleasure . . . that they never felt the like before." [14] The pleasure Crashaw finds in martyrdom is not wholly idiosyncratic.

The pleasure described by Pico, based on the Plotinian tradition, amounts to a divine *voluptas*, pleasure raised to a mystical level. On his personal medal, a succinct emblem of his most important beliefs, Pico chose to portray the Three Graces in their traditional postures: giving, receiving, returning, or *emanatio, raptio, remeatio.* These emblematic Graces are a paradigm of the relationship between God and man: divine giving, human receiving, and human movement back up toward God. On the rim of Pico's medal, however, is an unusual inscription: *"Pulchritudo Amor Voluptas."* As Wind explains, for

Pico the way back to God is through *voluptas* or pleasure.[15] It is uncertain whether Herrick knew his predecessors in the philosophy of pleasure or rediscovered this kind of Christian Epicureanism for himself. One should not underestimate the learning of a seventeenth-century poet. In any event, the philosophical line that can be traced through such writers as Plotinus, "Orpheus," Apuleius, Hermias, Valla, Ficino, Pico, Erasmus, and More is congenial with Herrick's poetry. It provides a philosophical basis for his failure to observe the Epicureanism of the golden mean in such poems as "A Country life" even at the moment he invokes it. It accounts for the constant movement in *Hesperides* out of swooning, sensuous pleasure toward heaven and the divine.[16] It also provides a means of understanding such obviously successful devotional poems as "The white Island."

2. *Vocal Devotions and Songs*

Herrick did not restrict himself to a single devotional mode. His favorite form was the epigram. Of the 272 poems in *Noble Numbers,* roughly 200 are epigrammatic and more than 100 are couplets.[17] Crashaw, who (in younger days) was equally fond of this form, typically employs it to astonish and amaze, though on occasion he achieves remarkable intensity of feeling in a short space, as in *"Sampson* to his *Dalilah":* "Could not once blinding me, cruell, suffice? / When first I look't on thee, I lost mine eyes." In Crashaw's hands, the epigram could become a poetic corollary to the popular affective ejaculation. Herrick, in contrast, usually neglects the affective possibilities, striving for simplicity and clarity rather than astonishment. His epigrams are usually more catechetical than devotional,[18] and in this respect truer to the normal spirit of the form. "Predestination" is typical: *"Predestination* is the Cause alone / Of many standing, but of fall to none." Milton makes the same point at considerable length in the *Christian Doctrine.*

Most readers prefer devotional to doctrinal poetry and turn with relief from the epigrams to the seventy remaining poems. These include a number of vocal devotions. "To God, on his sicknesse" is an excellent example of metrical psalmody:

> What though my Harp, and Violl be
> Both hung upon the Willow-tree?
> What though my bed be now my grave,
> And for my house I darknesse have?
> What though my healthfull dayes are fled,
> And I lie numbred with the dead?
> Yet I have hope, by Thy great power,
> To spring; though now a wither'd flower.

Herrick weaves a series of biblical images and verbal echoes into three couplet questions. After setting up a rhythm of expectations, he emphasizes the answer by unexpectedly employing enjambment and strong caesura in the final couplet, throwing full weight on his final images: the flower that withered but will "spring" once more.

Herrick also wrote a litany. Miriam Starkman calls "His Letanie, to the Holy Spirit" "an artful wedding of litany and meditation both." [19] The poem, in the tradition of meditation on the Four Last Things, evokes a series of conventional scenes: the deathbed, the doctor with no hopes "but of his Fees," the passing bell, the terrors of what comes after death. Unlike ordinary meditation, Herrick's poem continually returns to the petitionary mode in its refrain and has the appearance of a song text. It is first a vocal litany and only secondly a meditation:

> 6. When the passing-bell doth tole,
>   And the Furies in a shole
>   Come to fright a parting soule;
>   Sweet Spirit comfort me!

> 7. When the tapers now burne blew,
>   And the comforters are few,
>   And that number more then true;
>   Sweet Spirit comfort me! . . .

11. When the flames and hellish cries
    Fright mine eares, and fright mine eyes,
    And all terrors me surprize;
        Sweet Spirit comfort me!

12. When the Judgment is reveal'd,
    And that open'd which was seal'd,
    When to Thee I have appeal'd;
        Sweet Spirit comfort me!

The materials are similar to the "Holy Sonnets" but the devotional mode is different. Herrick seems less interested in analyzing man's predicament than escaping from it, and he assumes a much more passive role than Donne.[20] Yet behind the apparently simpler and more naive devotional method lies an equal poetic capability.

Herrick's interest in vocal devotions led him to write several poems unique among the poets discussed in this book: the two Graces and the Creed. "His Creed" is based only loosely on the Church's three traditional creeds. More devotional and less doctrinal, it centers on the emotion-laden alternatives of salvation and damnation. Its form owes much to the metrical psalm. Indeed, the poem may be described as a metrical creed in the affective and vocal modes.

The simple, childlike tone of the two graces may be ascribed to their ostensible speakers, who are children. But there is something childlike in many of Herrick's best religious poems. He is not active but passive. He prefers not to know but to trust. He need not pray to love but to love rightly. "Another Grace for a Child," with its misleading simplicity of manner, illustrates these qualities:

Here a little child I stand,
Heaving up my either hand;
Cold as Paddocks though they be,
Here I lift them up to Thee,
For a Benizon to fall
On our meat, and on us all. *Amen.*

The poem is so polished and controlled it seems artless. Its empathic qualities irresistably suggest Ben Johnson's great epitaph on his son. It is not surprizing that this is the most anthologized of Herrick's religious poems.

"A Thanksgiving to God, for his House" is also an essentially vocal devotion. The striking rhythms of this simple but highly accomplished poem may owe something to the Horatian Ode. The blessings for which Herrick thanks his God seem small: such as might please a contented Stoic in his country villa. Miriam Starkman calls the tone ironic: "Emerging from the thanksgiving is the most ingenuous questioning of the ways of God to man. See how little I ask, the poet seems to be saying, and how great my thanksgiving." [21] Irony there may be; humor there certainly is:

> Lord, Thou hast given me a cell
>   Wherein to dwell;
> And little house, whose humble Roof
>   Is weather-proof;
> Under the sparres of which I lie
>   Both soft, and drie. . . .
> Lord, I confesse too, when I dine,
>   The Pulse is Thine,
> And all those other Bits, that bee
>   There plac'd by Thee;
> The Worts, the Purslain, and the Messe
>   Of Water-cresse,
> Which of Thy kindnesse Thou hast sent;
>   And my content
> Makes those, and my beloved Beet,
>   To be more sweet.

Assuredly, what irony there is in this bears no grudge. One may scarcely read the poem, especially its final passages, without noticing the speaker's unmistakable tone of genuine enjoyment. He is no Stoic making do with little, but an Epicurean who has learnt where his true pleasures lie and thanks his God for them.

'Tis thou that crown'st my glittering Hearth
   With guiltlesse mirth;
And giv'st me Wassaile Bowles to drink,
   Spic'd to the brink.

I doubt that this echo of the Twenty-third Psalm is accidental. Paradoxically, Herrick's little becomes a fertile, teeming abundance, filled to the brim:

Lord, 'tis thy plenty-dropping hand,
   That soiles my land;
And giv'st me, for my Bushell sowne,
   Twice ten for one:
Thou mak'st my teeming Hen to lay
   Her egg each day:
Besides my healthfull Ewes to beare
   Me twins each yeare:
The while the conduits of my Kine
   Run Creame, (for Wine.)

The tone is celebratory, unstintingly joyful.

"An Ode of the Birth of our Saviour," "To his Saviour. The New yeers gift," and "To keep a true Lent" are holy-day songs or hymns. The last is especially fine, with a simplicity worthy of Herbert or Jonson but a manner unmistakably Herrick's. More pertinent to the present study, however, is a cycle of three carols sung before Charles I at Whitehall, at least two of which were set to music by Henry Lawes. Lawes, who set several of the secular songs, is commended by a poem in *Hesperides* entitled "To M. *Henry Lawes,* the excellent Composer of his Lyricks."

The first of these poems is "A Christmas *Caroll,* sung to the King in the Presence at *White-Hall.*" Parts are marked for four soloists and chorus with musical accompaniment. The poem opens with a burst of musical imagery:

What sweeter musick can we bring,
Then a Caroll, for to sing
The Birth of this our heavenly King?

Awake the Voice! Awake the String!
Heart, Eare, and Eye, and every thing
Awake! the while the active Finger
Runs division with the Singer.

The rest of the poem develops images of night turning to day,
darkness to light, and sterile winter to blossoming spring. A
note at the end tells us: "The Musicall Part was composed by *M.
Henry Lawes.*"

"The New-yeeres Gift, or Circumcisions Song, sung to the
King in the Presence at White-Hall" has a chorus and (apparently) five soloists. Lutes are invoked to "fill the roome" with
music. It is a ritual as well as a song. The celebrants are directed
to cast holy water about and to cense the room. The child Jesus
is brought in for the circumcision. The pitying priest hesitates
but must proceed, for without a baptism of blood "The Birth is
fruitlesse." The circumcision itself is brilliantly evoked in
imagery reminiscent of Crashaw yet more tender:

Touch gently, gently touch; and here
Spring Tulips up through all the yeare;
And from His sacred Bloud, here shed,
May Roses grow, to crown His own deare Head.

The carols, whose texts only survive, probably were acted out as
well as sung. The acting would have been stylized and ceremonial, as in the pageants, masques, and entertainments of the
period. The last chorus of the circumcision song suggests a
countermovement like that in *Comus* as the participants conclude their rites:

Back, back again; each thing is done
With zeale alike, as 'twas begun;
Now singing, homeward let us carrie
The Babe unto His Mother *Marie;*
And when we have the Child commended
To her warm bosome, then our Rites are ended.

Courtiers traditionally took part in such ceremonies acted in the royal presence. Perhaps Henrietta Maria played the small but exclusive non-speaking part of *"Marie."*

"The Star-Song: A Caroll to the King; sung at White-Hall" celebrates the Epiphany and marks the end of the Christmas-tide sequence. A "Flourish of Musick" introduces the song. Solo parts are sung by the Three Kings and the Star of Bethlehem, backed by a Chorus. This poem too has movement and counter-movement, its climax the moment that the Star reveals the Christ-child at his mother's breast. The Three Kings address the Star:

> 1   Tell us, thou cleere and heavenly Tongue,
>   Where is the Babe but lately sprung?
>   Lies He the Lillie-banks among?
>
> 2   Or say, if this new Birth of ours
>   Sleeps, laid within some Ark of Flowers,
>   Spangled with deaw-light; thou canst cleere
>   All doubts, and manifest the where.
>
> 3   Declare to us, bright Star, if we shall seek
>   Him in the Mornings blushing cheek,
>   Or search the beds of Spices through,
>   To find him out?
> *Star.*   No, this ye need not do;
>   But only come, and see Him rest
>   A Princely Babe in's Mothers Brest.

J. Max Patrick notes that Charles, Prince of Wales, was conventionally associated with the evening star, which appeared in the midday sky within an hour of his birth in 1630.[22] The event is obliquely referred to in Herrick's prefatory poem to *Hesperides.* Probably Henrietta Maria once more played the part of Mary in a *tableau vivant,* revealed in the fashion of the time by a sudden parting or falling of a curtain, and the young Prince of Wales sang the three lines assigned to the Star, which is complimented for its "cleere and heavenly Tongue." The date of performance is unknown, but he would have been less than ten years old. That is not impossible. Master Thomas Egerton played the much more demanding role of Younger Brother in *Comus* at age nine.

All this speculation may seem aside from the point. But a tentative reconstruction of a lost event emphasizes that these are not only fine poems but devotions of a peculiarly public and vocal character. The words, reinforced by instrumental music and singing, were probably supported by splendid costuming, flowers, dramatic lighting effects, and dancing in a "Round" at the moment of the dramatic epiphany or showing forth of the mother and child. To us, such an admixture of courtly compliment may distract from the poem's devotional nature; to Herrick and those who thought like him, it would have seemed to reinforce it.

3. Herrick in Meditation

Herrick, whose poetry is often celebratory, ceremonial, and social, and whose devotions are more affective than intellectual, wrote few primarily meditative poems. Yet among these are several we should be loath to lose, because they differ from any we have seen so far. "To his sweet Saviour," despite its multiple echoes from the Psalms, is more a meditation than a vocal prayer:

Night hath no wings, to him that cannot sleep;
And Time seems then, not for to flie, but creep;
Slowly her chariot drives, as if that she
Had broke her wheele, or crackt her axeltree.
Just so it is with me, who list'ning, pray
The winds, to blow the tedious night away;
That I might see the cheerfull peeping day.
Sick is my heart; O Saviour! do Thou please
To make my bed soft in my sicknesses:
Lighten my candle, so that I beneath
Sleep not for ever in the vaults of death:

Let me Thy voice betimes i'th morning heare;
Call, and I'le come; say Thou, the when, and where:
Draw me, but first, and after Thee I'le run,
And make no one stop, till my race be done.

This poem has the basic meditative structure of composition
and colloquy. Yet by linking the horrors of a sleepless night to
traditional meditation on death and the grave, Herrick achieves
something new and unexpectedly powerful. The intellect behind the poem conceals itself and emphasizes human affections.

The ending may remind us of an ending of Donne's: "Thy
Grace may wing me to prevent his art / And thou like Adamant
draw mine iron heart." While Donne prays to be a passive recipient of love, here and elsewhere, he does so actively, throwing
himself about in his efforts to escape his predicament. Herrick,
on the contrary, is passive. His life sinks to a low ebb; time
creaks to a halt; sickness is scarcely distinguishable from death.
The solution to a Donne sonnet typically is divine grace bringing peace and ending struggle. The solution to Herrick's poem
is God's "Call," the magnetism of his love, which will draw the
speaker from increasing immobility into renewed vigor and
motion: "Draw me, but first, and after Thee I'le run, / And
make no one stop, till my race be done." St. Paul's footrace,
which Donne uses in "Holy Sonnet 3" to evoke the last minute
and last stride pressing on to Judgment, here receives radically
different treatment.

"His Meditation upon Death" is another unusual poem.
Herrick begins as if with composition of place: "Be those few
hours, which I have yet to spend, / Blest with the Meditation of
my end." But he makes no further effort to set a specific scene
or meditate on it. Instead, he addresses a series of epigrams to
himself:

Nor makes it matter, *Nestors* yeers to tell,
If man lives long, and if he live not well.
A multitude of dayes still heaped on,
Seldome brings order, but confusion.

The tone and poetic form of this opening are Jonsonian; it is less a devotion than a series of moral apothegms. But the next lines move back to a variant of meditative technique:

> Which to effect, let ev'ry passing Bell
> Possesse my thoughts, next comes my dolefull knell:
> And when the night perswades me to my bed,
> I'le thinke I'm going to be buried:
> So shall the Blankets which come over me,
> Present those Turfs, which once must cover me:
> And with as firme behaviour I will meet
> The sheet I sleep in, as my Winding-sheet.
> When sleep shall bath his body in mine eyes,
> I will believe, that then my body dies:
> And if I chance to wake, and rise thereon,
> I'le have in mind my Resurrection,
> Which must produce me to that *Gen'rall Doome.*

Herrick uses a conventional devotional technique: everyday events as reminders of the spiritual life. Just so Vaughan advises, in *The Mount of Olives,* that we think of time and mortality when we hear a clock strike. In Herrick's poem, daily experiences of a particularly tactile kind are employed, such as the feeling of a sheet or blanket as one gets into bed. The devices Herrick mentions were probably common enough, but their employment in a meditative poem is strikingly effective. The end of the poem returns to the mode of the beginning, but the series of sensible or affective meditations at its heart lend urgency to its calm and balanced moral resolutions. The apothegms speak with Classical rationality, but to make the advice more emotionally real and put it into practice—"Which to effect," the middle section begins—affective meditation is Herrick's chosen tool. The poem is half meditation, half Horatian Ode.[23]

Noble Numbers concludes with a Holy-Week sequence, from Good Friday to Easter morning. It includes a variety of devotional modes from epigram to song, but all touched in some degree by meditation. The first poem, "Good Friday: *Rex*

Tragicus, or Christ going to His Crosse," is a meditation on the
Passion. In it, Herrick reveals that a major poet could still contribute powerfully to a well-worn genre. His approach is
suggested by the phrase *Rex Tragicus:* the poem is a direction to
the central actor in the Passion Play. In a moving variation on
composition of place, the poet describes the plot of the play that
the Divine Tragedian must enact:

> Put off Thy Robe of *Purple,* then go on
> To the sad place of execution:
> Thine houre is come; and the Tormentor stands
> Ready, to pierce Thy tender Feet, and Hands.

This indirect approach risks artificiality, yet, if anything, the
description of what-is-to-happen proves more moving than
another conventional description of what-is-happening. The
poem captures the terrors of anticipation.

> Long before this, the base, the dull, the rude,
> Th' inconstant, and unpurged Multitude
> Yawne for Thy coming; some e're this time crie,
> How He deferres, how loath He is to die!

The Crucifixion is real, but the multitude, looking upon it as an
entertainment, are bored by the principal actor's delay. Herrick
may have witnessed such behavior at English executions. Not
long after he published the poem, Marvell described a similar
event, when King Charles played his role on the "Tragick Scaf-
fold":

> While round the armed Bands
> Did clap their bloody hands.

As the poem develops, Herrick reveals that he as well as the
crowd views the Crucifixion as a drama. Those who think they
are spectators enjoying a diversion are in fact among the actors
of the tragedy. The true spectators are a larger and more distant body, whose attitude toward the drama about to take place
is utterly different:

The *Crosse* shall be Thy *Stage;* and Thou shalt there
The spacious field have for Thy *Theater.*
Thou art that *Roscius,* and that markt-out man,
That must this day act the Tragedian,
To wonder and affrightment: Thou art He,
Whom all the flux of Nations comes to see;
Not those poor Theeves that act their parts with Thee:
Those act without regard, when once a *King,*
And *God,* as Thou art, comes to suffering.
No, No, this *Scene* from Thee takes life and sense,
And soule and spirit, plot, and excellence.
Why then begin, great King! ascend Thy Throne,
And thence proceed, to act Thy Passion
To such an height, to such a period rais'd,
As Hell, and Earth, and Heav'n may stand amaz'd.

Hell, Earth, and Heaven; readers of the Bible and of the poem;
all who witness the Passion by meditating on it: these are the
audience for whom the play is acted.

And we (Thy Lovers) while we see Thee keep
The Lawes of Action, will both sigh, and weep;
And bring our Spices, to embalm Thee dead;
That done, wee'l see Thee sweetly buried.

The Passion is a tragic necessity in obedience to the plot and
rules of the Divine Dramatist. It cannot be altered without de-
stroying the play's unity, meaning, and effect on its audience.

The Renaissance and seventeenth century produced a
number of plays along classical lines with Christ as tragic hero.
Milton briefly considered writing such a play in the early 1640s.
The classical Passion tragedy may have suggested the central
conceit of *"Rex Tragicus"* to Herrick. Nevertheless, it is a strikingly original poem: a new variant on a traditional meditation.

Two minor poems that follow are colloquies addressed to
Christ. One is epigrammatic. When Christ was taken, the Disciples fled: "Let their example not a pattern be / For me to flie,
but now to follow Thee." The next, "Another, to his Saviour,"

develops the same theme. Herrick will follow Christ "hap what shall." If necessary, he will share in the scourging, but he would rather burn the rod. From one with Herrick's sensibility to pain the offer is touching, but the poem is slight.

"His Saviours words, going to the Crosse" is a brief *Improperia*. It begins, like the Good-Friday rite, with the Sufferer calling to passers-by in words that echo Lamentations i.12. It ends more metaphysically, urging the passing daughters of Sion not to fear that they must suffer the instruments of the Passion, the Cross, the cords, the nails, the spear:

> For *Christ,* your loving Saviour, hath
> Drunk up the wine of Gods fierce wrath;
> Onely, there's left a little froth,
>
> Lesse for to tast, then for to shew,
> What bitter cups had been your due,
> Had He not drank them up for *you.*

The next poem, "His Anthem, to Christ on the Crosse," responds to the Reproaches. As its title suggests, it is marked for singing, with versicles and chorus. The last lines suggest it might be sung before Holy Communion:

> *Chor.* Lord, I'le not see Thee to drink all
> 　　　The *Vineger,* the *Myrrhe,* the *Gall:*
>
> *Ver. Chor.* But I will sip a little wine;
> 　　　　Which done, Lord say, *The rest is mine.*

Following this meditative anthem is the last Good Friday poem, in the shape of a cross. It serves as a visual emblem to sum up the considerations of the series of six.

The Holy-Week sequence is concluded by three poems on the sepulcher, taking us to Easter morning. "To his Saviours Sepulcher: his Devotion" reveals Herrick at his characteristic best. The poem begins with a classical composition of place as the poet prepares himself and travels through imagination to the scene of the burial:

Haile holy, and all-honour'd Tomb,
By no ill haunted; here I come,
With shoes put off, to tread thy Roome.
I'le not prophane, by soile of sin,
Thy Doore, as I do enter in:
For I have washt both hand and heart,
This, that, and ev'ry other part;
So that I dare, with farre lesse feare,
Then full affection, enter here.

The style is marked by a limpid, balanced, Jonsonian simplicity of which perhaps only Herrick, of all Ben's many sons, was capable. This part is also marked by Herrick's wonderful capability of transforming a spiritual state or emotion into a ceremonious ritual.

Once in the tomb, the poet shows no desire to look about curiously in the Ignatian manner, to analyze the scene or his responses to it. Instead, he falls immediately into a characteristically affective mode, evoking pure senses and feelings:

Thus, thus I come to kisse Thy Stone
With a warm lip, and solemne one:
And as I kisse, I'le here and there
Dresse Thee with flowrie Diaper.
How sweet this place is! as from hence
Flow'd all *Panchaia's* Frankincense;
Or rich *Arabia* did commix,
Here, all her rare *Aromaticks.*
Let me live ever here, and stir
No one step from this *Sepulcher.*
Ravisht I am! and down I lie,
Confus'd, in this brave Extasie.
Here let me rest; and let me have
This for my *Heaven,* that was Thy *Grave*:
And, coveting no higher sphere,
I'le my Eternitie spend here.

"How sweet this place is!" This is not so great a poem as Keats's "Ode to a Nightingale," nor is Herrick's eternity the same as

Keats's. Yet in both poems one feels a shift out of present time into another, imagined place that becomes strongly realized as "here." In both the pressure of intense feelings and sense experience leads to a swooning and *extasis* of the soul into eternity.

Noble Numbers ends with two more brief poems that make the meditative voyage to the Sepulcher. "His Offering, with the rest, at the Sepulcher" is a brief, simple poem in which the poet offers a "Virgin-Flower" to dress his "Maiden-Saviour." "His coming to the Sepulcher" is all that Herrick gives us in the way of an Easter conclusion to the sequence. It is less triumphant than open-ended, as Herrick shares the doubts of Mary Magdalene and the Disciples as to where the vanished Savior has gone:

> Hence they have born my Lord: Behold! the Stone
> Is rowl'd away; and my sweet Saviour's gone!
> Tell me, white Angell; what is now become
> Of Him, we lately seal'd up in this Tombe?
> Is He, from hence, gone to the shades beneath,
> To vanquish Hell, as here He conquer'd Death?
> If so; I'le thither follow, without feare;
> And live in Hell, if that my *Christ* stayes there.

Modern critics as well as ancient philosophers and theologians express doubt about the religion of pleasure, with considerable justification. A man whose ultimate goal is pleasure in heaven—pleasure that can never fade—is only too likely to prefer that pleasure to its Giver. In his parting poem, however, Herrick reveals that if put to the choice, he prefers the Person to the place. His ladder of self-gratification leads finally to selfless love:

> I'le thither follow, without feare;
> And live in Hell, if that my *Christ* stayes there.

On this note, *Noble Numbers* ends.

Notes

1. See S. Musgrove, *The Universe of Robert Herrick* (Auckland University Press, 1950); Ronald S. Berman, "Herrick's Secular Poetry," *ES,* 52 (1971), 20–30; Robert H. Deming, "Robert Herrick's Classical Ceremony," *ELH,* 34 (1967), 327–348, and "The Use of the Past: Herrick and Hawthorne," *JPC,* 2 (1968), 278–291.

2. See Roger B. Rollin, *Robert Herrick* (New York: Twayne, 1966) and Earl Miner's pleasant study, *The Cavalier Mode from Jonson to Cotton* (Princeton: Princeton University Press, 1971).

3. See A. Leigh DeNeef, *"This Poetick Liturgie": Robert Herrick's Ceremonial Mode* (Durham: Duke University Press, 1974), pp. 109–125.

4. As noted by Paul R. Jenkins, "Rethinking what Moderation Means to Herrick," *ELH,* 39 (1972), 51–52.

5. Røstvig, *The Happy Man* (Oslo: Akademisk Forlag, 1954).

6. See D. C. Allen, "The Rehabilitation of Epicurus and His Theory of Pleasure in the Renaissance," *SP,* 41 (1944), 1–15.

7. Press, *Herrick,* Writers and their Work (London: Longmans, 1961), p. 9.

8. Rollin, *Robert Herrick,* p. 162.

9. Rollin, p. 162.

10. Ficino, *Apologi de Voluptate,* in Paul Oskar Kristeller, *The Philosophy of Marsilio Ficino,* trans. Virginia Conant (New York: Columbia University Press, 1943), p. 355.

11. Wind, *Pagan Mysteries in the Renaissance,* 2d ed. (New York: Barnes & Noble, 1968); I rely heavily on Wind's discussion of *voluptas.*

12. Erasmus, "The Epicurean," *Colloquies,* cited by Wind, p. 70.

13. More, *Utopia* (New Haven: Yale University Press, 1964), pp. 91–102.

14. See Roger L. Deakins' introduction to Ellis Heywood, *Il Moro,* trans. Deakins (Cambridge: Harvard University Press, 1972), p. xxxv. A useful study of Epicureanism in More and his predecessors (but unwilling to concede pleasure might be an ultimate good) is Edward J. Surtz's *The Praise of Pleasure* (Cambridge: Harvard University Press, 1957).

15. See Wind, pp. 43 ff. and Plates 10–11.

16. A tendency noted and condemned by H. R. Swardson, *Poetry and the Fountain of Light* (Columbia: University of Missouri Press, 1962), passim.

17. See Miriam K. Starkman, "Noble Numbers and the Poetry of Devotion," *Reason and the Imagination,* ed. J. A. Mazzeo (New York: Columbia University Press, 1962), p. 3.

18. See Starkman, pp. 2–3.
19. Starkman, p. 10.
20. See Starkman, p. 10.
21. Starkman, p. 10.
22. *The Complete Poetry of Robert Herrick,* ed. Patrick (New York: W. W. Norton, 1968), p. 9, note.
23. The latter is suggested by Starkman, p. 10, note.

8.

Andrew Marvell: The Soul's Retreat

1. Religious and Secular Poetry

The relation between religious and secular poetry in the seventeenth century was complex and uneasy. In the previous century, Spenser drew a clear line between Nature and Grace yet proceeded to mingle them inextricably in *The Fowre Hymnes* and *The Faerie Queene*. Religion is not a separate category but an essential part of living. Jonson's few religious poems rub shoulders with his other works and two of his favorite kinds, the epitaph and moral epistle, are neither wholly religious nor secular. Warfare between sacred and profane poetry was declared in the sixteenth century and earlier, yet few restricted themselves exclusively to one form. Donne's poems may be divided more readily than Spenser's into sacred and profane, a division not made in the first edition but encouraged by Walton's biography of 1640. But "Satire III" and the two Anniversaries do not lie easy in such categories. Herbert was first of the major poets to dedicate himself wholeheartedly to separating the two poetries: in the "Jordan" poems, in the sonnets to his mother quoted approvingly by Walton, and in the contents of *The Temple* itself.

Herbert's example especially exerted a powerful influence on the century's remaining religious poets, though one finds

235

conflicting signs. Crashaw segregated his secular and religious poems but published them between the same covers. Vaughan repudiated his secular works in *Silex Scintillans* (1655) but earlier and later he imitated Spenser and Jonson. Herrick segregated *Hesperides* and *Noble Numbers* but continued his pursuit of pleasure. All these poets, even Herrick, apparently felt somewhat guilty about their secular poems; while their artistic instincts pulled them one way, their consciences pulled them another. Ideally they might have followed Herbert's example and destroyed their profane works, dedicating themselves to God alone. But the flesh is weak and, luckily for us, they refrained from such drastic measures.

In contrast, there are few signs of these anxieties in the two great poets who begin and end the period, Spenser and Milton. Their commitment to religion is undoubted, yet they appear untroubled by this issue that so exercised their contemporaries. Those contemporaries were compelled, for substantial periods and sometimes to the ends of their lives, to repudiate the world. Donne turned from his dead wife to the pulpit, Herbert retreated to Bemerton and Vaughan to Newton. Crashaw was driven from his nest in Little St. Mary's to his last retreat at Loretto. Herrick reconciled himself to Dean Prior. Spenser and Milton, though forced to retire from time to time, turned those moments into opportunities for renewed attack. Although Spenser's Red Cross Knight glimpses the New Jerusalem and gains Una, these respites from his quest are short. Although Milton's Son of God retreats into the desert for forty days, it is to prepare himself to save mankind. Love, ethics, politics, and social relationships are not separate from religion in Spenser or Milton: rather they are informed by it.

Marvell's position, as one might expect, is ambivalent. On one hand is "The Coronet," one of the century's finest and subtlest poems on the difficult relationship between poetry and religion. In it, he begins like Herbert by repudiating former sinfulness and the writing of secular poetry. He promises to dismantle "all the fragrant Towers / That once adorn'd my Shepherdesses head" to weave a floral crown for Christ, whom his previous writings have crowned with thorns. But in vain:

Alas I find the Serpent old
That, twining in his speckled breast,
About the flow'rs disguis'd does fold,
With wreaths of Fame and Interest.

It is beyond man's power to free himself or his poetry from the world or sin; only God can do that. As it turns out, the wished-for transformation may only be accomplished by complete destruction—of life, of poetry:

But thou who only could'st the Serpent tame,
Either his slipp'ry knots at once untie,
And disintangle all his winding Snare:
Or shatter too with him my curious frame:
And let these wither, so that he may die,
Though set with Skill and chosen out with Care.
That they, while Thou on both their Spoils dost tread,
May crown thy Feet, that could not crown thy Head.

True religious poetry is the product of radical transformation. Disentanglement is an unlikely solution, destruction of poetry's very framework more likely. Marvell knows that the wheat and the tares of this world can be separated only at the harvest. This parable, often in Milton's mind, Marvell seems to confront: to destroy the tares he offers to destroy the wheat. As critics suggest, the poem requires its own destruction. But not quite: it is too noticeably "set with Skill and chosen out with Care."

However one resolves the paradox, Marvell clearly went on writing poetry and apparently abandoned the idea of separating the secular from the religious. Like Milton's, his poems habitually blend the two in varying proportions. Although he is customarily treated as a secular poet, almost half Marvell's better-known poems are partly or predominantly religious. Except for a few well-worn topics such as mysticism in "The Garden" or the problem of his religio-political sympathies, religion in Marvell's poems is largely ignored. There are secular elements in nearly all his poems. Given their predispositions, modern critics naturally fasten on them with some relief, which allows them to treat Marvell as the first Metaphysical Poet after Donne to return to the secular lyric. Since the interests of this book are different, I shall concentrate on the devotional elements in Marvell's poems and largely ignore the secular. This results in a partial reading, which is, however, balanced abundantly by what others say elsewhere. Like Herrick, Marvell is not primarily a devotional poet, but his contributions to devotional poetry, if few, are worthy of his stature.

2. "On a Drop of Dew"

"On a Drop of Dew" is a meditation or contemplation on the creatures. The terms were sometimes used interchangeably in the seventeenth century, although I prefer "contemplation" in its stricter sense. Meditation on the creatures can, however, become contemplation, as in Vaughan's case, when an object ceases to be a means to some intellectual or imaginative exercise and takes on visionary splendor as Eternity shines through it.

Sometimes it is hard to say whether a meditation on an object is secular or religious. The withered posie of Herbert's "Life" and the rose of "Vertue" are not very far from the central image in Waller's "Go, lovely rose." Herrick's nostalgic "To Meddowes" might be either a Christian or a classical elegiac. While Marvell's "The Picture of little T. C." is predominantly secular, "On a Drop of Dew" is predominantly religious. Yet its central theme, the relation between body and soul, matter and spirit, was a problem for medicine and practical living as well as theology. Similar problems are examined in Marvell's many lyrics on the conflict between ideal and physical love.

None of the meditations on the creatures by Herbert, Vaughan, or Crashaw really parallels Marvell's poem.[1] Its extensive examination of a single small object with minute particularity may be found in comical poems and tours de force, such as Donne's "The Flea" or Cleveland's "Fuscara," but the effect Marvell achieves is entirely different. Poetically, he employs an extended metaphysical conceit as his main technique. But the conceit has a devotional purpose. Critics, who often call the poem frigid, ingenious but lifeless, do less than justice to the intense emotions that lie just under its polished surface and emerge splendidly at its conclusion.

The first part of the poem concentrates on evoking the object, the drop of dew, but at the same time begins to move beyond it. The orient dew, the morning, the blossoming roses suggest beginnings, growth, beauty, and human youth. When the dewdrop "incloses" itself into a little globe, it imitates the heavenly spheres of its birthplace, traditional symbols of eternity and perfection. It also imitates a basic human reaction: the body shrinking and hugging itself out of fear of its surroundings. There are further human overtones. The dewdrop, which we contemplate, itself contemplates the heavens from which it came. Like a human eye it gazes upward, like a human tear it mourns its exile. Not a mere stationary emblem, it rolls about on its leaf and trembles with insecurity and fear of contagion.

If the first part goes beyond physical particulars, the second, ostensibly an explication of the allegory, is equally far from leaving particulars for abstract statement. It points the moral but continues the story. According to geometrical theory, a sphere resting on a plane touches it at only a single, dimensionless point, so paradoxically the two surfaces both touch and do not touch. Such is the relationship between the spiritual soul and material body, whose inexplicable combination makes man what he is. While, because of surface tension, the dewdrop imitates this inimicability to touch, its transparency enables it to welcome in the light at every point in its three-dimensional volume. Thus it is more intimate with the distant sun than the contingent leaf from which it shrinks.

The poem is a lengthy, remarkably detailed composition by similitude, which investigates the relationship of the soul to the body and at the same time to eternity by comparing it with a drop of dew. Marvell's method is brilliantly subtle. Because he begins with the dewdrop, he gives his reader the impression that he is conducting an inductive investigation rather than proceeding by deduction from dogmatic assumptions. If this is illusory, it is from such illusions that poetry is made. What seems missing, however, if the poem is viewed as a meditative exercise, is a proper close. Where are the affections raised by consideration of various points? Where is the resolution or closing colloquy? Above all, is a poem devotional if it never once mentions God?

One need only ask these questions to see their solutions. The appropriate affections, revulsion from the world and longing for eternity, run through the poem from its very first lines. Yet they express more than doctrinaire Neoplatonism, because the beauties of particularity are given full weight. No single moment marks the speaker's resolution, because his affections rise unforced, with apparent naturalness. The feelings conveyed by the poem seem to arise so directly from the speaker's character, to be so deeply part of him, that many critics cannot refrain from subjecting him to Freudian analysis, something they would be less prone to if the poem's underlying emotions seemed more forced or deliberate. No one would think of psychoanalyzing Vaughan's resolutions in "The Water-fall"— the devotional technique of which resembles "On a Drop of Dew"—because they are so obviously taken in full consciousness. The real difference in handling the devotional resolutions, however, is that Marvell works with greater subtlety and perhaps (to give the Freudians their due) found these particular affections easy to arouse in himself. There is little doubt that he knew what he was doing and, like other devotional writers, hoped his poem would arouse similar affections in his readers.

Not all meditative poems end in colloquies. All that is needed is a positive spiritual movement. At the least, this involves leaving some sin or evil, but usually it includes a movement explicitly toward God. Crashaw symbolized such a movement in "The Weeper" by the fall of Mary Magdalene's tears toward Christ's feet or, in more spiritual terms, by their ascent into heaven and transmutation into the wine of sacrifice and love. Direct prayer from Crashaw to God is replaced by indirection, but the devotional end is the same. This is equally true of Marvell's devotional technique: God is never mentioned in "On a Drop of Dew" but is pervasively present.[2] The ubiquitous imagery of circulation points toward him, suggesting (in Milton's words) the traditional belief that "one Almightie is, from whom / All things proceed, and up to him return, / If not deprav'd from good." God is also invoked by the pervasive light imagery. He is "the clear Fountain of Eternal Day," who preserves the soul in exile from the contagion of darkness. Above all, he is the Sun, who takes pity on the dewdrop and rescues it from its plight by transforming it from water to fire. Dewdrop, soul, and poem alike dissolve into the "Glories of th' Almighty Sun," attaining their ends through dissolution and rebirth. A concluding colloquy is unnecessary because the whole poem is an indirect colloquy that ends on a note of near-mystical exaltation. Indeed, while the poem employs the logical and imaginative techniques of meditation, it also displays the intense concentration on its subject, the sense of informing eternal beauty, and (at its close) surrender to a greater unity that characterize contemplation. Spiritual activity and passivity are perfectly balanced. Characteristically, Marvell accomplishes this with unstrained ease.

3. Two Dialogues

"A Dialogue between the Soul and Body" is much admired by New Critics because of its "tension" and ambivalence. It owes much to the Renaissance dialogue and indirectly the Socratic dialogue in that neither party has a monopoly of truth. Truth emerges from such dialogues—one thinks of More's *Utopia*—not by one party's victory over the other but by the rethinking forced on the reader by his realization that the issues are not so simple as he thought. The Soul's opening argument is telling:

> O who shall, from this Dungeon, raise
> A Soul inslav'd so many wayes?
> With bolts of Bones, that fetter'd stands
> In Feet; and manacled in Hands.
> Here blinded with an Eye; and there
> Deaf with the drumming of an Ear.
> A Soul hung up, as 'twere, in Chains
> Of Nerves, and Arteries, and Veins.
> Tortur'd, besides each other part,
> In a vain Head, and double Heart.

But the Body, which has the last word, is equally persuasive, logically and poetically:

> What but a Soul could have the wit
> To build me up for Sin so fit?
> So Architects do square and hew,
> Green Trees that in the Forest grew.

Neither party wins the argument. What emerges is a sense of man's nature and predicament, formed as he is from two principles, each seemingly out to destroy the other. The poem, part secular, part religious, is only negatively a devotion. That is, its theme is like "On a Drop of Dew," its method resembles meditation, but its viewpoint is such that the goal of meditation is not in sight. The poem argues that wholeness is impossible in the natural realm but no more than hints at a supernatural realm where answers might be found. There are sights that eyes keep the soul from seeing, truths that ears prevent it from hearing, but we are not shown what they are. If heaven exists for the soul, what about the poor, victimized body? The scribe who wrote "desunt multa" on one manuscript copy may have known something or may simply have been frustrated by the poem's refusal to commit itself.[3]

The more modern critics admire "A Dialogue between the Soul and Body," the more they disparage what seems another poem in the same genre, "A Dialogue Between the Resolved Soul, and Created Pleasure." There are few good words for this poem, though the editor of the first edition liked it well enough to put it first. Perhaps it is disliked because it is misunderstood. Unlike the debate of Soul and Body, it is only secondarily a dialogue but primarily a vocal devotion. Probably it is a text for musical recitative, since it is marked for a Prologue, the parts of Soul and Pleasure, and a Chorus.[4] As a sung devotion of a kind suitable for public performance, the poem avoids subtleties that would only be lost on an audience in such circumstances, in favor of broader and more massive effects.[5] Subtlety of argument is subordinated to a basic contrast, reinforced by imagery and diction, between two tones of voice or ways of speaking.

Pleasure speaks expansively, with four lines to each point in her argument. Her language is sensuous or (as Milton might say) in a Lydian mode:

> On these downy Pillows lye,
> Whose soft Plumes will thither fly:
> On these Roses strow'd so plain
> Lest one Leaf thy Side should strain.

The Soul's replies, each limited to a couplet, are necessarily more pithy. Sensuous imagery gives way to plain statement. The mode is Doric:

> My gentler Rest is on a Thought,
> Conscious of doing what I ought.

The Soul, chaster in her imagery and forced to work in half her opponent's space, seems at a disadvantage, but, of course, the opposite is the case. Nothing sets off Doric plain statement and quiet wit to better effect then overblown, overdecorated mannerisms. If the text were set to music, the contrast would be further underlined and strengthened.

The poem's structure involves traditional patterns of temptations: appeals to the five senses and then to four worldly desires: love, wealth, glory, and knowledge. All these, however, are subordinated to the more basic structure of seduction versus restraint. Pleasure speaks in the language of sensuous persuasion, the Soul the language of absolute faith and unquenchable determination. Readers familiar with Baroque recitative or oratorio may imagine (no more is possible) the contrasting music. The mode of Pleasure, with her concrete, persuasive use of imagery, is (by a series of historic accidents) almost precisely what modern criticism expects of lyric poetry, and so needs little explanation. The mode of the Soul, less familiar, is illustrated by the poem's heroic opening passage:

> Courage my Soul, now learn to wield
> The weight of thine immortal Shield.

Close on thy Head thy Helmet bright.
Ballance thy Sword against the Fight.
See where an Army, strong as fair,
With silken Banners spreads the air.
Now, if thou bee'st that thing Divine,
In this day's Combat let it shine:
And shew that Nature wants an Art
To conquer one resolved Heart.

Dressed in St. Paul's armor of salvation, the Soul prepares herself for spiritual combat. Marvell's imagery, ancient and traditional, may remind us of the opening meditation on the Two Armies in the *Spiritual Exercises*. But Marvell is not interested in analyzing subtle points; his is a massive vocal celebration: duty against pleasure, spirit against sense, spiritual joy against artistic beauty.

To some the poem may seem a negative exercise, a sour Puritan denial of beauty and pleasure. Denial is certainly there, yet the dominant note throughout is triumphant joy. That is the mood confirmed by the concluding choruses:

Earth cannot shew so brave a Sight
As when a single Soul does fence
The Batteries of alluring Sense,
And Heaven views it with delight.

"Brave" is a key word, with all its seventeenth-century meanings of brilliant color as well as admirable carelessness in the face of danger. Heaven's "delight" adds to the positive emotional tenor. Denial becomes affirmation.

That Marvell's mind was on music when he wrote this devotion is further suggested by the temptation of hearing:

Pleasure

Heark how Musick then prepares
For thy Stay these charming Aires;
Which the posting Winds recall,
And suspend the Rivers Fall.

Soul

Had I but any time to lose,
On this I would it all dispose.
Cease Tempter. None can change a mind
Whom this sweet Chordage cannot bind.

The importance of music is emphasized by the Soul's words, by its position as the climactic sense-temptation, and by the extra lines in the Soul's answer. Sight was regarded as the most important sense, touch as the most dangerous. Yet the Soul herself acknowledges the supremacy of music, perhaps a graceful reference to the kind of devotion with which Marvell is working.

4. "Bermudas"

The greatest of Marvell's vocal devotions in poetry, surely one of the best in the language, is "Bermudas." Its lyric qualities put it into the small class occupied by Jonson's near-perfect but very different "Hymn to Diana." Jonson or Herrick might equal its hard-won simplicity, but only Marvell or Milton (or in another language Horace) could achieve such heroic simplicity. "An Horatian Ode" is Marvell's celebration, thematically and stylistically, of heroic simplicity in the political realm; "Bermudas" is his celebration of heroic simplicity in the realm of faith. Although "Bermudas" was printed in tetrameter couplets, it falls naturally into four-line stanzas, and I take the liberty of thus dividing it. Among possible sources, Douglas Bush mentions the story of Richard More's landing in Bermuda in 1612, with its "description of men rowing and the singing of a Psalm of thankfulness." [6] "Bermudas" describes and is a metrical psalm or psalm-like hymn: full of biblical echoes, it is not a translation but an original re-creation of the psalms. As I suggested earlier, it is in poems like this, not translations, that the Metrical Psalm finds significant fulfillment in English.

"Bermudas" opens with an introductory frame-stanza that sets the scene and identifies the body of the poem as sacred song:

Where the remote *Bermudas* ride
In th' Oceans bosome unespy'd,
From a small Boat, that row'd along,
The listning Winds receiv'd this Song.

Scansion is a blunt tool, inadequate to analyze why the rhythms in a poem like this are so effective for most readers. Either the ear is taken from the opening lines or it is not. One reason for the rhythm's success is that it perfectly accommodates the spirit of the poem: its heroic simplicity. Whatever the term "Doric mode" meant to the Greek composers, Marvell captures what it meant to his friend Milton: deliberate valor, calm courage, cheerful resolution, marching music for wayfaring and warfaring Christians. Ideally the poetic texts for such music share the same technical and affective qualities, so voice and verse may cooperate harmoniously.

What the rowers in the boat sing is a psalm of praise, which magnifies God through his works.

What should we do but sing his Praise
That led us through the watry Maze,
Unto an Isle so long unknown,
And yet far kinder than our own?

Where he the huge Sea-Monsters wracks,
That lift the Deep upon their Backs.
He lands us on a grassy Stage;
Safe from the Storms, and Prelat's rage.

He gave us this eternal Spring,
Which here enamells every thing;
And sends the Fowl's to us in care,
On daily Visits through the Air.

He hangs in shades the Orange bright,
Like golden Lamps in a green Night.
And does in the Pomgranates close,
Jewels more rich than *Ormus* show's. . . .

Oh let our Voice his Praise exalt,
Till it arrive at Heavens Vault:
Which thence (perhaps) rebounding, may
Eccho beyond the *Mexique Bay*.

The brilliance of Marvell's visual imagery is justly admired; like Shakespeare, he also gives us an island "full of noises / Sounds and sweet airs." The hollow seas roar and proclaim their bounty; the rocks and sky echo to the pilgrims' song of praise.

In the concluding frame stanza, the poem's rhythm is compared to the movement of the boat in which the singers row:

Thus sung they, in the *English* boat,
An holy and a chearful Note,
And all the way, to guide their Chime,
With falling Oars they kept the time.

The Bermudas themselves "ride" the Atlantic swells like a boat at anchor. Although many of the poem's images are emblematic, few are stationary. Motion and sound are pervasive. Marvell does not give us fixed golden oranges in a green night but lets us witness the very act of an invisible God working at creation as he "hangs" them, sends his fowls in care, closes the jewels in the heart of the pomegranate, throws melons at our feet, sets out miraculous apples and cedars of Lebanon with his own hand, causes the ambergris to be proclaimed on shore. This dynamism balances the tetrameter couplet's natural tendency toward stasis and rest, resulting in an effect of controlled power. Such too is the effect of the rhythm, which suggests unstoppable determination disciplined by that strict control that is one facet of determination. It is like the "Deliberate valour" with which Milton's fallen angels march to the voice of flutes and soft recorders, except that to the music of "united force" and "fixed thought" Marvell adds the consciousness of doing right based on hope rather than despair: he calls the poem's mode "An holy and a chearful Note."

5. Miscellaneous Poems

Most of the devotions in *Miscellaneous Poems* (1681) are grouped together at the beginning of the volume. They include "Eyes and Tears," which argues that weeping is more important than seeing, because although tears cloud physical sight they sharpen spiritual sight and permit the soul to take an angle on Heaven. "Only humane Eyes can weep," for only human eyes have split vision and see into two worlds. Marvell's poem is inferior to Crashaw's "The Weeper" but confirms that, in such contexts, weeping is less a manifestation of sorrow than a participation in the divine.

Some critics interpret "The Nymph complaining for the death of her *Faun*" as a religious allegory, with the Fawn representing Christ or the Church of England. Although suggestive, none of these readings is wholly convincing. The most interesting passage in the poem from this point of view is the Nymph's description of her Fawn playing in the garden. It irresistibly suggests the *hortus conclusus* of the mystical tradition from the Song of Songs, which it frequently echoes.[7] But roses and lilies are symbols that echo several venerable traditions, secular as well as religious. The poetry of mystical love between the Soul and the Divine Spouse borrows heavily from the poetry of human love, and human love poetry as often returns the compliment and borrows from religion. Marvell's brilliant passage lies somewhere at the interchange of these two traditions; precisely where is still uncertain. The poem as a whole has a good claim to be called devotional, but the object of its devotion and its position on the sacred-secular axis have not been established. One cannot even be certain whether it is primarily a love poem, a political allegory, an ironic psychological analysis, or a religious devotion.

"A Dialogue between *Thyrsis* and *Dorinda*" was published with two musical settings in 1659 and 1675. Parts also survive in an autograph manuscript setting by William Lawes, who died in 1645. But there are puzzling circumstances. The poem is printed among the political poems in the 1681 volume, its text is faulty, and its authorship is questioned. It seems to begin as a Christian pastoral but ends with the two singers agreeing to kill themselves in order to reach a heavenly Elizium more quickly. If the poem is Marvell's it was evidently written before he was twenty-four. Its balance is tipped away from the devotional toward the secular or ironic by its troubling conclusion.[8] It would be gratifying to have at least one of Marvell's poems set to music by contemporary composers, but the evidence is inconclusive.

"Clorinda and Damon," another pastoral dialogue, also seems marked for singing, though no music survives. Clorinda invites Damon, in the first part, to make love with her. Damon refuses: the other day Pan met him, and since then everything is changed. "What did great *Pan* say?" Clorinda asks.

> D. Words that transcend poor Shepherds skill,
>   But He ere since my Songs does fill:
>   And his Name swells my slender Oate.
> C. Sweet must *Pan* sound in *Damons* Note.
> D. *Clorinda's* voice might make it sweet.
> C. Who would not in *Pan's* Praises meet?

Chorus

> *Of* Pan *the flowry Pastures sing,*
> *Caves eccho, and the Fountains ring.*
> *Sing then while he doth us inspire;*
> *For all the World is our* Pan's *Quire.*

Clorinda's conversion is underlined metaphorically by music. The two voices, high and low, harmonize after their initial disagreement, and the whole is rounded off by the Chorus, whose many voices suggest the world's universal choir. If the poem were set, the metaphor would easily become actual. Pan, god of nature and patron of pastoral, is also a traditional figure for Christ. Marvell preserves pastoral decorum, though Pan's name "swells" Damon's "slender Oate." Yet the morality his Pan inspires is Christian rather than Pagan. The pagan world is subsumed into the Christian, and this harmonious synthesis is symbolized and embodied by music. The poem is an excellent example of how Marvell mingles the secular and religious even in poems that celebrate the repudiation of worldly values for God. It reveals, in this respect, affinities with Milton rather than Herbert or Vaughan.

6. "The Garden"

If one had to name the most significant theme running through Marvell's poetry, an obvious choice would be commitment and withdrawal. In one way or another it enters nearly all Marvell's poems, sometimes in an amorous context, sometimes social, sometimes political, sometimes ethical, sometimes religious, most often a combination. The chief tradition behind this theme is an old debate, mainly religious, between the active and contemplative lives. There are many practical ramifications. One thinks, for example, of the debate in *Utopia* concerning whether a virtuous man should advise a corrupt government in hopes of improving it or dissociate himself from it for fear of complicity with evil. In Marvell's time, as in More's or ours, such questions had practical relevance.

Marvell sees both sides of the case. "An *Horatian* Ode" begins with a call to leave the retired life for active commitment to the national cause:

'Tis time to leave the Books in dust,
And oyl th' unused Armours rust:
    Removing from the Wall
    The Corslet of the Hall.

The balance of the poem shows that this call to action is not just politically expedient but has providential sanction. A key phrase needs emphasis, however: " 'Tis time." In Marvell's poetry there are times for action and times for contemplation. Neither is necessarily superior; time and circumstances must be considered as well.

"The Garden" is a poem of withdrawal and contemplation. It begins with a critique of ambition and love. The poet prefers to retire from the heat and dust of the world into the cool shade of the garden, where he leads an Edenic existence amid quiet, innocence, and solitude. Having abandoned the pursuit of fame and beauty, he is, in a manner, courted by the garden:

> What wond'rous Life in this I lead!
> Ripe Apples drop about my head;
> The Luscious Clusters of the Vine
> Upon my Mouth do crush their Wine;
> The Nectaren, and curious Peach,
> Into my hands themselves do reach;
> Stumbling on Melons, as I pass,
> Insnar'd with Flow'rs, I fall on Grass.

As Stanley Stewart remarks, the speaker "remains in a passive, receptive state." Not only do fruits drop about him, crush themselves on his mouth, reach themselves into his hands, but even his mock Fall is passive and in no way sinful. It is not a willed act but something the garden does to him.[9] Stewart refers to what happens in this poem as meditation, but an apter term is contemplation.[10] From the moment the speaker makes his choice of abandoning active pursuits and "uncessant Labours" for the garden's peace, his experience resembles not the active, strenuous exercise of intellect in meditation but the passive receptivity to something larger that characterizes contemplation.

Nature in Marvell's garden, as Patrick Cullen persuasively argues, is not opposed to the divine realm of grace.[11] Beginning with contemplation inspired by nature, the speaker insensibly progresses to contemplation of God through the creatures and perhaps even to direct contemplation. Stewart suggests that Marvell borrowed his helpful fruits from an ode by Casimire Sarbiewski that imitates the Song of Songs.[12] But the central theme of the stanza, fruits that offer themselves for man's use, belongs to the Paradise of Genesis. This topos is easily employed, as Casimire shows, in a celebration of the mystical love between God and the Soul, thus drawing strands from Genesis and the Song of Songs together. Marvell's stanza suggests that, in the course of a mystical experience, man's prelapsarian state of innocence is momentarily restored, and that nature helps inspire and shares in that innocence. This return of Eden occurs not through the speaker's mental efforts or meditative exercises but as a free gift pressed upon him with comic but pleasant insistence.

From his rural retreat, the poet retires still further, into the realm of his own mind. He does not reject the garden, which helped prepare him for this journey, but moves from a lesser but real pleasure to a greater, from a lesser to a greater kind of contemplation.[13]

> Mean while the Mind, from pleasure less,
> Withdraws into its happiness:
> The Mind, that Ocean where each kind
> Does streight its own resemblance find;
> Yet it creates, transcending these,
> Far other Worlds, and other Seas;
> Annihilating all that's made
> To a green Thought in a green Shade.

"Annihilation" is a technical term sometimes used to describe mystical prayer.[14] One way of reading the stanza is to see it as a description of the poet's creative imagination. But poetry is only one product of such experience: recreation of the self and the world, or one's perception and relation to it, are more important and immediate.

As Marvell progresses toward the heart of his poem, the focus on the mind and its capabilities gives place to what appears to be a picture of the soul engaged in contemplative ecstasy:

> Here at the Fountains sliding foot,
> Or at some Fruit-trees mossy root,
> Casting the Bodies Vest aside,
> My Soul into the boughs does glide:

There like a Bird it sits, and sings,
Then whets, and combs its silver Wings;
And, till prepar'd for longer flight,
Waves in its Plumes the various Light.

In the *Ancrene Riwle,* cloistered nuns are called "birds of heaven that . . . sit merrily in the green boughs, that is they meditate upwards and upon the bliss of heaven that . . . is evergreen." [15] Joachim Camerarius, in his popular *Symblorum et emblematum centuriae tres,* shows a picture of a bird preening itself in a tree under the rays of the sun as an emblem of renovation of youth (*renovata juventus*). The accompanying text explains that just as hawks renew their youth by means of the sun's rays, so the devout Christian can, in St. Paul's phrase, exchange the "old man" for the new by turning to God. Through the divine will, wickedness and depravity are replaced by true innocence and purity. [16] It is doubtful that Marvell knew the *Ancrene Riwle,* though he may have known Camerarius. Similar experience and familiarity with common traditions and ways of thinking are sufficient to explain a similar image.

As many critics argue, Marvell almost certainly describes a mystical *extasis* of the soul, which anticipates the longer, permanent flight it will make to heaven after the body's death. [17] This brief flight is a preparation for the longer flight, as in Camerarius' emblem. The bird renews its youth, the soul renovates itself, as the last couplet suggests. Such is the basic *raison d'etre* of contemplation: to bring the soul closer to God, acclimate it to heaven, and prepare it by anticipation for the life to come. St. Thomas Aquinas writes: "The active life ends with this world, but the contemplative life begins here, to be perfected in our heavenly home." [18] Aristotle makes the same point. The chief question, less a difficulty than a matter of emphasis, is how one is to interpret Marvell's "various light." Because it is various, critics argue that it cannot represent the unmediated light of eternity. The very fact that the soul sits in a tree in the midst of the garden suggests a kind of nature mysticism. [19] But nature in "The Garden" is not the nature of Wordsworth and the nineteenth century. It is the Book of God, and through it God can be contemplated. The contemplator in the garden is brought to where he is by means of nature's active assistance, but his ultimate goal is beyond nature. Having annihilated all that's made by retreating into his mind and then progressed still further by flying forth from his body, it seems that with nature's initial assistance he transcends the natural realm. The transition is not obvious because, in "The Garden," nature and grace are not at war.

The poem, especially its first stanzas, repeatedly contrasts the poet's state in the garden with those who are in the world. From his former passions he has come "hither." He is "here" and now, they are there and "then." The simple present tense and what we may call present place are reserved for his experiences in the garden. As in Herbert's "The Flower" and Vaughan's "The Night," this use of present tense reflects, in the climactic stanzas, the soul's participation in and union with the timeless moment of eternity. But such moments, though in one sense eternal, cannot last. Like Herbert and Vaughan, Marvell falls back into the world. The mystical experience recedes into the past. For a moment, it pointed toward a "longer flight" to heaven; after its departure it seems more like Eden, the paradise man has lost.

> Such was that happy Garden-state,
> While Man there walk'd without a Mate:
> After a Place so pure, and sweet,
> What other Help could yet be meet!
> But 'twas beyond a Mortal's share
> To wander solitary there:
> Two Paradises 'twere in one
> To live in Paradise alone.

Even before the Fall, the creation of Eve introduced a worldly love that distracted Adam from his pure contemplative relation with God. Marvell's double paradise is like Milton's "paradise within": a paradise each man attains in his own soul by conformity with God's grace. The emphasis is not on misogyny but on the value of solitude and the contemplative relationship with

God, as opposed to even the most legitimate involvements in the world.

Here, as elsewhere in the poem, Marvell's touch is light and witty and has a comic bite. It is argued that the poem cannot simultaneously be gracefully civilized and deeply religious. It is hard to see why not. If Donne can write serious love poems based on ingenious jokes—such as "The Canonization"—then Marvell may be allowed to write a serious poem on the contemplative experience that nevertheless retains his characteristic tact and humor. I have said little about the humor in Marvell's poems, assuming that readers would rather perceive it for themselves. It need not conflict with serious implications. A poet who does not abandon his humor when courting a mistress or contemplating death need not abandon it in his devotions.

The poem's last stanza completes the descent from mystical ecstasy back to the everyday world.

How well the skilful Gardner drew
Of flow'rs and herbes this Dial new;
Where from above the milder Sun
Does through a fragrant Zokiack run;
And, as it works, th' industrious Bee
Computes its time as well as we.
How could such sweet and wholsome Hours
Be reckon'd but with herbs and flow'rs!

Ann Berthoff persuasively argues that the formal flowerbeds and floral sundials some critics read into these lines are their own invention.[20] From everything we have read in the poem to this point, Marvell's garden is a place of natural beauty, which, like Milton's Paradise, the hand of man has improved but not cramped into "Beds and curious Knots." The "Dial new" is not a circular flowerbed but the natural process in which one flower gives place to another as the seasons progress. The sun runs through the zodiac over the course of the year, and the bee computes its time over the summer season as it lays in its stock for winter.[21] Marvell describes a world in which time and nature are redeemed. Bacon observes in his essay on gardens that "God Almighty first planted a Garden": a commonplace. Although human gardeners may have planted the flowers in question, and Lord Fairfax may have supervised their laying out (not a consideration the poem encourages), God is the author and ultimate creator of this "Dial new."

Considered from a devotional standpoint, "The Garden" is akin to Vaughan's "The Night." Both poems describe a movement from the world into an inner or higher world of contemplation and then back again. For Vaughan, much as nature attracted and refreshed him, the boundaries between heaven and earth, the night of the soul and everyday business, are more firmly drawn. His is a world torn by sectarian strife, given to vain pursuits, from which the soul longs to escape to her true home. The cessation of the contemplative moment is for him a terrible disappointment and he repeatedly seeks to recapture it. (I speak, of course, of the poet revealed in *Silex Scintillans*.) Marvell, in contrast, characteristically presents nature and supernature as a continuum rather than an opposition.[22] In "On a Drop of Dew," though the drop shrinks from possible contamination, the rose petal is perceived in all its beauty and the sun is at once a part of the natural scene and a figure for God. In "Clorinda and Damon," the world is not rejected by the shepherds after their conversion, but transformed. In "Bermudas," the island and its flora embody the providential divinity that underlies and shapes nature. In "The Garden," nature actively helps prepare the mind and soul for the journey out of nature toward God. Once human passions and ambitions are rejected, the poem reveals a natural world that is redeemed, and redemptive, even before the soul experiences its transforming contemplative ecstasy. After that climax recedes, nature and time retain a redeemed aspect. Unlike Vaughan or Herbert, Marvell does not apparently need to reject one world for the sake of the other. When he falls back from the greater pleasure to the lesser, he rests in it until the time comes for longer flight. Disappointment is momentarily signaled in stanza eight by an unobtrusive shift in tense, a lightly touched-on reminder that paradise after all is lost, and a wry turn in the

poem's humor. But by the last stanza equanimity and contentment are regained.

Although they are complex and subtle poems, "The
Coronet" and "An *Horatian* Ode" reveal that Marvell can, when
appropriate, commit himself ruthlessly. But the preferred
course in his devotional poetry is to draw God into the world
rather than reject the world for God. Even in mysticism, the
most extreme devotional mode, this moderation prevails. It
sounds paradoxical. Yet many great mystics act similarly, and
are as practical and down-to-earth as they are visionary. Among
English poets, different as they otherwise are, Marvell, Milton,
and Traherne arrive at syntheses of heaven and earth without
confusing these realms. They share an appreciation for the
very taste and texture of natural objects with a simultaneous
awareness of an all-important, transcendant God beyond them.

Notes

1. See J. B. Leishman, *The Art of Marvell's Poetry* (London: Hutchinson, 1966), pp. 196–203; he finds no closer parallel than Vaughan's
"The Water-fall."

2. See Patrick Cullen, *Spenser, Marvell, and Renaissance Pastoral*
(Cambridge: Harvard University Press, 1970), pp. 177–178.

3. See *The Poems and Letters of Andrew Marvell*, ed. H. M. Margoliouth, 3d. edn. rev. by Pierre Legouis with E. E. Duncan-Jones
(Oxford: The Clarendon Press, 1971), I, 249.

4. Douglas Bush calls it "a miniature oratorio," *English Literature
in the Earlier Seventeenth Century* (Oxford: Clarendon Press, 1962), p.
169; Leishman speculates that "Marvell intended it to be set to music"
but draws back (pp. 208, 204).

5. This accounts for a stylistic problem raised by Rosalie Colie,
"My Ecchoing Song" (Princeton: Princeton University Press, 1970), pp.
77–78.

6. Bush, p. 187. Many echoes from the Psalms are cited in Tay
Fizdale's "Irony in Marvell's 'Bermudas,' " *ELH*, 42 (1975), 203–213,
with which I otherwise part company.

7. See Karina Williamson, "Marvell's 'The Nymph Complaining
for the Death of Her Fawn': A Reply," *MP*, 51 (1954), 268–271.

8. On provenance, see Margoliouth, pp. 247–249; Cullen proposes an ironic reading with naive speakers, pp. 200–201.

9. Stewart, *The Enclosed Garden* (Madison: University of Wisconsin Press, 1966), p. 158; also pp. 154, 159, 171.

10. Stewart, pp. 156, 167, 169, 170, 177–178, 180, 181; see also Cullen, pp. 153–161.

11. Cullen, passim, esp. pp. 153–161.

12. Stewart, pp. 159–160; on the fruits of Eden, see my "Angels and Food in *Paradise Lost*," *Milton Studies*, 1 (Pittsburgh: University of Pittsburgh Press, 1969), pp. 136–139.

13. See Pierre Legouis, "Marvell and the New Critics," *RES,* 8 (1957), 382–383.

14. See William L. Godshalk, "Marvell's *Garden* and the Theologians," *SP*, 66 (1969), 648; also Margoliouth, pp. 268–269.

15. Cited by Katharine Garvin, "Andrew Marvell the Anchorite," *TLS* (11 August 1950), p. 508.

16. Camerarius, *Symbolorum et emblematum centuriae tres* (1605), Book III, foll. 33ᵛ-34ʳ (plate xxxiv); the plate without text is reproduced (from the 1654 edn.) in Colie, *"My Ecchoing Song,"* Plate 18.

17. Godshalk, 649–651; Stewart, pp. 177–180, Margoliouth, pp. 268–270; other critics disagree.

18. *Summa Theologica*, trans. Fathers of the English Dominican Province (New York: Benziger Brothers, 1947), II, 1941 (Pt. II-II, Q. 181, A. 4).

19. As Legouis argues, "Marvell and the New Critics," pp. 386–387.

20. Berthoff, *The Resolved Soul* (Princeton: Princeton University Press, 1970), pp. 158–163, 229–233.

21. Descartes writes: "Doubtless, when swallows come in the spring, they act in that like clocks. All that honey-bees do is of the same nature." Letter to the Marquis of Newcastle (1646), *Descartes: Selections*, ed. Ralph M. Eaton (New York, 1927), p. 357; cited by Daniel Stempel, *"The Garden:* Marvell's Cartesian Ecstasy," *JHI*, 28 (1967), p. 113.

22. This chapter was headed toward its present conclusion when I read Patrick Cullen's *Spenser, Marvell, and Renaissance Pastoral* which doubtless has helped me clarify it. See also Geoffrey H. Hartman, "Marvell, St. Paul, and the Body of Hope," *ELH*, 31 (1964), 175–194.

9.

Thomas Traherne: Mystical Hedonist

1. Traherne's Uniqueness

Thomas Traherne's religious poetry has had more attention, as religious poetry, than that of either Donne or Herbert, to name only two of his more prominent fellows. Only Milton has been more seriously investigated as a philosopher and religious thinker. Recent studies have been so fruitful it may seem strange to say he is a writer who resists systematic analysis; yet such is the case. Much light has been thrown on the background, but the major works have been only tentatively illuminated. It is a commonplace that Traherne "evades labels" and, in spite of many debts, remains "an original." [1] The style and structure of his works and his devotional methodology are agreed to be essentially non-logical. Agreement ends in determining what organizational principles replace logic. Symptomatic of the difficulties in coming to grips with Traherne is Martz's remark that "the most notable effect" of reading the *Centuries* is "mental fatigue." [2] Other critics extend the observation to the poems. Yet reading these works as such is not fatiguing. When only a little background is sketched in, students take to the poetry enthusiastically. No fatigue results from reading as Traherne presumably intended, with emotional engagement. This may involve both passive submission to ideas and experiences and active cooperation in working them out.[3] Trouble begins when one reads with a continuous effort to analyze or make organized notes. Then fatigue comes quickly: a common experience with imaginative writers that is aggravated because Traherne's methods resist logic or summary.

John M. Wallace views the Dobell poems as a traditional meditative sequence.[4] His perception of interrelationships among the poems is valuable but the Ignatian model proves inadequate. Martz reads the *Centuries* as Augustinian or Bonaventuran meditations.[5] His discussion is best when it describes Traherne's iterative, circulating method and weakest when it relates that method to historical schools of devotion. A. L. Clements, taking the Dobell poems for his text, argues that Traherne's basic organizing principle is not meditation but mysticism.[6] That Traherne is a mystic many critics agree, although Clements' is the first systematic analysis. His book is the best effort yet to describe Traherne's devotional methodology; its weakness is the assumption that one devotional method rather than several suffices to understand a seventeenth-century poet. Mysticism underlies the poems and the *Centuries,* but it does not exclude other devotional modes or combinations.

We learn from Vaughan and Crashaw that the way to contemplation may involve vocal prayer, meditation, or sensible affection, in varying proportions depending on the poet's devotional and poetic genius. Here too Traherne is something of an original. Instead of beginning with elementary forms and working upward—from meditation to contemplation like Vaughan, or from affection toward contemplation like Crashaw—he begins with mystical experience and descends to various lower regions. Clements notes that he characteristically "writes out of, not toward, the mystical experience" and uses a "ladder of ascent" to accommodate mystical experience to his audience.[7] Mystics commonly descend from the heights in any case, so the desire to draw others up to share his own state may be only one reason for Traherne's mixed technique. The very act of writing poetry or putting experience into words and images is possible only after the writer is separated from the mystical experience he later evokes.

The "I" of the *Centuries* speaks in several tones of voice and from several points of view.[8] Sometimes he is a fallen sinner, sometimes an innocent child, sometimes a redeemed visionary. But typically it is from the midst of vision that we first hear him speak. "I will open my Mouth in Parables: I will utter Things that have been Kept Secret from the foundation of the World. Things Strange yet Common; Incredible, yet Known; Most High, yet Plain; infinitly Profitable, but not Esteemed" (C I.3).[9] The Dobell poems too begin with "Wonder," in which the speaker overlooks a gap of sinfulness from a vantage of later redemption and recalls the innocent vision of childhood.[10] At the beginning of his sequence the poet has already reached his goal and from there recapitulates his spiritual journey.

2. Mystical Experience: "Wonder"

Clements prefaces his study with the "fine" but "extremely important" distinction that he will demonstrate not that Traherne was a mystic but that "the speaker in at least one of his voices was a mystic or, better and more precisely, that the poetry is mystical." [11] The disclaimer sums up the constraints on an investigation that has few biographical facts to go on and is bounded by modern critical doctrine that strictly separates the poet from his poem. While modern critics rightly teach us not to rush in and confuse the writer with his protagonists, it is increasingly evident that the two are seldom wholly separate either. Mysticism, as mystics agree, is a matter of experience, not book learning. Poetry cannot be an authentic reflection of mysticism unless its writer is a mystic; or, if one wishes to make the fine distinction, the writer must give his reader the impression he has experienced what he writes of. As Vaughan notes, it is a curious dishonesty to claim experience in an area like this falsely.

Traherne goes further. The truths he wants to convey to his reader, the "Gifts" of God he wishes to pass on, can only be understood by experience. "They are unattainable by Book, and therfore I will teach them by Experience. Pray for them earnestly: for they will make you Angelical, and wholy Celestial" (C III.1). Baker agrees: In mystical matters "no trust is to be given to learning without experience, but much to experience though without learning." Or as Herbert puts it in a moment of experiential desolation: "Now I am here, what thou wilt do with me / None of my books will show." [12] It is an appeal to experience that introduces Traherne's Third Century, in which he recalls the visionary experience of childhood in his best-known words. His prose style is such as to make the experience seem real and present to the reader and evoke similar experiences in his breast if not recall them from his past.[13]

The Corn was Orient and Immortal Wheat, which never should be reaped, nor was ever sown. I thought it had stood from everlasting to everlasting. The Dust and Stones of the Street were as Precious as *Gold*. The Gates were at first the End of the World, the Green Trees when I saw them first through one of the Gates Transported and Ravished me; their Sweetnes and unusual Beauty made my Heart to leap, and almost mad with Extasie, they were such strange and Wonderfull Thing: The Men! O what Venerable and Reverend Creatures did the Aged seem! Immortal Cherubims! And yong Men Glittering and Sparkling Angels and Maids strange Seraphick Pieces of Life and Beauty! Boys and Girles Tumbling in the Street, and Playing, were moving Jewels. . . . Eternity was Manifest in the Light of the Day, and som thing infinit Behind evry thing appeared: which talked with my Expectation and moved my Desire. The Citie seemed to stand in Eden, or to be Built in Heaven. The Streets were mine, the Temple was mine, the People were mine, their Clothes and Gold and Silver was mine, as much as their Sparkling Eys Fair Skins and ruddy faces. The Skies were mine, and so were the Sun and Moon and Stars, and all the World was mine.
(C III.3)

The writing conveys a sense of experience or autobiography. Some of Traherne's earlier critics tried to deduce from it facts about his life and upbringing; one can agree with those who criticize such an approach yet still insist that these passages are autobiographical.[14] As Stanley Stewart remarks, Traherne's is not the sort of autobiography that gives us birthdate and father's occupation.[15] The center of his interest is elsewhere, in the spiritual or mystical experience. One may allow for the possiblity that Traherne might manipulate facts or dates, like Walton in his *Lives*, to bring out the essential truths of experience more clearly. But he would be unlikely to tamper with that experience itself or claim experiences he had not had.

The Dobell manuscript opens with a sequence of poems that evoke childhood mystical experiences. "The Salutation," "Wonder," "Eden," and "Innocence" treat the same autobiographical materials found in the Third Century. These experiences offer glimpses of felicity, the goal toward which Traherne means to draw his reader:

> At that we aim; to th' end thy Soul might see
> With open Eys thy Great *Felicity*,
> Its Objects view, and trace the glorious Way
> Wherby thou may'st thy Highest Bliss enjoy.

These lines from "The Author to the Critical Peruser" were probably meant to introduce another sequence but describe a technique and purpose that characterize all Traherne's later devotional works.

"Wonder," with its vivid evocation of childhood experience, is typical of these first poems in the Dobell sequence:

1

> How like an Angel came I down!
>   How Bright are all Things here!
> When first among his Works I did appear
>   O how their *Glory* me did Crown?
> The World resembled his *Eternitie*,
>   In which my Soul did Walk;
>   And evry Thing that I did see,
>   Did with me talk.

2

The Skies in their Magnificence,
    The Lively, Lovely Air;
Oh how Divine, how soft, how Sweet, how fair!
    The Stars did entertain my Sence,
And all the Works of *God* so Bright and pure,
    So Rich and Great did seem,
As if they ever must endure,
    In my Esteem.

3

A Native Health and Innocence
    Within my Bones did grow,
And while my *God* did all his Glories shew,
    I felt a Vigour in my Sence
That was all *Spirit*. I within did flow
    With Seas of Life, like Wine;
I nothing in the World did know,
    But 'twas Divine.

Although the voice that speaks is not identical with the childlike, unanalytic "I" of the past, the distinction is not pressed at first. The past tense is used, but the experience seems immediate. At one point Traherne slips into the present tense ("How Bright are all Things here!") and when he admires the air he further blurs considerations of time by omitting the verb. The implication is either that he can slip into his past and identify with his former self or that similar experiences occur in his present. Yet use of the conditional subtly hints at a potential for change: These wonders "So Rich and Great did *seem, / As if* they ever must endure, / *In my Esteem.*" The last ambiguous phrase may signify either that, in his childish estimation, worldly things would endure for ever or that they would be ever thus *in his estimation.* He, as well as they, would never change.

The possibility of change or imperfection is hinted more strongly in the next stanza, though mostly by denial:

4

    Harsh ragged Objects were conceald,
        Oppressions Tears and Cries,
    Sins, Griefs, Complaints, Dissentions, Weeping Eys,
        Were hid: and only Things reveald,
    Which Heav'nly Spirits, and the Angels prize.
        The State of Innocence
    And Bliss, not Trades and Poverties,
            Did fill my Sence.

The charge that Traherne did not believe in original sin or evil
does not survive close reading.[16] Ugliness, oppression, grief,
and sin exist, but were "conceald" and "hid" from his infant-
eye. When he was a child, the "State of Innocence, / And Bliss"
filled his senses and left no room for contrary impressions.
Paradoxically, although this childish vision is partial, it is ultimately truer than the vision of what Blake later called "experience." "Evry Creature is indeed as it seemed in my infancy: not
as it is commonly apprehended. Evry Thing being Sublimely
Rich and Great and Glorious. Evry Spire of Grass is the Work of
His Hand" (C III.62). Evil is real, purity of vision more real still.
    Negative elements disappear from the poem which returns
to immersion in the childhood experience:

5

    The Streets were pavd with Golden Stones,
        The Boys and Girles were mine,
    Oh how did all their Lovly faces shine!
        The Sons of Men were Holy Ones.
    Joy, Beauty, Welfare did appear to me,
        And evry Thing which here I found,
        While like an Angel I did see,
            Adornd the Ground.

6

    Rich Diamond and Pearl and Gold
        In evry Place was seen;

Rare Splendors, Yellow, Blew, Red, White and Green,
    Mine Eys did evrywhere behold,
Great Wonders clothd with Glory did appear,
    Amazement was my Bliss.
That and my Wealth was evry where:
    No Joy to this!

The reader knows the streets were not literally paved with gold
or the houses built of diamonds and pearls. Yet the experience
is real. Traherne suggests this double meaning—the streets
only seemed golden yet, while he was in his mystical state, were
golden—by his verbs. The streets "were pavd"; faces "did . . .
shine": statements of fact. At the same time, these wonders only
"appear"; "'Mine Eys did evrywhere behold": the miracle is in
the beholder not the object. The value of his vision is still felt by
the speaker: "like an Angel I did see." The stanza ends in
another timeless exclamation: "No Joy to this!"
    More negatives enter to be dismissed:

7

Cursd and Devisd Proprieties,
    With Envy, Avarice
And Fraud, those Feinds that Spoyl even Paradice,
    Fled from the Splendor of mine Eys.
And so did Hedges, Ditches, Limits, Bounds,
    I dreamd not ought of those,
But wanderd over all mens Grounds,
    And found Repose.

8

Proprieties themselvs were mine,
    And Hedges Ornaments;
Walls, Boxes, Coffers, and their rich Contents
    Did not Divide my Joys, but shine.
Clothes, Ribbans, Jewels, Laces, I esteemd
    My Joys by others worn;
For me they all to wear them seemd
    When I was born.

For Traherne, sin is chiefly an acquired characteristic; the growing child learns its ways from the corrupting influence of parents, friends, or society. It entails a change in the individual's perception of the world, whose wonders begin to be seen in terms of ownership and exclusion. This change, Traherne tells us, was impressed on his original innocence with difficulty: "So that with much adoe I was corrupted; and made to learn the Dirty Devices of this World" (C III.3). Not only did his eye skip over "Hedges, Ditches, Limits, Bounds," the signs of "Cursd . . . Proprieties"; it converted them into things of beauty. "Proprieties themselvs were mine, / And Hedges Ornaments." The rich clothes worn by others, perhaps in pride or to excite envy, seem to be worn for his pleasure and delectation. But the poem ends conditionally: things were thus "When I was born." By implication, they were not so later.

One virtue of "Wonder" (as well as "Eden" and "Innocence") is that Traherne acknowledges the potentiality of evil yet preserves the integrity of his innocent vision. His poetry is neither blinkered nor disingenuous; if the narrator is more experienced than the child he describes, he is not ironic with his earlier self. He knows evils exist but values the perception that passes over them or converts them into good.

"Wonder" may not seem to be a devotional poem. It is neither meditation nor vocal prayer, and has neither colloquy nor resolution. It is certainly a poem of feeling and experience, so that to call it affective seems closer to the mark. Traherne does not evoke the senses in anything like the same way as Crashaw or Herrick. Although the poem is a paean to objects, things, and colors, a love poem for the world as well as the God whom it manifests, no attempt is made to visualize or sense those objects with any specificity. This kind of poetry is only explicable if, as Clements argues, we assume Traherne is writing "out of" mystical experience, or more precisely remembering and trying to recapture a mystical experience in order to lead his reader toward a similar experience and so toward felicity. To accomplish this end, the essential point is not to enable the reader to visualize particular trees seen through a city gate or particular objects, but to enable him to seize hold of the kind of vision that makes objects fresh, new, and splendid.

Critics compare Traherne's descriptive powers unfavorably with Marvell's. His "Rare Splendors, Yellow, Blew, Red, White and Green" are not directly comparable to Marvell's "golden Lamps in a green Night." The function of the images in their contexts differs radically. One need not excuse Traherne for being vague because he is in a mystic trance. Rather, he takes precisely the line that may best produce the effects he wants. "I will teach . . . by Experience." The experience in question is not of objects but perception, the "Wonder" of a kind of childlike vision. This perception turns whatever it meets, whether a paving stone or color and light, into reflections of divinity.

"Wonder" has the passivity that characterizes affective and mystical poetry. Things "talk" to the poet. The stars "entertain" his sense. He is caressed by the "Lively, Lovely Air." Health and innocence grow in his bones, without effort on his part, and his body flows "With Seas of Life, like Wine." Ugliness and sin "were conceald," "Were hid." The agency in these passive verbs is unspecified: perhaps it is nature, perhaps God, perhaps youth; in any event, he is the passive recipient. His senses are filled. He finds, sees, beholds, wanders, esteems: his activities are really responses. All he does in the poem that is noticeably active is to come down like an angel into the world, but by the poem's end this arrival is also seen as passive. Everything wonderful happened to him "When I was born," the ultimate in unwilled, passive acts.

Of course, Traherne describes a state of bliss proper to infancy, before discursive meditation and intellectual volition are possible. Corruption comes with intellect and speech, though not necessarily caused by these new abilities. But Traherne does not only describe his childhood. The key to felicity, the right devotional method for him and readers whose minds work like his, is to recapture this early state. "Innocence," the last of these recollective poems, concludes: "I must becom a Child again." He must "unlearn" the world's dirty devices and "becom as it were a little Child again, that I may enter into the Kingdom of *God*. . . . Our Saviours Meaning . . . is Deeper far then is generaly believed" (C III.3, 5).

The requisite childlikeness consists of simplicity, peace and purity of soul, nakedness from evil habits and customs. "Grit in the Ey or the yellow Jandice will not let a Man see those Objects truly that are before it. And therfore it is requisit that we should be as very Strangers to the Thoughts Customs and Opinions of men in this World as if we were but little Children" (C III.5). That is how Traherne characterizes the vision of "experience" or disillusionment: jaundice or grit in the eye.

In some ways Traherne anticipates Blake (who did not know him), but he values the state of innocence more highly. His adult voice never undercuts the child's experience or turns against it with irony and bitterness. The adult state of regained felicity is not identical with the child's, but unlike Blake's it incorporates little of the transitional, "fallen" state. This difference is not a result of naivete or ignorance of evil, but a difference of poetic and devotional bent. The revolution from custom is not seasoned with bitterness; he prefers to forget, except in passing, what he regards as false paths taken, the better to begin again.

3. The Argument from Want:
"Poverty" and "Insatiableness (II)"

The Dobell Manuscript, written and corrected in Traherne's own hand, is probably a complete poetic sequence. The Burney Manuscript, written by Thomas's brother Philip, runs the Dobell poems into another sequence, which (I hope to show elsewhere) is probably only partly complete.[17] Because Philip revised the Burney poems, one is tempted to avoid them. I have decided against this for several reasons, of which the most important is that some poems available only in Philip's version are among Traherne's best. I mention these technical matters because, regrettably, these poems have been tampered with to an unknown extent.[18] Yet even as they stand they are remarkable.

A reader of Traherne's works learns to expect problems in their structures and devotional methods. The two poetic sequences begin with the vision of childhood, yet the first poems contain much that is only developed later, including most obviously the question of who is speaking and from what vantage point. In *Centuries of Meditation,* Traherne follows a different order, reserving the childhood experiences until the third Century. He begins with the present—his reader's present rather than his own—and gradually prepares the ground for a backward step into a new beginning. What begins the *Centuries* is a certain condition that Traherne asks his reader to look for in himself: infinite desires and wants, powerful urges to possess and enjoy, unwillingness to settle for anything less than perfection and infinity. This omnipossessiveness is revealed in the first poems of the sequences. "The Boys and Girles *were mine,*" says the poet in "Wonder": "*my Wealth* was evry where." A reader coming on these assertions without some grounding in Traherne's methods might find them puzzling. His "system" is like a seamless web. One must begin somewhere, but the decision where to begin is somewhat arbitrary: a problem for the poet, reader, and critic.

One unique aspect of Traherne's devotional method is his brilliant presentation of the state of innocence or infant's vision. Another is his use of infinite desire as the starting point for the spiritual quest. "Do you not feel yourself Drawn with the Expectation and Desire of som Great Thing?" (C I.2), he abruptly asks. "Is it not a Great Thing, that you should be Heir of the World?" (C I.3). He circles around the point and returns to it again and again. "The Noble Inclination wherby Man thirsteth after Riches and Dominion, is his Highest Virtu, when rightly Guided" (C I.23). "Your Enjoyment of the World is never right, till you so Esteem it, that evry thing in it, is more your Treasure, then a Kings Exchequer full of Gold and Silver" (C I.25). God "made us to Want like *Gods,* that like *Gods* we might be satisfied" (C I.41). "God gav Man an Endless Intellect to see All Things, and a Proneness to covet them, becaus they are His Treasures" (C III.42). "Felicity must be perfect, or not Felicity. . . . And unless in these I could be satisfied I should never be contented" (C III.57).

The *Centuries* tell us that Traherne's longings went back to his childhood and were coterminous with the state of infant bliss.[19] But the best evocation of these childhood wants is "Poverty":

> As in the House I sate
> Alone and desolate,
> No Creature but the Fire and I,
> The Chimney and the Stool, I lift mine Ey
> Up to the Wall,
> And in the silent Hall
> Saw nothing mine
> But som few Cups and Dishes shine
> The Table and the wooden Stools
> Where Peeple us'd to dine. . . .

The adult voice intervenes, gently suggesting that the child has certain possessions which, for the moment, he forgets: ease, health, hands, eyes, sun, moon, stars, other people. He does not imply, however, that the child is too greedy for wanting so much. Infinite desires are legitimate, we learn:

> Som greater things I thought
> Must needs for me be wrought,
> Which till my pleased Mind could see
> I ever should lament my Poverty:
> I fain would have
> Whatever Bounty gave;
> Nor could there be
> Without, or Lov or Deity:
> For, should not He be Infinit
> Whose Hand created me?
> Ten thousand absent things
> Did vex my poor and absent Mind,
> Which, till I be no longer blind,
> Let me not see the King of Kings.
>
> His Lov must surely be
> Rich, infinit, and free;
> Nor can He be thought a God

Of Grace and Pow'r, that fills not his Abode,
    His Holy Court,
  In kind and liberal sort;
    Joys and Pleasures,
 Plenty of Jewels, Goods, and Treasures,
(To enrich the Poor, cheer the forlorn)
    His Palace must adorn,
     And given all to me:
    For till *His* Works *my* Wealth became,
    No Lov, or Peace did me enflame:
    But now I have a *Deity.*

God is not God unless he pours treasures on his subjects; there is neither love nor peace until all is Traherne's. Such is the child's insight, such the adult's. Somehow, these infinite desires have been satisfied, for the poem ends with the one-line reassurance worthy of Herbert: "But now I have a *Deity.*" Instead of giving up the impossible, the poet realizes it.

The four complex stanzas begin and end alike, but the rhyme pattern varies in the middle from one stanza to the next. In the first three there is an unrhymed line, but the last, whose pattern is more regular, rhymes throughout.[20] The effect is movement from discord to harmony: a pattern Herbert often employs, and Milton in "Lycidas." The poem seems to begin with composition of place. But no attempt is made to describe the objects in the room. Critics dispute whether Traherne refers to his father's house or an inn owned by a putative relative, the Mayor of Hereford. What seems a description of literal poverty turns out to be an evocation of a mood or a psychic state. In his effort to delineate this state, Traherne seems to have telescoped two actual incidents described in the *Centuries:* his sense of spiritual poverty as a four-year-old in his father's house and his sense of desolation in a banqueting hall in the absence of the feasters. If so, the poem is another illustration that he is concerned to recapture the experience and not the outward circumstances.

The simplicity of the images resembles "Wonder," but bare description need not always have the same force. In "Poverty," the main effect, of course, is to emphasize the poverty of the child's vision. Some of the furnishings actually suggest wealth—a painted cloth, a glass window—but it is as if the child's eye is too uninterested to consider these things. Where "Wonder" suggests a flooding of the senses "Poverty" suggests sensory deprivation. The difference is in the beholder's state. But in both poems the devotional method is to throw the emphasis on feelings and perceptions.

Another major poem on the theme of infinite want is "Insatiableness (II)":

> This busy, vast, enquiring Soul
>   Brooks no Controul,
>   No Limits will endure,
> Nor any Rest: It will all see,
> Not Time alone, but ev'n Eternity.
>   What is it? Endless sure.
>
> 'Tis mean Ambition to desire
>   A single World:
>   To many I aspire,
> Tho one upon another hurl'd:
> Nor will they all, if they be all confin'd,
>   Delight my Mind.
>
> This busy, vast, enquiring Soul
>   Brooks no Controul:
>   'Tis hugely curious too.
> Each one of all those Worlds must be
> Enricht with infinit Variety
>   And Worth; or 'twill not do.
>
> 'Tis nor Delight nor perfect Pleasure
>   To have a Purse
>   That hath a Bottom of its Treasure,
> Since I must thence endless Expense disburse.
> Sure there's a *God* (for els there's no Delight)
>   One Infinit.

This poem too has a complicated rhyme scheme: the third stanza recapitulates the first, and the fourth the second. But the last stanza has two lines with extra feet: "That hath a Bottom of its Treasure, / Since I must thence endless Expense disburse." The expansion underlines the meaning and points toward the conclusion: "Sure there's a *God* . . . / One Infinit."

The legitimacy of egotism, of following one's desires without limit, is a theme common among Romantic poets but rare in the seventeenth century. Ordinarily it would only be expressed to be condemned, or put in the mouths of dramatic figures like Marlowe's heroes and Shakespeare's villains, or Milton's Satan (not yet perceived as heroic). But Traherne is not a Romantic poet. Although he insists on unlimited desire in pursuit of felicity, he also insists that it be reconciled with traditional Christian values.

We have seen something approaching Traherne's philosophy in Crashaw and Herrick. Herrick's concentration on the pursuit of pleasure especially resembles Traherne. In Herrick's case, I suggested that a philosophical tradition underlies the poetry. If Pico, Ficino, and More did not influence him directly, they at least resemble him. With Traherne, the case is clearer. His interest in philosophy, which he pursued at Oxford, continued afterward. Two authorities we know he consulted in detail were Pico and Ficino.[21]

"Felicity" is a favorite term of Traherne's, but he also speaks often of delight, happiness, and joy. Significantly, he is not afraid to speak of "pleasure," that favorite term of Herrick and More. "You will feed with Pleasure upon evry Thing that is His. So that the World shall be a Grand Jewel of Delight unto you: a very Paradice; and the Gate of Heaven" (C I.20). "For Lov implies Pleasure, becaus it is ever pleased with what is Beloved" (C I.80). "And shall we prize the sun less then it [gold], which is the Light and fountain of all our Pleasures?" (C II.7). In the poems "pleasure" appears again and again, often rhyming, as it does in "Insatiableness," with "treasure." A treasure is anything that satisfies Traherne's desires and gives him joy and pleasure. The *Centuries* offer a useful gloss on "Insatiableness":

The Image of God implanted in us, guided me to the maner wherin we were to Enjoy. for since we were made in the similitud of God, we were made to Enjoy after his Similitude. Now to Enjoy the Treasures of God in the Similitud of God, is the most perfect Blessedness God could Devise. For the Treasures of *God* are the most Perfect Treasures and the Maner of God is the most perfect Maner. To Enjoy therfore the Treasures of God after the similitud of God is to Enjoy the most perfect Treasures in the most Perfect Maner. Upon which I was infinitly satisfied in God, and knew there was a Dietie, becaus I was satisfied. For Exerting Himself wholy in atchieving thus an infinit felicity He was infinitly Delightfull Great and Glorious, and my Desires so August and Insatiable that nothing less then a Deity could satisfy them.

(C III.59)

A basic premise of many traditional philosophical systems is that man's final end is happiness. Differences arise from defining that happiness and the best path to it. The path of intensified pleasure, not denied but raised, and culminating in the beatific vision, characterizes some Christian humanists and Neoplatonists, but is most accurately called Christian Epicureanism.

Because of Epicureanism's proneness to abuse, few serious thinkers in the Renaissance trusted it. Even Herrick felt obliged to bridle his immoderate hedonism with the golden mean, though he is unable to repress it for long. Traherne is perhaps the first major English writer to follow the path of Christian hedonism to its limits and yet not fall into the obvious pitfalls.

Another strain that may have helped Traherne refine his thinking was the school of Descartes. The new philosophy spread quickly among University and intellectual centers in England, and it would be odd if Traherne did not know of it.[22] Stewart suggests that Traherne's devotional method, whereby one "knows and loves the infinite by knowing and loving the infinite in himself . . . is the Trahernean analogue to Descartes' *'Cogito.'* "[23] To start with oneself as the most immediately knowable and progress outward and upward is very much in accord with the Cartesian revolution. There are other resemblances as well, such as Descartes' refusal to suppress the passions and his interest in creating new worlds in the mind. But if Traherne borrowed from Descartes, he characteristically took only what he wanted and left the rest.

Another movement that might have influenced Traherne was radical Puritanism, the belief in an "experimental" or experiential Christianity. Traherne, a convinced Anglican and monarchist, would not have sympathized with Puritans as such; yet we have seen that devotional methods cross the boundaries of doctrinal difference. The leading characteristic of the experimentalists was that they believed that religion should be "based on or derived from experience as opposed to mere testimony or conjecture." [24] It was not what the bishops, or the Fathers, or even the Bible said, but what one felt within with utter convincement that mattered. Another idea that often accompanied experimentalism was the belief that one enjoys heaven on earth in this life, that heaven is a state of mind or inner condition rather than a place, and even that there is no life after death.[25] The reward of the elect is present bliss. Traherne would not have agreed. He speaks of man enjoying a "fourfold Estate of Innocency, Misery, Grace and Glory" (C III.43), the last attained only after the Last Judgment. A major part of his present felicity is the knowledge that it will last forever (C III.57). There is no happiness in a purse with a bottom. Yet in his state of Grace, from which he looks back on the state of Innocence over the state of Misery, is a present felicity that lacks little of the state of Glory.

Traherne's method of recapturing perceptions and feelings from the past and encouraging his reader to see and feel them too, in some ways similar to Crashaw's affective methods, also looks something like what Cotton Mather later called the "Affectuous way" of psalm singing and scripture reading, which involves "an *Experimental Taste,* of the *Piety* which was working in the Hearts of the Writers at the Time of their Inspiration." [26] According to Kenneth Silverman, Mather derives this mode of

devotion from a type of biblical exegesis among whose propo-
nents were Luther, Philipp Jakob Spener, and the German
pietist August Hermann Francke. The method is to "enter into
the Affections of the Inspired Writers with sacred attention and
perseverance . . . as it were, raise the Writer from the dead." [27]
Given the prevalent habit of converting scripture readings into
devotions, it is easy to see how this method of getting into the
hearts of Moses and the Prophets could become a devotional
technique. These are unlikely sources for Traherne, but they
illustrate how an interest in affective methods appears at the
fountainhead of Protestantism and among Puritans as well as
Anglicans and Roman Catholics.

Another influence on Traherne's experimentalism may be
mentioned, and with it we come full circle. The radical Puri-
tans, Anabaptists, Familists, and others who flourished in
England were greatly influenced by such unorthodox mystics as
Meister Eckhart, Heinrich Suso, and Johannes Tauler. The
Quaker Robert Barclay was influenced by the Catholic Augustine Baker.[28] The line separating orthodox from unorthodox
Catholic mystics was often thin. Many of the beliefs for which
Eckhart was attacked are duplicated by St. John of the Cross.
What finally distinguishes the orthodox mystic from his het-
erodox brethren is willingness, not under pressure but freely,
to balance extreme emphasis on personal, internalized, experimental religion with orthodox beliefs. Such a position is
obviously Traherne's. It may have been a difficult stance for
him to achieve since, as we noted in discussing Vaughan, there
was no recognized place for an Anglican mystic in the seventeenth century. But mystics may expect such difficulties in any
time. Traherne may have been encouraged to take the path he
did by what he learned from the Cartesians, Puritan Experimentalists, and Luther, but the major philosophical support for his method of infinite want is Christian Epicureanism.
Want is a devotional method as well as a philosophical concept,
and it is as an Anglican mystic that Traherne's employment of
the method, with combined vision and orthodoxy, is best
explained.

4. Songs of Praise

Mystical writers in the seventeenth century agreed that, once an individual reaches the level of contemplation, he is unlikely to have much further need of meditative techniques. Meditation may in some cases be a road to contemplation, but it is not an end in itself. Nevertheless, mystics commonly continue to use vocal prayer. This return to elementary prayer and neglect of an intermediate form may seem odd, until one realizes that by its nature meditation is a laborious method for climbing upward on the spiritual journey but that vocal prayer (which also has this function) may be used to express the joys of contemplative experience. Emerging from contemplation, which is ineffable, the mystic seizes on vocal prayers and hymns to give thanks for his experience or convey it to others. Many of the Church's hymns were written by mystics. Henry Vaughan, who found meditation ultimately fruitless, continued to employ vocal prayer and hymnology. Traherne was evidently less inclined to music than his predecessors, yet he too turned to vocal devotion as a means of praise.

"The Church's Yearbook," based on the traditional calendar of feasts from Easter to All Saints (another part is probably lost) attests to Traherne's interest in properly observing holidays. It contains a variety of meditations, devotions, litanies, and prayers. Although at least half the contents are borrowed from other writers,[29] this does not detract from the manuscript's value as evidence of Traherne's devotional practices. As Carol M. Sicherman points out, parts of the notebook seem taken from "material prepared for oral delivery," while others might be used for private or group devotions.[30] Among the vocal works are a number of collects from the Book of Common Prayer, including those for St. Barnabas, St. Peter, St. James, St. Bartholomew, St. Matthew, St. Michael, St. Luke, and Ss. Simon and Jude.[31] From Lancelot Andrewes Traherne borrows a litany and several selections from the *Sermons*.[32] The evidence for his interest in vocal prayer is considerable, but there are few hymns. There is a reworking and abridgement of an English version of St. Peter Damian's "Ad Perennis Vitae Fontem," published in Paris in 1631.[33] There is "An Hymne upon St Bartholomews Day" and an abridged translation of "Veni Creator Spiritus" that may be Traherne's. Only the last may be called notable poetry and its ascription is uncertain. What "The Church's Yearbook" suggests is that Traherne had a considerable interest in vocal devotions but was not much interested in extending it to hymn texts.

Traherne's carelessness about regularity in his stanzas implies that he did not design most of his poems for musical setting. Such devices as lengthening lines for poetic effect, while legitimate, disqualify poems like "Insatiableness (II)" as potential musical texts. In the years between 1640 and 1660, when Traherne's poetic sensibilities were formed, political conditions made difficult the performance of literary hymns or cathedral music of the kind Donne and Herbert grew up with. Most of Traherne's stanza forms, unlike those of his predecessors, do not seem directly shaped by musical influence or the hope of musical setting. For the most part, they are purely literary forms.

There are exceptions. As one might expect of an Anglican poet who grew up in the Civil War, one of Traherne's poems, a hymn by literary genre if not musical setting, was inspired by Christmas, a holiday banned by the Puritans. "On Christmas-Day" celebrates the feast as a public occasion and a manifestation of the established order. The poem, pervasively musical, is built on the rhyme words "sing" and "King," generally used twice in every stanza. There is room only to quote two verses, but that may show how, in this vocal, public devotional mode, Traherne sounds very like Spenser in "Epithalamion" or Herrick in *"Corinna's* going a Maying":

Shake off thy Sloth, my drouzy Soul, awake;
    With Angels sing
    Unto thy King,
And pleasant Musick make;

Thy Lute, thy Harp, or els thy Heart-strings take,
And with thy Musick let thy Sense awake.
  See how each one the other calls
  To fix his Ivy on the walls,
  Transplanted there it seems to grow
  As if it rooted were below:
    Thus He, who is thy King,
      Makes Winter, Spring. . . .

Hark how remoter Parishes do sound!
    Far off they ring
    For thee, my King,
  Ev'n round about the Town:
The Churches scatter'd over all the Ground
Serv for thy Prais, who art with Glory crown'd.
  This City is an Engin great
  That makes my Pleasure more compleat;
  The Sword, the Mace, the Magistrate,
  To honor Thee attend in State;
    The whole Assembly sings;
    The Minster rings.

The resemblance between this poem and "Epithalamion" or "Corinna" results not from direct influence but from similarities in occasion and mode. They are, in their different ways, holiday poems and ritual celebrations.

"Bells," which follows "On Christmas-Day," is in a similar public vocal mode, though it goes further in making a personal, affective application of the feelings raised by the music and festivities:

Bells are but Clay that men refine
  And rais from duller Ore;
Yet now, as if they were divine,
They call whole Cities to adore;
Exalted into Steeples they
Disperse their Sound, and from on high

Chime-in our Souls; they ev'ry way
  Speak to us throu the Sky:
    Their iron Tongues
    Do utter Songs,
And shall our stony Hearts make no Reply! . . .

Doth not each trembling Sound I hear
  Make all my Spirits dance?
Each Stroak's a Message to my Ear
That casts my Soul into a Trance
Of Joy: They're us'd to notify
Religious Triumphs, and proclaim
The Peace of Christianity,
  In *Jesus* holy Name.
    Authorities
    And Victories
Protect, increas, enrich, adorn the same.

The musical sounds "Chime-in our Souls": bring them into the pattern as the change-ringing bells go through their courses toward their final peal. Even stony hearts are affected. As for the poet, each sound makes his spirits—the subtle distillations that link body and soul—dance within him, while the soul is cast into a trance of joy. The poem's imitative effects recapture metaphorically these aural experiences and perhaps elicit similar affections in the reader.

Among the most original of Traherne's writings are the *Thanksgivings*. These works, neither poetry nor prose in the ordinary sense, are probably attempts to imitate biblical or Hebraic poetry, particularly the Psalms, various canticles, and the Song of Songs. The Psalms, which are quoted extensively, are the primary model. One may agree with Stewart that the "formal characteristics" of the *Thanksgivings* "reveal the speaker's desire to imitate the psalmist as a poet" but question whether this influence reveals a pervasive "meditative mode" in these works.[34] It might be better to speak of a vocal mode. That is what Traherne suggests, when he refers to his model:

O that I were as *David*, the sweet Singer of *Israel!*
    In meeter Psalms to set forth thy Praises.
Thy Raptures ravish me, and turn my soul all into
        melody.[35]

A long discussion of David and the Psalms in the Third
Century reveals that Traherne found these works perfect ex-
pressions for his own ecstatic experiences, especially with regard to the wonders of creation. Here too he emphasizes the
Psalmist as a holy singer:

His fingars touchd his Trembling Lyre,
And evry Quavering String did yeeld,
A Sound that filled all the Jewish Quire
    And Ecchoed in the Field.
No Pleasure was so Great to Him
As in a Silent Night to see
The Moon and Stars: A Cherubim
Abov them even here He seemd to be.
Enflamd with Lov it was his great Desire,
To Sing Contemplat Ponder and Admire.
                            (C III.69)

Singing is linked with affection and contemplation of the creatures, but "Melodie" is the poem's dominant image and vocal
devotion its dominant mode.

Traherne believed that one of the best ways to express
gratitude to God is by right and appreciative use of the senses.
The material universe was created toward this end, and even
angels derive pleasure from sensible things at secondhand
through man. Honey, milk, and butter gratify the taste, gold
and silver the eye, music the ear:

Thy Angels have neither ears nor eyes,
    Nor tongues nor hands,
Yet feel the Delights of all the World,
And hear the Harmonies, not only which

Earth but Heaven maketh.
The melody of Kingdoms,
The joys of Ages,
    Are Objects of their joy.
They sing thy Praises for our sakes;
    While we upon Earth are highly exalted
      By being made thy Gifts,
        And Blessings unto them.[36]

Traherne had only a limited interest in composing hymn texts but keenly appreciated the importance of music in the divine praises and of vocal devotions in general.

5. Mysticism and Sensible Affection

Most mystics agree that, in true mystical prayer, reason is left behind, while the soul approaches God under the dark cloud of unknowing. In terms of traditional faculty psychology, it was common to say that contemplation is a function of will rather than reason: *"Ibi non intrat intellectus, sed affectus."* [37] According to scholastic theologians, will is the seat of love, and man approaches nearest to God in this life by love, not knowledge. Protestant theologians, while speaking of grace rather than contemplation, agreed.

Nevertheless, Traherne respects the intellect. He acknowledges that philosophical studies played a large part in his search for felicity and treats the intellect as an important aspect of man's ability to transcend limitations and be like God. His description of intellect and imagination at work is reminiscent of Vaughan:

When my Soul is in Eden with our first Parents, I my self am there in a Blessed Maner. When I walk with Enoch, and see his Translation, I am Transported with Him. . . . I can visit Noah in His Ark, and swim upon the Waters of the Deluge. I can see Moses with his Rod, and the children of Israel passing thorow the Sea. . . . I can visit Solomon in his Glory, and go into his Temple, and view the sitting of His servants, and Admire the Magnificence and Glory of his Kingdom.

(C I.55)

There are many similar passages in the *Centuries*. They are not, in most cases, meditations in the ordinary sense. Typically, there is no elaboration of the imagery, no effort to dwell on objects or scenes with systematic application of intellect or imagination. For Traherne, such sights as Noah in his Ark and Solomon in his Temple need no elaboration; immediately, without further effort, they evoke the desired affections and responses.

The closest Traherne comes to systematic meditation is his treatment of the Crucifixion in the *Centuries*. The Crucifixion was important to him; he recognizes it as the event that enabled man to progress from the state of sin to grace and glory. He holds up the figure of Christ crucified before the reader's eyes through many paragraphs. Yet even here, he constantly moves from meditation to other devotional forms: affective prayer, perhaps contemplation. To cite two brief examples:

O Let me so long Eye Thee, till I be turned into Thee, and look upon me till Thou art formed in me, that I may be a Mirror of thy Brightness, an Habitation of thy Lov and a Temple of thy Glory.

As therfore we see thy Flesh with our fleshly Eys, and handle thy Wounds with our Bodily Sences, let us see thy Understanding with our Understandings, and read thy Lov with our own. Let our Souls hav Communion with thy Soul, and let the Ey of our Mind enter into thine. (C I.87, 88)

Constantly moving from Christ's humanity to his Godhood, the prose in these passages resembles Baroque art. More immediately, it reflects a devotional method closer to Crashaw's than Donne's or Herbert's. Intense concentration on and through the senses points toward mystical union. There is a progression from flesh and sense to understanding, from understanding to love, and from love to communion of souls. On this road toward mysticism, meditation plays a part, but the main connecting link is sensible affection.

The recovery of felicity in the mature state of grace is, for Traherne, a result of divine love. In three poems emphasizing this point that lead up to the concluding group in the Dobell sequence, the devotional method moves between affection and contemplation. "The Recovery" and "Another" constantly refer to "conjugal pleasures . . . set in appropriately sensuous surroundings." [38] A third poem, "Love," exemplifies the devotional thrust from sensible affection toward contemplation. Its closing images, working like those in the Song of Songs, have a potential to shock that goes well beyond the famous love metaphors of Donne's "Batter my heart" and "Show me deare Christ":

3

Did my Ambition ever Dream
Of such a Lord, of such a Love! Did I
   Expect so Sweet a Stream
As this at any time! Could any Ey
   Believ it? Why all Power
    Is used here
Joys down from Heaven on my Head to shower
And Jove beyond the Fiction doth appear
   Once more in Golden Rain to come.
   To Danae's Pleasing Fruitfull Womb.

4

His Ganimede! His Life! His Joy!
Or he comes down to me, or takes me up
   That I might be his Boy,
And fill, and taste, and give, and Drink the Cup.
   But these (tho great) are all
    Too short and small,
Too Weak and feeble Pictures to Express

> The true Mysterious Depths of Blessedness.
> I am his Image, and his Friend.
> His Son, Bride, Glory, Temple, End.

The justification for such daring imagery derives from the mystical tradition, though Traherne borrows his specific materials from classical myth. Not only is the speaker visited and impregnated by God as lover, he is taken up into heaven to be Jove's Ganymede: "And fill, and taste, and give, and Drink the Cup." Whether visitation or *extasis,* these spiritual events are painted in vivid affective metaphors that seem out of place to describe anything less than mystical experience or union.

The poems on divine love lead into a series of poems entitled "Thoughts," which argue that felicity resides not in objects but the thoughts that comprehend them. These poems too reflect the mature speaker. Their titles suggest intellectual activity, but their method continues to be affective or contemplative. Significantly, as Stewart remarks, "In these closing poems Traherne draws upon the iconographic and literary association of *hortus conclusus* and the New Jerusalem." [39] When these poems descend from mystical rapture, it is typically into a mode of devotion that is intensely affective and sensuous.

> Ye Thoughts and Apprehensions are
> The Heavenly Streams which fill the Soul with rare
> Transcendent Perfect Pleasures.
> At any time,
> As if ye still were in your Prime,
> Ye Open all his Heavenly Treasures. . . .

> O ye *Conceptions* of Delight!
> Ye that *inform* my Soul with Life and Sight!
> Ye Representatives, and Springs
> Of inward Pleasure!
> Ye Joys! Ye Ends of Outward Treasure!
> Ye Inward, and ye Living Things!
> The Thought, or Joy Conceived is
> The inward Fabrick of my Standing Bliss. . . .

Like Bees they flie from Flower to Flower,
Appear in Evry Closet, Temple, Bower;
   And suck the Sweet from thence,
     No Ey can see:
   As Tasters to the Deitie.
   Incredible's their Excellence.
   For ever-more they will be seen
Nor ever moulder into less Esteem.
   They ever shew an Equal face,
   And are Immortal in their place.
Ten thousand Ages hence they are as Strong,
Ten thousand Ages hence they are as Yong.

Traherne's "thoughts" in these culminating poems do not analyze, they feel and know. They are springs of pleasure, joys, the quintessence and cream of objects. They are bees that suck sweets, tasters to the Deity. The mode of apprehension and devotion is still similar to Herrick and Crashaw. Traherne's thoughts, like the prayer of contemplation, will endure unchanged into the next life; they are not dependent on the body, the senses, or the object perceived.

The goal toward which Traherne's prose and poetic sequences move is the fourth state of man: glory. From his preoccupation with the past—his youth and man's biblical past—which is the source of his earlier devotions, he turns to the present—the natural universe and the loving God behind it—and to the future—the state in which his felicity will be perfect, infinite, and eternal. Present felicity, especially the contemplative experience, is the closest that the state of grace comes to the state of glory in this life. Therefore it is not surprising that, when Traherne turns to that future state, he uses the contemplative mode and employs traditional mystical imagery.

When he turns to this highest theme, Traherne does not leave sense imagery behind. A major expression of the state of glory is a poem inserted into "Thanksgivings for the Body," inspired by contemplation of the glorious body after the general resurrection (Philippians iii.21):

Then shall each Limb a spring of Joy be found,
And ev'ry Member with its Glory crown'd:
While all the Senses, fill'd with all the Good
That ever Ages in them understood,
Transported are: Containing Worlds of Treasure,
At one Delight with all their Joy and Pleasure.
From whence, like Rivers, Joy shall overflow,
Affect the Soul, though in the Body grow.
Return again, and make the Body shine
Like Jesus Christ, while both in one combine,
Mysterious Contacts are between the Soul,
Which touch the Spirits, and by those its Bowl:
The Marrow, Bowels, Spirits, melt and move,
Dissolving ravish, teach them how to love.

(ll. 430–43)

Although contemplation, like its fruition in glory, is imageless, only the most intense images seem useful to describe it. Contemplation and sensible affection form, in a manner of speaking, a resonant cycle like the mutual reinforcement Traherne describes between the glorified body and soul. He is influenced, of course, by the doctrine of bodily resurrection, which results in an attitude opposite to Platonic scorn of the body as matter: "For God designs thy Body, for his sake, / *A Temple of the Deity* to make" (ll. 464–65).

In "Goodnesse," the last poem in the Dobell sequence, the poet speaks from the state of grace toward which the whole sequence points.[40] By following the method of egotism, desire, and want, he arrives paradoxically at an unselfish desire to include others in his happiness. The property of God's treasures is to multiply the more widely they are shared. The method of devotion—vocal, affective, contemplative—approaches the highest of possible devotional modes: beatific vision.

I

The Bliss of other Men is my Delight:
  (When once my Principles are right:)
  And evry Soul which mine doth see
    A Treasurie.

The Face of *God* is Goodness unto all,
And while he Thousands to his Throne doth call,
  While Millions bathe in Pleasures,
  And do behold his Treasures
    The Joys of all
    On mine do fall
And even my Infinitie doth seem
A Drop without them of a mean Esteem.

As the poem progresses, the imagery grows ever richer, more sensuous, and more sensual:

5

The Soft and Swelling Grapes that on their Vines
  Receiv the Lively Warmth that Shines
  Upon them, ripen there for me:
    Or Drink they be
Or Meat. The Stars salute my pleased Sence
With a Derivd and borrowed Influence
  But better Vines do Grow
  Far Better Wines do flow
    Above, and while
    The Sun doth Smile
Upon the Lillies there, and all things warme
Their pleasant Odors do my Spirit charm.

6

Their rich Affections me like precious Seas
  Of Nectar and Ambrosia pleas.
Their Eys are Stars, or more Divine:
    And Brighter Shine
Their Lips are soft and Swelling Grapes, their Tongues
A Quire of Blessed and Harmonious Songs.
  Their Bosoms fraught with Love
  Are Heavens all Heavens above
And being Images of *God,* they are
The Highest Joys his Goodness did prepare.

The image of the celestial vine, like Crashaw's in "The Weeper," is derived from the Bible (especially John xv). It is Traherne's equivalent of Dante's mystical rose in the *Paradiso*. The saints of God, grafted onto the divine stem and ripened by warmth from the sun/Son, receive and reflect the beatific vision. They are the poet's spiritual food and drink; other than God, of whom they are "Images," they are the greatest treasures God has prepared for us.

The imagery of these last poems in the sequence, like the first, is kaleidoscopic and elliptical, more evocative than descriptive. A reader of the earlier poems may compose pictures including golden streets and shining youths, though that is not (apparently) the poet's primary intention. Rather he wishes to recapture a mode of vision. It is harder for a reader to picture the heaven of the last poem, filled with saints, stars, lilies, and grapes, as a consistent whole, because these are shifting metaphors for the same thing. When Traherne makes the transition from representative material objects remembered from youth and set in ideal landscapes, which by their nature are susceptible to the reader's habit of composing pictures, to shifting metaphors that embody spiritual states and unimaginable heavenly realities, he employs images more rather than less fully realized and sensuously described. "Love" notes that, however vivid the metaphors one chooses, they are too "short and small" and paint "Too Weak and feeble Pictures" to express "The true Mysterious Depths of Blessedness." Paradoxically but logically, Traherne's poetry becomes more material as it approaches nearer his ideal. The logic of this paradox is poetic strategy and devotional exigency. It is similar to the paradox of Crashaw's Teresa poems, which, like the whole course of his poetic development, grow more sensuous as they grow more mystical.

There are two ways of regarding Traherne's final poems as devotions. One is that he employs, more and more intensely, the techniques of sensible affection in order to break through into the ecstasy of mystical contemplation. The other is that his mysticism, like that of St. Teresa or St. John, blossoms with sensuous and luxuriant imagery as an effort to express the inexpressible. The latter seems more probable though unprovable. Without entering into biographical judgments, one may say that the poems give the impression of a speaker who has attained the mystical state of extraordinary grace and felicity. From that state his devotions overflow into vocal praise, affections, and occasional brief meditations. But they consistently point back up toward contemplation. Just as consistently, they ask the reader, whether by direct address or poetic enticements, to follow the author up the same path.

Notes

1. Carol L. Marks, "Thomas Traherne and Cambridge Platonism," *PMLA*, 81 (1966), 534.
2. Louis Martz, *The Paradise Within* (New Haven: Yale University Press, 1964), p. 44.
3. On reader cooperation see Stanley Stewart, *The Expanded Voice* (San Marino: Huntington Library, 1970), pp. 105–109.
4. Wallace, "Thomas Traherne and the Structure of Meditation," *ELH*, 25 (1958), 79–89.
5. Martz, *The Paradise Within*, pp. 33–102.
6. Clements, *The Mystical Poetry of Thomas Traherne* (Cambridge: Harvard University Press, 1969).
7. Clements, p. 7.
8. See Joan Webber, *The Eloquent "I"* (Madison: University of Wisconsin Press, 1968), pp. 219–247.
9. References to the *Centuries* as printed by Margoliouth.
10. See Clements, pp. 7–8, 61–62, et passim.
11. Clements, p. viii.
12. Baker, *Sancta Sophia* (Douai: John Patte and Thomas Fievet, 1657), I, 71 (I.ii.2.5); Herbert, "Affliction (I)."
13. The intensity of Traherne's childhood experiences and his ability to express them are unusual, but many readers may have experienced something similar. See Michael Pafford, *Inglorious Wordsworths: A Study of Some Transcendental Experiences in Childhood and Adolescence* (London: Hodder & Stoughton, 1973). Pafford draws doubtful conclusions, but his data are interesting and support those seventeenth-century writers (a minority) who argue that the ability to contemplate is potentially commoner than the ability to meditate.
14. Gladys I. Wade, *Thomas Traherne* (Princeton: Princeton University Press, 1944); contra, Rene Wellek and Austin Warren, *Theory of Literature*, 3d edn. (New York: Harcourt, Brace & World, 1956), pp. 207–208.

15. Stewart, pp. 105–106 et seq.

16. See William H. Marshall, "Thomas Traherne and the Doctrine of Original Sin," *MLN,* 73 (1958), 161–165; George R. Guffey, "Thomas Traherne on Original Sin," *N&Q,* 14 (1967), 98–100; Patrick Grant, "Original Sin and the Fall of Man in Thomas Traherne," *ELH,* 38 (1971), 40–61.

17. Stewart, pp. 105ff., argues otherwise; see Margoliouth, I, xii–xvii for data.

18. Philip's revisions of poems found in both MSS are conveniently studied in Margoliouth: some are minor, others extensive.

19. See especially C III.16, 23, 27.

20. As line 9 of Stanza 4 is squeezed in, Margoliouth (p. 367) speculates Philip inserted it. But it brings the stanza to 14 lines and is wittily applicable to vehicle and tenor of the metaphor.

21. See Carol Marks (Sicherman), "Thomas Traherne and Hermes Trismegistus," *Renaissance News,* 19 (1966), 118–131; "Thomas Traherne's Commonplace Book," *PBSA,* 58 (1964), 458–465; "Traherne's Ficino Notebook," *PBSA,* 63 (1969), 73–165. Traherne quotes extensively from Pico's *De Dignitate Hominis* in the *Centuries* (C IV.74–78, 81).

22. See Sterling P. Lamprecht, "The Role of Descartes in Seventeenth-Century England," *Studies in the History of Ideas* (New York, 1935), 111, 198.

23. Stewart, p. 64; see also pp. 72, 129.

24. *OED,* s.v. "experimental"; cited by Norman T. Burns, *Christian Mortalism from Tyndale to Milton* (Cambridge: Harvard University Press, 1972), p. 48; see also Ronald Knox, *Enthusiasm* (New York: Oxford University Press, 1950).

25. Burns, pp. 45ff.

26. Mather, *The Accomplished Singer* (Boston: B. Green, 1721), p. 13; cited by Kenneth Silverman, "Cotton Mather and the Reform of Puritan Psalmody," *SCN,* 34 (1976), 55.

27. Franck[e], *A Guide to the Reading and Study of the Holy Scriptures,* trans. William Jacques (Philadelphia: David Hogan, 1823), pp. 126, 128; Francke quotes first Spener, then Luther; cited by Silverman, p. 55. On exegesis see also H. G. Haile, "Luther and Literacy," *PMLA,* 91 (1976), 925, for " 'Nacherleben des Inhalts', intense imaginative participation."

28. Barclay, *An Apology for the True Christian Divinity* (London, 1678), pp. 256–257.

29. Carol Marks, "Traherne's Church's Year-Book," *PBSA,* 60 (1966), 31–72.

30. Marks, p. 38.

31. Marks, p. 44.

32. Marks, p. 57.

33. Margoliouth, II, 401–403.

34. Stewart, p. 97; the chapter is called "Traherne and the Meditative Mode."

35. "Thanksgivings for the Body," 11. 341–343.

36. "Thanksgivings for the Body," 11. 405–416.

37. "Here enters not intellect but will" (Hugh of St. Victor), *The Cloud of Unknowing,* ed. Justin McCann (Westminster: Newman Press, 1952), pp. xiii–xv.

38. Stewart, p. 194.

39. Stewart, p. 198.

40. See Clements, pp. 184–189; Stewart, pp. 204–207.

10.

Conclusion

1. Poet and Reader

The poet critics of the Renaissance, such as Sidney and Spenser, or of the seventeenth century, such as Milton and Herbert, were confident that a prime duty of the poet is to instruct, move, and change or convert his readers. The Romantic and Modernist movements viewed didacticism with suspicion—somewhat paradoxically, since the great English Romantics thought of themselves as teachers and prophets, as did the Victorians, as did the Moderns. Nonetheless, as heirs of these movements, we may prefer poetry of self-expression or self-examination to poetry the purpose of which is too obviously rhetorical or doctrinal. The poet's eye should not be on his readers but on himself and his experiences. An illustration of this view is Helen Vendler's recent book on Herbert. In it she consistently argues that Herbert is best when he expresses himself and worst when he addresses an audience, conveys a doctrine, sings a hymn of praise, or otherwise departs from self analysis. "To approach such private poetry as an exercise in public communication with an audience is to misconstrue its emphasis." [1]

One need not separate self-expression from communica-

294

tion. The seventeenth century was a great age of spiritual autobiography and inward-looking analysis, but these analyses
were undergone in order to change and renovate the self, with
God's grace, and were published to reach and convert others.
Fox and Bunyan, Montaigne and Descartes, like St. Augustine
before them and Wordsworth after, found self-examination to
be a powerful means of persuading others. Poets teach by the
method of fiction, using living examples, including themselves,
rather than dead rules. If the office of the poet resembles the
pulpit, it is, Milton argues, more immediate, more passionate,
and therefore more effective.

The more Donne puts himself, or fictional derivatives of
himself, into his poetry, the more effectively he sways his
readers. This may be why he put himself into his sermons so
often, most notably in *Deaths Duell.* He was not the only devotional poet to realize that experience is a prerequisite of poetry
and that, in Vaughan's phrase, "true, practick piety"—with
truthful admission of faults—is the best source a religious poet
can draw on. To seem natural, a poet must be artful; yet in the
end he probably must be as he wishes to seem. The English
devotional poets, fortunate in their talents and spiritual gifts,
were also equipped, by their religious and humanistic educa-
tions, both to be and by their arts to seem. To this it seems
appropriate to add that public forms, litanies, psalms, hymns,
songs of praise, are also reflections of the poet's experience and
the life of his times and that, when they are well written, they
deserve as much respect or liking as those more introspective
poems our time prefers.

2. Varieties of Devotion

The great variety of style and spirit within the "schools" or
movements of seventeenth-century English poetry has always
been evident. It extends to devotional methodology. We have
examined four main types: vocal, meditative, affective, and contemplative. All the major poets we have looked at employ several of these types in one poem or another or within single

poems. There are also varieties of emphasis. Donne, beginning with vocal, liturgical poems, moves into a middle period of striking meditation, then closes his career with three great hymns. Herbert's lyrics, whatever the history of their composition, reveal no such progression as he left them. Instead, *The Temple* is ordered on the principle of variety itself: rhyme schemes, poetic genres, devotional methods. More than most poets, Herbert was influenced by music, but this element like others is subordinated in his final text so that a larger devotional harmony emerges.

Crashaw too was a musical poet and perhaps a mystical one. But what distinguishes him most is his use of sensible affection. Vaughan, a skilled meditator when he chose and a brilliant composer of dynamic, music-like verse, was chiefly a mystic, not because the majority of his poems are mystical but because that is where his genius or uniqueness lies. When Herrick turned to devotional poetry, he gave the meditative poem several new turns and broadened the holiday song in his court compositions. But his chief contribution was to baptize Epicurus, to take sensible affection and marry it to the philosophy of pleasure. Marvell, with Crashaw, developed the religious lyric toward the oratorio. With Vaughan he helped move meditation on the creatures toward Wordsworthian contemplation of single objects. His witty contemplation in "The Garden" and his grave but joyous music in "Bermudas" are perhaps closest to the heart of his originality. Finally, Traherne touches on music and meditation, but his chief mode is an interplay between contemplative ecstasy and sensible affection, with support from the philosophy of pleasure.

Martz long ago demonstrated how many kinds of meditation alone are found in English poetry.[2] There are two main branches of vocal prayer, "said or sung," and many further varieties within those branches, from the collect to the litany, from the hymn (various in itself) to the metrical psalm. This is not to speak of combinations, such as the meditative hymns of Donne, the affective hymns of Crashaw, or the mystical hymns of Vaughan, or those rarer poems that begin in one mode and end in another. Sensible affection too is varied. And while mysticism points toward one goal, it follows many paths. Its spirit varies from the fires and passions of Crashaw to the disciplined darkness and negation, issuing into clear light, of Vaughan. In Traherne's mystical poetry, a reader may find something of Vaughan's cool spirit and style and something of Crashaw's or even Herrick's passionate attachment to pleasure. In short, while each poet found his own devotional path, it was seldom a simple one. None relied on a single devotional authority or method. Poets of their caliber were no more likely to impose such a limitation on themselves than to rely on a single literary theorist—Puttenham, let us say—for their poetic techniques.

The proof of literary criticism is whether it sends the reader back to the poems. If my discussion of devotional modes has any worth, that is where it may be tested. One of the greatest pleasures in writing this book was to reread all the poems, and to discover some that I always neglected because they were not quite what habit taught me to value. I hope this may be a communicable experience.

Notes

1. Vendler, *The Poetry of George Herbert* (Cambridge: Harvard University Press, 1975), p. 5; see also pp. 23, 79, 122, 127, 151–153, 164, 178, 190, 197. While I disagree with this view, I admire many of the individual explications.

2. Louis Martz, *The Poetry of Meditation* (New Haven: Yale University Press, 1954; rev. 1962).

Texts of the Poetry

Unless otherwise noted, quotations are from the following texts. "U" and "v," "i" and "j," "w," and "&" are regularized. Contractions are expanded and small capitals in Crashaw and Traherne are normalized as italics. I thrice prefer Grierson's text of Donne (in "Satire III," "This is my playes last scene," and "Batter my heart") and, using Margoliouth's apparatus, restore revisions made by Thomas Traherne.

John Donne. *The Divine Poems.* Ed. Helen Gardner. Oxford: The Clarendon Press, 1952; repr. 1969.

George Herbert. *The Works.* Ed. F. E. Hutchinson. Oxford: The Clarendon Press, 1941; repr. 1964.

Richard Crashaw. *The Poems, English, Latin and Greek.* Ed. L. C. Martin. Oxford: The Clarendon Press, 1957.

Henry Vaughan. *The Works.* Ed. L. C. Martin. Oxford: The Clarendon Press, 1957; repr. 1963.

Robert Herrick. *The Poetical Works.* Ed. L. C. Martin. Oxford: The Clarendon Press, 1956; repr. 1963.

Andrew Marvell. *The Poems and Letters.* 3d Edition. Ed. H. M. Margoliouth, rev. Pierre Legouis with E. E. Duncan-Jones. 2 vols. Oxford: The Clarendon Press, 1971.

Thomas Traherne. *Centuries, Poems, and Thanksgivings.* Ed. H. M. Margoliouth. 2 vols. Oxford: The Clarendon Press, 1958.

I have used the Oxford English Texts out of old habit and for the sake of consistency. Equally authoritative are the New York University Stuart Editions (paperbacks by Norton): Donne, ed. J. T. Shawcross; Herbert, ed. J. M. Patrick (forthcoming); Crashaw, ed. G. W. Williams; Vaughan, ed. F. Fogle; and Herrick, ed. J. M. Patrick. Also recommended: Herbert, ed. C. A. Patrides, and editions of Marvell by E. S. Donno and G. deF. Lord. Donne's other poems are edited by H. Gardner, W. Milgate, T. Redpath, and F. Manley; the complete poems by H. J. C. Grierson and A. J. Smith.

Index